Educator's Survival Guide
for Television Production
and Activities

Educator's Survival Guide for Television Production and Activities

Keith Kyker
Christopher Curchy

LIBRARIES
U N L I M I T E D

A Member of the Greenwood Publishing Group

Westport, Connecticut • London

British Library Cataloguing in Publication Data is available.

Copyright © 2003 Keith Kyker and Christopher Curchy

All Rights Reserved

ISBN 1–56308–983–1

First published in 2003

Libraries Unlimited
A Member of Greenwood Publishing Group, Inc.
88 Post Road West
Westport, CT 06881
1–800–225–5800
www.lu.com

Printed in the United States of America

The paper used in this book complies with the Permanent Paper Standard issued by the National Information Standards Organization (Z39.48–1984).

10 9 8 7 6 5 4 3 2 1

This book is dedicated to all my former news crew students,
elementary through high school, who helped
turn possibilities into realities.
—Christopher Curchy

This book is dedicated to June Leonard Kyker
and Rose Hagy Leonard Hendrix.
Individually and collectively, two of the best ever.
—Keith Kyker

Contents

Introduction

Welcome to *Educator's Survival Guide for Television Production and Activities.* Of course, for some of you, "welcome back" may be more appropriate.

In 1998 we published *Educator's Survival Guide to TV Production Equipment and Set-Up,* our fourth book for Libraries Unlimited. Back then, the video format choice was between VHS and S-VHS, computers and TV equipment didn't communicate very well, and nonlinear digital video editing was well above the price range of most schools. Now, it's common to find digital video formats like MiniDV and DV8mm in schools, computer displays integrated into the school news show, and a video editing system included with your new laptop computer. Times have changed!

And media educators need to keep up with all of these changes. It's not just about buying the neatest, coolest equipment. It's about wisely spending your school television production budget. Not only are digital camcorders and nonlinear editing systems much more powerful than their twentieth-century analog counterparts—they're much less expensive, too! In today's marketplace, it's possible to spend *more* money for outdated technology. Nobody wants that—especially your students.

Therefore, for this work, a simple update or revision of the 1998 book just wouldn't do. In many chapters, we had to start from scratch. And every chapter contains new sections, pictures, or diagrams to drive the points home. Here is a rundown of what you'll find.

In chapter 1, "Video Equipment: Description and Selection Criteria," *digital* is the buzzword. We explore the new digital format camcorders, digital videotape, and even the digital capabilities of character generators and video mixers. This is definitely the direction in which school video production is going. Chapter 1 explains it all.

Chapter 2, "Audio Equipment: Description and Selection Criteria," explains microphone selection. You'll also find information about the wide range of microphone formats on the market, including surface mounts, pressure zone microphones, and wireless microphones. And don't forget to read the section about avoiding copyright problems by using buy-out music in your video productions. You can even learn about creating your own royalty-free production music. It's easier than you think!

Chapter 3 is an all-new chapter, "Nonlinear Digital Video Editing." Here you can find a complete explanation of the nonlinear, computer-based editing system, as well as selection criteria for purchasing your nonlinear editing system. We even walk you through the planning and editing of a hypothetical project.

Once you've determined the equipment you'd like to buy, read chapter 4, "Buying Television Production Equipment and Services for Schools." Equipment purchase and rental is given the full treatment. You'll also learn about blank videotape purchases and about obtaining video duplication service.

Chapter 5, "Creating Your Video Production Studio," is your guide to configuring your school's audio and video equipment into a working television facility. It includes step-by-step instructions—complete with diagrams—to guide you through this process.

You've selected and purchased your equipment and configured it into a working studio. Now what? Chapter 6 is all about "Producing School News Shows." Topics include selecting your students (sample applications included), designing and building sets, organizing your classes, and creating a show that your students, faculty, and administration will love.

Chapter 7, "Video Production Activities," is another entirely new chapter. It contains a dozen ready-made video projects suitable for elementary through high school students. Each project includes a student project plan, a teacher guide, and a grading rubric.

Chapter 8, "Presenting Your Television Programs," gives practical advice on using multiple monitors, big-screen televisions, video projectors, and sound systems to create the professional atmosphere your productions deserve. Have you ever shown your school orientation videotape at the parent-teacher association (PTA) meeting or school open house? Then you know how important this chapter can be.

Chapter 9, "Questions from the Floor," presents some of the most commonly asked questions (and answers) from our workshops, presentations, and Web site, SCHOOLTV.com. Chances are that if one person asks, then someone else probably wants to know, too!

Our guide ends with a glossary, covering school television production terms from *adapter* to *zoom lens.*

So, this book is more than just an update or revision. In 1998, *Booklist* said of *Educator's Survival Guide to TV Production Equipment and Set-Up,* "It seems to address almost every question a school media specialist or others involved in television production in a school setting might ask." That's a tough act to follow, and we've done our best to present a current and accurate guide.

Good luck, and stay in touch!

Christopher Curchy
Keith Kyker
2003

Chapter 1

Video Equipment
DESCRIPTION AND SELECTION CRITERIA

There will probably be no more exciting time in your video production class than when your students see themselves and their work on the television screen for the first time. Video has a magical quality—combining the visual impact of photography with the immediacy of a quick glance in the mirror. Can anyone resist a shy shrug when they see themselves on camera for the first time? Of course, to create this magic, your students must have access to the proper tools of television production.

Purchasing video and audio equipment for your school is an arduous task, best approached with an arsenal of selection criteria, a knowledge of your school's video production goals, and a firm understanding of each component's role in the television process. In this chapter, we'll briefly explain the function of video equipment and recommend certain features that should be present on the equipment that you buy.

The following equipment is described in this chapter:

- **camcorder**—the basic tool for recording videotape in schools,
- **tripod**—a support for the camera that helps steady the shot,
- **monopod**—a single-legged camera support,
- **dolly**—wheels for the bottom of the tripod used to facilitate advanced camera movements,
- **industrial/professional videocassette recorder (VCR)**—a full-feature VCR for recording and postproduction,
- **video mixer (also known as a special-effects generator or an A/V mixer)**—a component that allows the selection and manipulation of video sources,
- **television or video monitor**—a component that allows the user to see the production in progress and view the finished project, and
- **character generator**—an electronic device that allows graphics to be typed onto the screen and perhaps even be superimposed over video.

(Editing equipment is covered in chapter 3.)

Although the equipment described in this chapter can be categorized as "video" equipment—it all involves the visual image—each item performs a unique task. Furthermore, each item can also function as part of an integrated video production system. When deciding to purchase video production equipment, consider not only the stand-alone features of the item but also its place in your production system.

Your finished video production will only be as good as the weakest item in your video production system allows. Imagine that your students have worked hard to create an orientation tape for your school media center. They have used creative camera angles, reinforced important points with graphics, and edited the project to eliminate mistakes and provide a steady pace. Now imagine that orientation video created with poor-quality equipment. Think about a camcorder that doesn't white balance or that has no manual iris control. How about a character generator that creates poor-quality graphics that are too small to read? As you can see, it is important to buy equipment that facilitates good video production in your school.

But we're getting a bit ahead of ourselves here. Let's go back to that workhorse of school video production, the camcorder.

Evaluating the Camcorder

The camcorder—the most basic item in a school-based television production program—allows students to record the audio and video of school activities and community events (see fig. 1.1). The features of a camcorder suitable for the school setting allow students with minimum training to produce excellent recordings. Many schools use camcorders as their studio cameras in a small- or portable-studio configuration. Camcorders are quite visible at local consumer-electronics

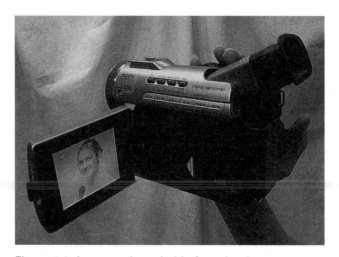

Figure 1.1 A camcorder suitable for school use

dealerships and discount houses and on the Internet. But not all camcorders represent good value for schools. Some media specialists make the mistake of investing in underdeveloped, underpowered camcorders, whereas others buy budget-busting equipment better suited for the local broadcast television station.

When buying a camcorder for your school, you are applying a different set of criteria than the home or hobby customer uses. The typical camcorder customer is buying a camcorder to use at family or community functions: picnics, volleyball matches, vacations, and the like. They are looking for quick, easy operation, as well as a good value. They want a camcorder that is easy to pack in a suitcase or carry-on—one that won't create a burden at a tourist attraction or a family gathering. They want some nice advanced features, but they also want something simple enough for the younger family members to use. They want to watch the videotape they make on their home TVs, and they probably won't edit the footage or add narration and music. They will probably appreciate a button that creates a "Happy Birthday" graphic when pressed. Chances are that they will never connect the camcorder to another item of production equipment.

You, on the other hand, are buying a camcorder for a completely different setting: the school production setting. You're looking for a camcorder with more-advanced production features. You want something easy to use, but you also want to make sure the camcorder has a microphone jack and a headphone jack for conducting interviews. Instantly watching your videotape is probably not your primary goal. You will, however, be connecting your camcorder to other items of video production, such as a video mixer and a character generator. You will probably also want to edit the video that you shoot, and you may even use your camcorder as a VCR in that process. And you will groan if a student accidentally presses that "Happy Birthday" button while videotaping an interview with the principal!

So, don't be surprised if the salesperson and the print advertisements are geared toward the typical camcorder customer. When looking for a camcorder for your school, realize that the most popular (and least-expensive models) may not be the best choices. You may even have to educate the salesperson on the features that you want. When a salesperson says, "Gee, nobody ever asked about that before," consider it a victory for media educators everywhere, and press onward! Here are the criteria that we recommend when selecting a camcorder for your school.

Image Processor

Every new, "factory-fresh" camcorder will have a charge-coupled device (CCD) as an image processor. Most camcorders affordable to schools will have a single CCD. Several industrial/professional camcorders are available with two or three CCDs. The multi-CCD camcorders offer superior picture quality—at a price three to five times that of the single-CCD camcorder. However, secondary schools teaching professional videography techniques to students who will enter the broadcast workforce or study television production in college may want to invest in multi-CCD camcorders.

Format

Format refers to the videotape format used by the camcorder. In other words—what kind of videotape do I need to buy? Camcorders appropriate for school use are available in several formats: VHS, S-VHS, VHS-C, S-VHS-C, 8mm, DV8mm, and MiniDV (see fig. 1.2). When deciding which format best suits your needs, you should consider the way that you will use the camcorder in the school. Also, consider potential applications, not just the way you currently use equipment.

VHS

The VHS (video home system) format is still quite common in schools. VHS dominates the home video scene, allowing many parents to view completed projects at home. A full-size VHS camcorder mounts on the shoulder, providing a steady shot. However, the size may make it difficult for smaller students to use. Only a few VHS camcorders are still available on the market as customers have shown a preference for other formats.

Although declining in popularity in the home market, VHS still has a place in the school setting. Teachers like to use VHS camcorders in the classroom because blank tapes are cheap—about a dollar each—and easily available, and the finished video will play in their classroom VCR. Some schools continue to use VHS cam-

Figure 1.2 Videotape formats include (left to right) VHS, VHS-C, 8mm, and MiniDV.

corders for video production activities, although more attractive options now exist. VHS's biggest drawback is the picture quality, which is average at best.

S-VHS

The S-VHS (super VHS) format was developed for videographers who desire a higher-quality picture. A program shot with an S-VHS camcorder on an S-VHS tape and played on an S-VHS VCR is broadcast quality. However, such a tape cannot be played on a VHS VCR. Blank S-VHS videotapes sell for about five dollars each. (S-VHS equipment can also use regular VHS tapes, but with only VHS quality as a result.) S-VHS VCRs also can be quite costly, although newer models are becoming less expensive. An attractive feature of an S-VHS camcorder is the presence of an S-VHS output jack. In other words, the S-VHS camcorder not only records a high-quality video picture; it also sends that high-quality signal down the line for input into a video mixer or VCR with an S-VHS input.

An S-VHS industrial-professional camcorder can be purchased for about $2,000. Expect those prices to drop as S-VHS becomes more prevalent in the home market.

VHS-C

The VHS-C (VHS-compact) format couples the VHS market saturation with a smaller-size camcorder. The VHS-C camcorder is held in one hand and uses VHS-C videotapes, which are about half the size of regular VHS tapes. These tapes can be played in regular VHS VCRs using a special videocassette adapter. These features—smaller camcorder and programs compatible with the home VCR—make VHS-C an attractive option for the family videographer. However, picture quality is equivalent to VHS (which is average), and the necessary adapter is downright inconvenient in the school setting.

S-VHS-C

The S-VHS picture quality is also available on a VHS-C cassette. Few S-VHS-C models are available, and most are aimed at the high-end consumer market. Although the picture quality produced by these camcorders is attractive in the school setting, the need for an adapter is a mark against this format. Blank S-VHS-C videotapes are also rare in the consumer marketplace.

Hi-8 and 8mm

The Hi-8 and 8mm formats, which use a small videotape 8 millimeters wide, are making an impact in the educational setting. Picture quality rivals S-VHS for resolution and clarity. Hi-8 and 8mm camcorders usually are designed to be operated in the palm of the hand, although some larger, shoulder-mounted models are on the market. Hi-8 and 8mm VCRs are required for playback and editing and may

Figure 1.3 IEEE-1394 connectors on a DV camcorder

not be as readily available as VHS and S-VHS equipment. Typically, the camcorder is connected to the TV or VCR using audio and video cable, making the camcorder the "play" VCR. Because of the VHS saturation of the home video market, most student projects will have to be transferred to VHS for home viewing. However, many schools find the small, feature-packed camcorders and high-quality video picture worth that inconvenience.

Two Digital Formats: MiniDV and DV8mm

The two newest videotape formats offer astounding picture quality and prices that are very attractive to schools. The two formats are MiniDV (mini digital video), and DV8mm. Both formats use a very small videotape to record broadcast-quality picture and digital-quality sound. The audio and video, recorded as digital information on the videotape, produce 480 lines of resolution (twice the quality of VHS) and sound that rivals a compact disc. Most, but not all, MiniDV and DV8mm camcorders have VHS and S-VHS quality outputs for connection to your existing equipment. They also feature a computer connector known as IEEE-1394. Two trade names for this type of connector are FireWire® (Apple) and i.LINK® (Sony). Using this connector with video equipment and editing appliances maintains the digital quality (see fig. 1.3). Manufacturers of video mixers and character generators now include IEEE-1394 inputs and outputs on their equipment, too.

The only disadvantages to using MiniDV and DV8mm formats in the school setting are 1) the relative expense of blank videotapes—about five dollars for a 60-minute blank tape—and 2) the lack of affordable playback VCRs. Schools using these formats will find themselves using the camcorder as the VCR until afford-

Table 1.1 **Videotape Formats**

Format	Advantages	Disadvantages
VHS	Availability of equipment; ease of use	Average picture quality; limited choices in the marketplace
S-VHS	Excellent picture quality; S-VHS outputs	Requires S-VHS VCR and S-VHS videotape
VHS-C	Small camcorder size	Average picture quality; adapter required for playback
S-VHS-C	Excellent picture quality; S-VHS outputs; small camcorder	Limited camcorder selection; limited blank videotape availability; adapter required for playback
Hi-8 and 8mm	Good picture quality; small camcorder size	Not compatible with most school VCRs
Digital formats (MiniDV and DV8mm)	Outstanding picture and sound quality; IEEE-1394 connector (compatible with nonlinear editing devices); small camcorder size; high-quality outputs	Lack of affordable digital VCR; expensive blank videotapes

able VCRs become available. Still, for schools desiring a high-quality video signal, and planning to edit using a nonlinear editing system, the two digital formats represent the best decision. (Nonlinear editing is discussed at length in chapter 3.)

Table 1.1 provides a summary of the format choices.

Technical Picture Quality

Two measurements included in equipment descriptions indicate the technical quality of the video recorded by the camcorder: lines of resolution and signal-to-noise ratio.

Lines of Resolution

The lines-of-resolution measurement indicates the number of electron lines that make up the television picture. The more lines of resolution, the better. The following list shows the various video formats with their lines of resolution.

Format	Lines of Resolution
VHS and VHS-C	240 lines
S-VHS and S-VHS-C	400 lines
8mm	240 lines
Hi-8mm	400 lines
MiniDV and DV8mm	480 lines

Keep in mind that these standards are produced in optimum situations and represent the maximum achieved by the format. Still, it is startling to note the drastic difference between VHS and the two digital formats—twice the picture quality. A good MiniDV or DV8mm camcorder suitable for school use can be purchased for less than $1,000. Never before has such a high-quality image been available at the school level.

Signal-to-Noise Ratio

The signal-to-noise ratio measures the strength of the good video signals against the bad video signal, or "noise," present in the video picture. This ratio is expressed in decibels (dB). A signal-to-noise ratio of 46–50 dB represents a good-quality picture.

As they say in the video production field, the best measurement is the interocular method. In other words, *look at it*. Make a sample videotape with each of the camcorders that you are evaluating. Watch the tape on your existing school VCRs. After two or three viewings, you will notice subtle differences in the way that each camcorder processes brightness and color. Compare your "interocular" evaluation with the technical measurements described earlier to select the best camcorder.

Lens

The camcorder lens gathers light from the physical environment, and the camcorder turns the light into electrical signal. For that reason, a quality lens is a critical component to a quality camcorder.

Zoom Lens

All camcorders currently on the market have a variable-strength, or zoom, lens. Zoom lens strength is expressed by a numeral followed by the "times" symbol ($\times$). This measurement indicates the magnification of the lens, relative to normal vision. (A lens of $1\times$ would indicate normal vision.) A 12×1 zoom lens would allow the user to zoom in 12 times the normal range of vision. Zoom lens strength on camcorders ranges from 3×1 on very inexpensive consumer camcorders to 20×1 on more expensive camcorders. Zooming in all the way greatly exaggerates any slight camera movement; few camera operators can provide a steady shot on the 20×1 setting. Still, a 10×1 zoom strength is the minimum a media specialist should consider.

Many camcorders also feature a digital zoom. The digital zoom is not really a function of the zoom lens at all; it is a digital effect produced by the camcorder's internal electronics. When activated by the user, the digital zoom electronically analyzes the signal produced by the CCD, crops the outer portion on all sides, and enlarges the resulting image to standard picture size. Using this process, many camcorders boast digital zoom strength of 300 × 1 and more. On some of the lower-quality camcorders, the resolution suffers greatly with a high-digital zoom setting, as the picture becomes mosaiclike. Higher-quality camcorders compensate with advanced electronic circuitry. Also, as you can imagine, it is very difficult to hold a steady shot with the camcorder zoomed in to 300 times your normal vision. For that reason, electronic image stabilization (discussed in the next section) should accompany a digital zoom lens. A powerful digital zoom may provide occasional service in an educational setting but should not be considered a chief criterion for camcorder selection.

Electronic Image Stabilization (EIS)

Electronic image stabilization (EIS) is a digital camcorder function that takes the "shake" out of your video shots. Sometimes it's hard to hold the camcorder steady. Back in the old days (the 1990s), most camcorders were larger and held on the shoulder. Video shot with shoulder-mounted camcorders was usually pretty steady. But when the camcorder went from the shoulder to the hand, the problem of shaky video came with it. Soon after, EIS became a common camcorder feature. When the EIS feature is engaged, the camcorder examines each frame of video shot (that's 30 frames each second) and compares it to the previous frame. If the shots are reasonably close around the edges, but not exactly matched, the camcorder adjusts the images to make them match. Of course, all of this happens so quickly that the user can't see the process, only the product. EIS really works—to a point. Try this feature out when you're shopping for your next camcorder.

Focus

Most camcorder lenses can be focused two ways: manually or automatically. Examine the ease and smoothness of the camcorder's manual focus. With the camcorder out of focus, turn on the automatic focus control and determine how quickly the camera focuses. Out-of-focus shots are often desirable in advanced video production; consequently, look for camcorders that offer manual focus.

Iris

The iris is a mechanism within the lens that controls the size of the lens opening. Although the front of the lens is several inches across, the lens is rarely completely open. On most camcorders, the lens automatically adjusts to the proper setting. This function, called automatic iris, determines the iris size based on the brightest part of the picture. Many professional camcorders have both manual and automatic settings. This feature is rarely seen on camcorders used in the school setting. Instead, camcorders offer automatic gain control and backlight functions as a way to control the brightness of the shot.

Automatic Gain Control and Backlight

Automatic gain control (AGC) and backlight are operation controls that brighten the video shot to compensate for low-light situations or to bring out the detail in a subject who is in front of a bright background. Some camcorders offer on or off settings for AGC and backlight. Others offer three-step (low, medium, high) AGC. Also, different manufacturers have different ways of defining these features. For example, on a Panasonic MiniDV Palmcorder, AGC is a digital function; a video shot with AGC has a slightly jerky and mosaic look. The backlight function on this camcorder simply brightens the shot. AGC and backlight functions are easily field tested in an electronics store or at a media conference. Select a camcorder that offers one or both of these functions.

White Balance

The white-balance function controls how the camcorder processes color. In the automatic setting, the white balance continuously monitors the ambient light and adjusts the color to the appropriate level (so that greens look green and blues look blue, etc.). However, this automatic white balance does not account for nuances in lighting environments, and the factory settings can deteriorate over time. For this reason, all camcorders selected for use in your school should offer the option for adjusting the white balance. Some camcorders offer a true manual white-balance option, whereby the camera operator points the camcorder at something white (a note card, T-shirt, etc.) and pushes a white-balance button. Other camcorders instead offer preset choices, such as "indoor" or "outdoor," and "incandescent light," "sunlight," or "fluorescent light." Whether you are physically setting the white balance or selecting from a menu of choices, white balancing the camcorder always results in truer color recording. Make sure that your camcorders offer at least one, if not both, of these white-balancing options.

Minimum Illumination Required (Lux Rating)

Because a camcorder converts light into electrical signal, it follows that the camcorder requires some minimum amount of light to produce a good-quality video picture. The lux rating of a camcorder is the measure that indicates the minimum amount of light that the camcorder needs to operate. Most camcorders will operate with a lux rating of 5 lux. (Some multichip camcorders require at least 25 lux.) Most school videotaping situations will offer at least 15 lux of light. However, if you plan to videotape in low-light situations, select a camcorder that can operate at 5 lux or less. Note: Lux ratings generally include the use of the AGC setting.

Fade Control

Most camcorders on the market have a fade control, which allows the videographer to fade in and out of shots. However, not all fade functions are user friendly. Some fade controls require a simple tap of the fade button. Others require the user to hold the button down during the entire fade, which may cause the user to stop recording before the fade is complete. Select a camcorder that provides a simple fade function.

High-Speed Shutter

If your plans for school videography include videotaping fast-moving objects (like baseball-bat swings and model-rocket blastoffs), you should consider a high-speed shutter function as a criterion for camcorder selection. When activated, the high-speed shutter functions like a high-speed shutter on a 35mm still camera. Each frame of video can be paused during playback to reveal a crisp recording. Without the high-speed shutter, which exposes 30 individually focused frames per second, a model-rocket liftoff would be a blur of white smoke.

Digital Effects

Because camcorders process digital signals from the CCD, it is natural that many camcorders now feature a selection of digital effects. These effects may include freeze-frame, strobe, picture-in-picture, and digital transitions from one shot to the next. Such features are especially helpful if no other video equipment capable of producing digital effects (such as a video mixer or a nonlinear editor) is available. Consider these effects a plus for purchase.

Viewfinder

Videographers use the viewfinder to see what they are videotaping. Most viewfinders feature screens that measure about 1-inch diagonal and are accessed using the camcorder's eyepiece. Some camcorders include a 2.5-inch or 3-inch LCD screen that flips out from the side of the camcorder body. This is a useful feature, especially when accessing the camcorder functions via on-screen display. Color viewfinders are usually found on better camcorders; lower-quality models usually have the black-and-white eyepiece-only viewfinder.

The viewfinder also contains useful information for camcorder operation, such as the battery-power indicator, the record indicator, the tape counter, and so on. Before buying a camcorder, make sure that the viewfinder will display all of the information that you need for its operation.

Record Review

The record-review function (also known as "camera search" or "tape search") allows the videographer to watch the last few seconds of videotape in the camcorder viewfinder while the camcorder remains on "record/pause." This feature is quite useful when the videographer needs to make sure the last shot was actually recorded. However, abuse of this feature can lead to accidental tape erasure because it cuts off the last second of the program recorded. This is a valuable feature, but it should be used carefully.

Graphics

Many camcorders feature a series of on-screen graphics-production capabilities. These include a day/date graphic on the tape and the typing of simple messages. Some camcorders even offer an optional handheld character generator that connects directly to the camcorder. Generally, these graphics are undesirable in the educational setting because they have a way of popping on at the most inopportune moments. Many otherwise-perfect videos have been ruined by the (usually incorrect) date or the time flashing in the lower right-hand corner of the picture. Title pages and credits produced on these camcorders are rarely of sufficient quality to evoke pride from the user. In the school setting, the most important consideration for these unwelcome guests is to figure out how to turn them off.

Internal (Installed) Microphone

The microphone installed on the camcorder is usually designed to record ambient sound—the sound of a family picnic or a birthday party. In other words, don't expect to find an internal microphone that will effectively record an on-camera interview (you'll need an external microphone for that—see chapter 2). A few of the higher-end camcorders feature internal microphones with wide-angle and shotgun (long-distance) settings. Although these adjustable microphones may still not be powerful enough to record a guest speaker across the classroom, they are much better at collecting sound from a specific source than are their omnidirectional forerunners. The presence of such an internal microphone is a plus for camcorder purchase.

Microphone Jack

Any camcorder purchased for school use should have an external microphone jack. An external microphone is critical for recording interviews, guest speakers, and news reports. The microphone jack should be positioned near the front of the camcorder for easy access by the talent. Most camcorders affordable to schools feature 1/8-inch minijacks, like those used in personal stereos.

Headphone Jack

If you are using a microphone, you will need headphones to monitor the microphone audio. Make sure that the camcorder you select has a headphone jack. (A volume adjustment for the headphone jack is a rare bonus.) When your student reporter forgets to turn on the microphone, and no sound is heard through the headphones, you'll really appreciate this feature.

Built-In Speaker

Some camcorders feature a small speaker on the side of the camcorder. An adjustable volume control is essential to this function. Often this feature is only active when the camcorder is used for playback and is automatically muted during the recording process. This feature frequently accompanies the LCD-screen viewfinder. Using the LCD-screen viewfinder and the built-in speaker together, your student production team can watch its program on location, and make sure that it has captured the audio and the video as intended.

Tape Speed

Some camcorders record on only one tape speed—usually SP (standard play, the fastest speed) or equivalent. Other camcorders offer a choice of two or even three tape speeds. For the sake of quality, videotape should always be recorded at the fastest speed possible. However, for those times the school play lasts more than the expected two hours or the soccer match goes into double overtime, it is nice to have a camcorder that will make your remaining tape last twice as long. Consider multiple tape speeds a bonus on your camcorder.

Editing Functions

Many schools just beginning video production programs may need the camcorder to serve double duty as a VCR for postproduction. This feature is quite useful and often goes unexplored by school media specialists. Two editing functions are frequently available on camcorders: audio dub and video insert.

Audio Dub

Audio dub means replacing old audio with new audio. Many camcorders facilitate this process. A microphone, mixer, or other audio component is connected to the camcorder's microphone jack or audio input jack, the audio-dub button is pressed, and the audio-dub process begins.

Video Insert

Video insert, also known as video dub, allows for the replacing of video without destroying the audio track. If you connect a VCR to the video inputs of the camcorder, video cutaways can be inserted during long interviews and narrations. This feature is also very important if the camcorder is to be used as a postproduction VCR.

Audio and Video Outputs

In the school setting, the ability to output the audio and video signals is a critical feature for your camcorder and should be considered a requirement for purchase. Easy access to these outputs is essential if the camcorder is to be used for playback or postproduction functions (see fig. 1.4). Audio and video outputs may be mounted

Figure 1.4 Camcorder outputs include (top to bottom) headphones, IEEE-1394, A/V, and S-video.

on the back or side panel of the camcorder or may require the use of an A/V line adapter included as a camcorder accessory. In either case, make sure that these outputs are available before you purchase your camcorder.

With the development of higher-quality camcorders available for reasonable prices, it's not unusual to see several different outputs on a camcorder. For example, the Panasonic MiniDV camcorder has the following outputs: composite audio/video (for VHS-quality signal), S-VHS, IEEE-1394 for direct digital connection to an editing computer, and a USB (universal serial bus) connection to access still images recorded on a separate multimedia card.

Some camcorders include audio and video inputs as well. Of course, the microphone jack is an audio input. And the IEEE-1394 jack is both an input and output for both audio and video. Be aware of the audio and video input/output capability of any camcorder that you plan to buy.

Ergonomics

Ergonomics refers to the camcorder's ease of use. Consider two questions. First, how does the camcorder feel while it is being used? A camcorder should fit comfortably in the hand or on the shoulder. The weight of the camcorder should be balanced so that it does not naturally pull forward, backward, or to one side during use. Make sure that the camcorder is comfortable for your students, too.

Second, how difficult is it to access the features mentioned in this chapter? The user should be able to access camcorder features and functions easily while videotaping. A feature that requires the operation of more than one or two buttons is practically useless in the field. Buttons should be clearly labeled and easily accessible.

The Camcorder Case

Another important feature of the camcorder is the case. If you plan on taking your camcorder outside the studio, you'll probably want to purchase a case or camera bag to put it in. Imagine a social studies teacher wants to take the camcorder on a class field trip to a historic landmark. Do you plan to just hand over the camcorder as is or perhaps use the cardboard box the camcorder arrived in? Of course not! You'll want (and the teacher will expect) a nice carrying case.

Some of the more-expensive camcorders come with their own carrying cases, but this is a rarely found added feature. Sometimes, a custom-made case is available for purchase, but the cost is excessive (especially when a sizable amount of money has just been spent for the camcorder!). Fortunately, there are several generic camcorder carrying bags on the market. Most discount chain stores and electronics dealers that sell camcorders also sell a collection of camcorder bags.

Over the years, we've seen a variety of valises—from carry-on luggage to padded toolboxes—serve as camcorder bags. A sturdy, well-insulated (well-padded) cooler can make a wonderful camcorder case! (See fig. 1.5.) Whether you're planning to spend the extra money for the custom case or buy a generic model, or even improvise a solution, make sure that you have some way to safely transport your camcorder to remote locations.

Paying attention to the preceding criteria will help you to find a good-quality camcorder that will provide many years of valuable, versatile service to your school video production program. But the camcorder is just one, albeit important, item of video production equipment. Read on to select the rest of your equipment.

Evaluating the Tripod

A tripod is a three-legged mounting device for the camera. A tripod provides a steady platform for the camcorder and relieves the videographer of any fatigue that comes from holding it. Tripods are essential for successful school-based television production. Prices for good-quality tripods from manufacturers like Davis-Sanford and Bogen begin at about $125. Because the tripod is a simple instrument, many upper-level consumer tripods available at retail stores can be used in schools. Follow the criteria listed here to select the best tripod for your camera.

Figure 1.5 A well-padded cooler can make a great inexpensive camcorder case.

Weight-Support Capacity

Read the tripod's manual to determine the maximum weight the tripod can support. Some cheaper tripods cannot support the weight of larger camcorders. Your camcorder's weight should appear in the camcorder operations manual. Make sure to add the weight of the battery.

Collapsed Size

A tripod is designed for remote shooting. Make sure your tripod collapses into a size that is manageable for your videographers. Ideally, a student should be able to carry both the camcorder and the tripod.

Height Range

Determine the highest and lowest camera positions that your tripod can achieve. These high and low angles are often desirable for dramatic effect, and the lower position may be necessary if small children are operating the camcorder.

Quick-Release Mounting System

A quick-release mounting system includes a plastic or metal plate that screws into the mounting hole of your camcorder. The quick-release plate with camcorder attached mounts onto the top of the tripod in one or two easy steps (see fig. 1.6). Most

Figure 1.6 Quick-release system for mounting a camcorder on a tripod

tripods have this system as a standard feature, but the quick-release functions vary greatly; some are easy to use and others are quite difficult. Practice mounting your camcorder on the tripod using the quick-release system.

Tripod Head

The tripod is divided into two parts: the head and the legs. The camcorder attaches to the head. The head also controls pans and tilts. First, make sure the tripod you are evaluating includes a panning/tilting head. Some tripods are à la carte—the legs and head are purchased separately. A tripod designed for a 35mm still camera may not include a panning/tilting head. Also, ask about a panning handle, which may or may not be included on the tripod head.

More-expensive tripods will have a fluid head. A thick, oily substance is sealed into the tripod head, which allows the user to achieve smooth pans and tilts. A non-fluid head requires more skill to execute smooth movements. A fluid tripod head may be worth the extra expense for your program.

Finally, experiment with the tripod head to determine how difficult it is to operate. Some tripods allow panning, tilting, and locking (securing the tripod in one position) by twisting a single screw or handle. Others are more complex.

Small Tripod Parts

Some tripods rely on screws or wing nuts to adjust leg length or move the tripod head. If these screws can be removed completely from the tripod, they will likely become lost. When possible, select a tripod that doesn't shed parts. Tripod replacement parts are expensive and may not be readily available in your area.

Leg Tips

Carefully evaluate the tips at the end of the tripod legs. Tripod leg tips should keep the tripod securely in place. Rubber leg tips work best; plastic leg tips can be quite slick. Some tripod leg tips recede to reveal short metal spikes, which videographers find quite useful for using outside in the grass. Don't forget to check your tripod where the rubber meets the road.

Mini-Tripods

Several years ago, a high-quality camcorder meant a big, heavy camcorder. Now, camcorders that produce broadcast-quality signals can fit in the palm of the hand. Do you really need large professional tripods? Not always. Several companies

Figure 1.7 A mini-tripod designed for table-top use with a small digital camera or camcorder

make and sell mini-tripods for smaller camcorders (see fig. 1.7). The cost is minimal—usually around $10—and they can be purchased at discount stores. These tripods can sit on a desktop during interviews, or on a bleacher during a ball game. As with all tripods, make sure you test the mini-tripod's ability to hold your camcorder securely.

Evaluating the Monopod

A monopod is a single-legged camera support. Obviously, the monopod can't defy gravity; the videographer still has to steady the shot. However, the monopod bears the weight of the camcorder, which can be an important task during longer shoots. A good-quality monopod sells for about $75. This can be a wise investment if you own a heavy camcorder and typically videotape at sporting events and pep rallies.

Evaluating the Dolly

A dolly is a set of wheels or casters mounted to a frame that attaches to the legs of the tripod. Using a dolly with a tripod allows new camera movements and offers a degree of portability to the tripod-mounted camcorder. As with the tripod, determine the weight rating of the dolly. Most dollies are made for the industrial/professional market and will have no problem supporting your camcorder.

Carefully examine the dolly's wheels. Are they large rubber wheels or sliding metal casters? The larger and softer the wheel, the more fluid the dolly's movement as it rolls across the floor. Remember, part of the dolly's function is to roll while the camcorder is making videotape. A bumpy dolly is really no better than having no dolly at all. Also, examine the brakes on the wheels. The user must be able to independently lock down each wheel or caster on the dolly. Brakes can vary from an actual wheel-contact brake to a metal rod that is depressed to lift the wheel from the floor. Examine how the lock-down affects the sturdiness of the dolly. Many otherwise-steady dollies become unstable when the brakes are applied.

Make sure that the dolly is adjustable to fit varying tripod leg widths. Diverse videotaping situations require higher or lower camera positioning. Fully extended tripod legs atop a small dolly create an unstable, top-heavy platform for the camcorder.

Examine how the dolly is attached to the tripod. This can vary from a strip of rubber, which quickly but tenuously connects the two, to a nut-and-bolt assembly, which is quite secure but time consuming. Consider your videotaping situations and determine your need for security and convenience.

Digital Video, IEEE-1394, and Your School TV Studio

Digital video is making a big impact on the school video market. Earlier in this chapter, we discussed the digital camcorder formats—MiniDV and DV8mm—and their ability to output a digital video signal via an industry-standard connection called IEEE-1394 (also known as FireWire® and i.LINK®). One of the first applications for IEEE-1394 was connecting the digital camcorder to a computer to input video footage to be edited on the computer. The IEEE-1394 connection is required to transfer the excellent image quality—at least 480 lines of resolution—to the computer. To capture that high-quality signal, the latest models of other video production tools also include IEEE-1394 connections. The character generators, video mixers, and VCRs discussed in the following paragraphs can now be purchased with IEEE-1394 inputs and outputs. IEEE-1394 cable can totally replace the S-VHS and composite video cable you are now using. The result is outstanding picture clarity. The price, for now, is a bit high. Expect to pay almost twice the amount for character generators, video mixers, and VCRs that will send and receive the IEEE-1394 signal. But, as with all electronic items, that price should drop over the next few years. If you are reading this book because you are building a school TV studio from scratch (perhaps at a new school), we strongly encourage you to buy video production components that facilitate IEEE-1394 connections. When you see the image quality, you'll be glad you did!

Evaluating the Videocassette Recorder

Most VCRs in schools are used to play prerecorded educational programs. These VCRs may be located in classrooms or placed on A/V carts for circulation by the library media center. A high-quality consumer model will probably suffice for this application. However, most schools involved in video production will find an industrial/professional VCR to be a valuable tool.

Many of the features that once appeared only on industrial/professional VCRs—four-head recording and playback, a jog/shuttle wheel—are now found on many models designed for the home market. A good industrial/professional VCR will cost approximately $1,200. However, price alone cannot determine the usefulness of the VCR in the production setting. Many high-end, feature-packed VCRs cost hundreds of dollars but are virtually useless in video production. Let's examine some important features of VCRs that will help you produce outstanding video programs.

Format

Industrial/professional VCRs record in a high-quality format, such as S-VHS or MiniDV. Dual-deck VCRs are also emerging, as more schools begin to use a combination of video formats. For example, JVC makes a VCR that has two videocassette slots—one for MiniDV and the other for VHS/S-VHS tapes. Can you imagine the application? A student shooting an interview or a class project using a MiniDV camcorder can easily dub the footage onto VHS videotape for viewing at home or in the classroom. And the dual deck could also be used as a source deck in a school news show configuration, playing videotapes in the MiniDV, S-VHS, and VHS formats. List price for a dual deck is currently around $1,300 (with a "street price" of about $1,000). Expect those prices to drop over the years, well into the affordability range of schools serious about TV production.

Jog/Shuttle Wheel

A jog/shuttle wheel is a control that allows the user to cue videotape accurately and obtain a clear still pause. A jog/shuttle wheel is a dial within a dial and is usually activated by pressing a button near the wheel. Make sure that your purchase includes this feature.

Audio and Video Inputs and Outputs

A true industrial/professional VCR will have at least two audio and video inputs and outputs to allow you to connect several pieces of equipment to the VCR at the same time and access that equipment with the flip of a switch. Often, a consumer or classroom VCR uses only one output—the connection to the TV—and no inputs. A videotape is simply played in the VCR. But in the production setting, other equipment must be connected to the VCR. Here's an example. Your industrial/professional VCR is the segment VCR for your school news show. Students record and edit interviews and reports around school, and those segments are included in your school news program. The output of this VCR must go to the video mixer so that the segments can be rolled in to the news show. But another output must be sent to a TV/monitor so the VCR operator can see the videotape and cue it to the beginning of the segment. In this application, at least two outputs are needed. The audio follows the same path—one output to the recording VCR and another output to the TV/monitor.

Number of Heads

The four-head configuration is standard on industrial/professional VCRs. The head configuration may vary by manufacturer, but the presence of four heads dedicates one head to the clear still/pause necessary for precise cueing and simple editing (audio dubbing and video inserting).

Audio-Dub Feature

An industrial/professional VCR used in schools should be able to perform the task of audio dubbing (putting new audio over old video). Audio dubbing is the first step in teaching (and learning) postproduction skills. Students can videotape scenes around school, return to the classroom to write a script, and then audio dub their script and music onto their footage. Make sure that your VCR facilitates this important process.

Video Insert

Just as an audio dub replaces the audio with new audio, the video insert replaces the existing video with new video. Long interviews can include video cutaways while maintaining the original audio.

Microphone Jack

Although it is not included in all industrial/professional VCRs, look for a microphone jack on the front control panel. The ability to quickly plug in a microphone and perform a voice-only audio dub may be an often-used feature in your production program.

Headphone Jack

Some, but not all, industrial/professional VCRs have a headphone jack. Although not critical to every production situation, this feature may prove useful during news show production, as the producer monitors the audio signal being recorded.

Adjustable Audio-Recording Levels

Audio-recording controls allow the editor to boost or decrease sounds being recorded and perform simple fade-ins and fade-outs. Look for dials or fader bars on the control panels of industrial/professional VCRs.

Hi-Fi/Stereo Audio Recording

Most industrial/professional VCRs can record audio in hi-fi and stereo modes. Audio recorded on S-VHS, Hi-8mm and the digital formats using these settings rival compact disc audio. This extra feature can add a touch of class to your special productions.

Time-Base Corrector

Although not a required function, many industrial/professional VCRs have a built-in time-base corrector (TBC). A TBC converts the naturally unstable and weak signal generated by a VCR into strong, solid video signal. Video signal that looks great on a TV/monitor may suffer when connected to a video mixer. If you plan to integrate the VCR into a system that includes upper-level industrial/professional or broadcast-quality video components, the TBC may represent good value. However, the advent of digital video makes TBC unnecessary in many video situations. Consult with your vendor to determine if TBC is necessary.

The Manual

As you can see, an industrial/professional VCR represents a substantial investment not only of school funds but also of time. Spending $1,000 for a VCR and using only the "play" and "record" buttons is a real waste of money and educational opportunity. A thorough, easy-to-read, illustrated manual is essential. Look at the manual *before* you decide to buy the VCR. Unless the salesperson agrees to follow you home and live at the school, the manual will be your guide to accessing all your VCR's features.

Alternatives to the Industrial/Professional VCR

At this point you may be thinking, "Do I really need to spend $1,000 for a VCR? A regular VCR that I can buy for one-tenth that cost records just fine. We're an elementary school recording on VHS. And we have so many other needs." In this case, the industrial/professional VCR takes a lower priority. Fortunately, many consumer-level VCRs are now incorporating many of these features. For example, JVC makes a VCR that, for about $250, will audio dub, video insert, and record on S-VHS. True, there's no headphone jack or microphone jack, but there is a jog/shuttle wheel, and the picture looks great.

As you continue in school video production, you will eventually see the need for an industrial/professional VCR for your school. It is not unusual for a true industrial/professional VCR to provide service for 10 years or more. Although other alternatives are available, consider planning to buy one of these work-horses eventually.

Carefully examine your prospective purchase to determine if it meets your production needs. We can relate several stories of colleagues who spent hundreds of dollars on high-quality VCRs, only to find out that the machines could not audio dub, video insert, or record in an advanced format. Spend your money wisely, and buy not only for the present but also for the future of your program.

Evaluating the Video Mixer

A video mixer enables the user to select and combine several different video sources. The simplest video-mixer functions allow the user to press a button to select input #1 (a camcorder) and then press a different button to select input #2 (perhaps a screen of graphics), and maybe even a third button to select input #3 (perhaps a videotaped segment). The output is sent to a VCR for recording.

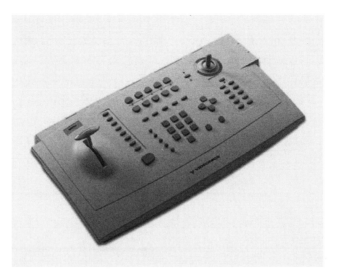

Figure 1.8 Videonics MX-Pro Digital Video Mixer.
Picture courtesy of Focus Enhancements.

Of course, most video mixers are much more complex and feature laden. You can expect a video mixer in the $1,200 price range to provide up to four inputs, more than 100 transitions, and digital effects such as picture-in-picture and chroma key (see fig. 1.8).

Before continuing, let's make sure we distinguish between a true video mixer and a simple video selection switch. With home video equipment available and relatively inexpensive, it is not unusual for a living room system to include a VCR, a DVD player, a cable TV input, and even a digital satellite receiver—all going to a single television. Consumers usually buy a video selection switch to choose between these sources. Although the concept of video mixing is there—one button pushed yields a new input—the video switch does not offer the signal synchronization necessary for seamless video mixing. In other words, the picture will jump every time a switch is made. This jump is not important to the home viewer who is simply selecting another video source. But, of course, the jump is not acceptable in a production setting. Make sure that you're buying a true video production mixer—not just a glorified living-room switch.

Let's take a look at some of the evaluative criteria.

Video Inputs

One of the most important criteria for evaluating a video mixer is the number of video inputs that the device allows. In other words, how many sources can be plugged in to the video mixer? To be used as a primary mixer in schools, the video mixer should accommodate at least four inputs: two video cameras, graphics, and a source VCR. Video mixers with fewer than four inputs will severely limit your production power, forcing you to make decisions that affect quality or to creatively "rig" your equipment to compensate for the mixer's inadequacies. Even if you don't own a character generator, and you've never added video from a source VCR to your news program, still look for at least four inputs. As you gain experience and add more equipment to your television studio, your four-input video mixer will continue to provide valuable service. Prices for four-input video mixers begin at about $1,200 and continue upward as units become more powerful and offer more inputs.

Another criterion for video inputs is the format of those inputs, which relates directly to picture quality. It doesn't matter how high the quality of the source video signal is if the video mixer's video inputs aren't capable of relaying and processing that signal. Advanced-format camcorders (S-VHS, Hi8mm, and digital) usually offer a variety of outputs. Digital models also have IEEE-1394 digital video outputs. A video mixer with only composite (regular video) inputs is not taking full advantage of your camcorder's capabilities and will produce a signal no better than VHS quality. A video mixer for the school setting will have at least one higher-quality format available for input, such as S-VHS, or IEEE-1394. Video mixers with only composite inputs are not capable of superior picture processing. The following factors also affect picture quality.

Lines of Resolution

Make sure that your video mixer produces enough lines of resolution to conform with your other equipment. Check the owner's manual to determine the number of resolution lines that the video mixer produces. (A video mixer's lines of resolution are often referred to as *passing lines* because the video mixer is passing the lines from the video sources to the recording VCR or broadcast system. A question to a vendor may be worded, "How many lines will it pass?") Consider the following situation. A school has a simple studio configuration. The outputs of two S-VHS camcorders are connected to the inputs of the video mixer. The output of a character generator is connected to the third input, and a source VCR (used for rolling in campus interviews) is connected to the fourth input. Each camcorder is capable of producing 400 lines of resolution. The character generator produces a broadcast-quality signal, and the interview was recorded in S-VHS, which also consists of 400 lines of resolution. To maintain the excellent quality of the video signal for the viewing audience, the video mixer must also be able to pass 400 lines of resolution. A lower-quality video mixer may pass only 200 lines, which results in a loss of resolution, brightness, and color for the viewer. Don't let the video mixer be the weak link in your production chain.

Preview Capability

The student operating the video mixer (the technical director) must be able to see each source before it is selected. In other words, the technical director should see camera 2 on a preview monitor before deciding to switch from camera 1 to camera 2. Generally, the video mixer provides this ability with preview-monitor outputs. Some video mixers require a separate preview monitor for each video input—one for camera 1, one for camera 2, one for the character generator, and one for the source VCR that contains the interview segment. (This explains the mountain of monitors in sophisticated production studios.) The outputs to the monitors are usually located near the inputs on the back of the video mixer. Other video mixers require only one preview monitor. In these systems, the technical director can select the preview signal by pressing the corresponding button on the video mixer. Although this setup saves on the number of monitors needed by the production system, it adds an extra task for the technical director and becomes quite confusing in production systems. Another type of preview output puts all four preview images on a single screen, combining the total-vision option of the multimonitor configuration with the economy of the single-monitor mixers. Although the picture quality of this four-in-one preview monitor is somewhat inferior to its full-screen counterparts, it is generally acceptable for entry-level school-production needs.

Line Outputs

The video mixer processes the video inputs so that the resulting program can be viewed by an audience or recorded for later use. The line output of the video mixer must be connected to the input of the broadcast modulator for distribution or to a VCR for recording. Some video mixers have only one line output, whereas others have two or three. One line output usually suffices for broadcast or recording, but a second output may be desirable for more-advanced situations.

Transition Capabilities

The primary reason most schools buy a video mixer is to improve the "look" of their shows. Unsophisticated, single-source programs can be produced with a single camcorder. You buy a video mixer if you want to add another camera, graphics, and a source VCR. You also buy a video mixer if you want to perform professional transitions from one source to another. Most video mixers accommodate this desire for increased visual sophistication by offering the following effects.

Background Colors

Most video mixers allow you to select from several background colors instead of just the standard fade to black.

Transitions

A variety of transitions are available on most video mixers. Simple transitions include fades (from video to a background color) and dissolves (fading one video source into another). Wipes are often popular with students. New video sources can appear to fly in, push the old source off the screen, or bounce in from one corner. As computer technology continues to merge with video production, the number of wipe patterns grows.

Key Features

Two popular key features are often included with video mixers: chroma key and luminance key. Chroma key removes one color from a video signal and replaces it with a second video signal. The most common example of chroma key is seen on the local news each evening, as the weather anchor walks in front of the weather map. The anchor is really standing in front of a blue or green screen, while a VCR or graphics computer provides the weather map. Luminance key operates on the same principal but uses brightness, not color, as the signal that is substituted. The darkest or lightest part may be selected for substitution. Students can usually think of creative applications for key functions.

When evaluating video mixers, remember that transition capabilities are only part of the equation. Don't let fancy wipes and chroma key capabilities distract you from signal quality and the number of video inputs that the video mixer provides.

The Learning Curve

Make sure that your students can learn to operate the video mixer that you are evaluating. Take a student to a product demonstration or ask the vendor to demonstrate your potential purchase to your students. A video mixer that is too confusing to operate or has a very steep learning curve may not be useful in the educational setting, where the task of teaching is at least as important as the measure of competence.

The video mixer represents a substantial purchase for a school video production program. This single piece of equipment will process most of the programming viewed by your audience. For this reason, the video mixer is definitely a "try it before you buy it" item. Make sure that your current equipment and the equipment that you plan to buy in the future is compatible with the video mixer. Be sure that your students can learn to operate the equipment. And finally, make sure that the bells and whistles available on many video mixers do not distract you from the consideration of picture quality.

Evaluating the Television and Video Monitor

Students who are working on video production programs need to see the video that they are creating. And for this, you need to provide monitors. Although evaluating a monitor may not be as complex as evaluating a video mixer or camcorder, you should look for several important features.

First, let's distinguish between a monitor and a television. A video monitor is a picture tube (cathode-ray tube) that provides a video image. This image may be in color or monochrome (black and white). A monitor usually has basic picture controls, such as vertical, horizontal, brightness, and contrast. If you add an RF (radio frequency) tuner and an audio speaker to that monitor, you have a television. In other words:

video monitor + RF tuner + audio speaker = television

The RF tuner receives the television signals either through broadcast (using an antenna) or through a cable TV system or satellite-dish system. The RF signal contains both the audio and video signals. The video is sent to the picture tube for display, and the audio is sent to the speaker. By adjusting the tuner, the viewer can select from several different channels.

Is it correct to use the terms *television* and *monitor* as synonyms? No. As noted, a video monitor is only part of the television set. In addition to the extra components that distinguish a television from a monitor, there is another basic difference. Monitors process video signal, and televisions process RF signal. It is important to know the difference between these two types of signals.

There are four major differences between video signal and RF signal:

Power. The RF signal is much more powerful than the video signal. An RF signal can travel through cable all the way across the school. A video signal starts to lose strength after 30 or 40 feet.

Cable requirements. The RF signal is so powerful that it requires heavy-duty, insulated cable, commonly referred to as coaxial cable. The video signal can travel through ordinary shielded cable like that used to connect stereo components.

Content. The RF signal contains both the audio and video portions of the program. The video signal contains only the video portion.

Point of origin. The RF signal is produced by transmitters at television stations; it can also be modulated by VCRs and satellite-dish systems. The video signal is produced by video cameras and other video sources, such as character generators, video mixers, videodisc players, computers, and video games.

Again, the monitor requires a video signal, and the television requires an RF signal. Monitors cannot process RF signal, and televisions cannot process video signal. Here's an example. One media specialist was building a production system piece by piece. He had saved enough money to buy a video mixer and had only $100 to buy the two monitors that the video mixer required. He went to a local discount store and purchased two 9-inch black-and-white TVs for $49 each. Did the TVs work as monitors? No. The TVs require RF signal, and the video mixer was providing video signal. Fortunately, a TV can perform the duties of a video monitor if an RF modulator (about $25) is connected. This modulator converts the video signal to RF signal that the television can process (usually on channel 3). So, did the purchase of the two black-and-white TVs represent value to the media specialist? No. Even with the addition of two RF modulators, the resulting signal was black and white, and the monitors were probably of less quality than any other item in his system. In this case, as in most others, it would have been better to spend more money and buy the appropriate equipment.

Apart from the signal-processing factor, TVs and monitors differ in price and picture quality. Even though they contain fewer components than TVs, monitors are generally more expensive—about $250 for a 13-inch color video monitor, compared to about $80 for a 13-inch color TV. This is because monitors usually provide better picture quality. This increased quality is probably the result of the intended use of monitors. Whereas a TV is designed to be watched across a living room, a monitor must meet the strict resolution demands of up-close viewing because the production technician is only a couple of feet from the monitor.

Most television manufacturers market combination TV/monitors. These special sets, available at appliance stores, have two sets of inputs in the back: the regular RF input and inputs for video and audio signals. The picture quality may not be quite monitor level, but the price is attractive. These combination units sell for about $100 for the 13-inch model, which is appropriate for school use. The TV/monitor combination represents a wise purchase for schools that are involved in limited television production.

After you have made the choice—monitors or TV/monitor combinations—you still need to consider a few other criteria.

Number of Inputs

Many monitors have two or more video inputs, accessed by A-B buttons on the front panel, which allow two video sources to share the same monitor. TV/monitor combinations generally have only one video-signal input. This input is usually accessed by tuning the television one notch below channel 2, to a channel marked "A/V in."

Types of Input Jacks

Most video monitors feature BNC input jacks for composite video input. This twist-lock connector is common on industrial/professional equipment and is valued because of its security. A BNC connection will not become accidentally unplugged. Lower-priced monitors and most TV/monitor combinations feature RCA (phono) input jacks, which are much less secure.

Higher-quality monitors also have S-VHS inputs. This feature allows for connection of higher-quality video component and yields a better-quality image.

Ease of Control Adjustment

If monitor brightness, contrast, or color must be adjusted, you should be able to do it quickly and efficiently. The easiest controls are the manual knobs mounted on the front of the monitor. However, as the years pass, fewer and fewer monitors offer manual knobs. Most monitors and TV/monitor combinations instead have electronic adjustments that must be accessed using an on-screen menu and the "+" and "–" buttons. Although this adjustment may have high-tech appeal, it is neither quick nor convenient.

Housing

Because video monitors are built for the industrial/professional market, they usually feature metal or hard-plastic housings. This strong material may help if the equipment is dropped. Less-expensive monitors and TV/monitor combinations may have thinner plastic housings.

Careful monitor selection may not seem as critical as selection of other equipment, but it is not to be overlooked. A correct TV/monitor purchase can make previewing and viewing activities easier, allowing you to concentrate on the more technical and creative aspects of television production.

Evaluating the Character Generator

A character generator is a video component that allows the typing of words and simple graphics onto the TV screen (see fig. 1.9). Character generators are sometimes called video titlers or video typewriters. Most schools that engage in regular production will want to own a character generator. Adding simple graphics gives a program a professional touch and increases its content. For example, announcements about club activities, PTA meetings, and sporting events can be enhanced with typed information.

Character generators have different capabilities and are available at very different prices. Models with limited features designed primarily for hobbyists can cost less than $300. High-end industrial/professional character generators cost thousands of dollars. By using the following descriptors as guidelines, you should be able to purchase a model that is packed with many features yet not too expensive.

Fonts and Character Quality

Because a character generator is meant to create high-quality graphics and text, you should carefully examine the letters and symbols created by each character generator that you evaluate. Create a page of graphics and stand across the room to read the graphics on the TV. If the graphics are difficult for you to read, they will probably be equally difficult for your classroom viewers. Many character generators

Figure 1.9 Videonics Titlemaker 3000. Picture courtesy of Focus Enhancements.

have a demonstration program that will display the machine's capabilities. Also, investigate the different fonts (type styles) that can be created on the character generator. Years ago, the best that one could hope for in an industrial/professional character generator was a single font that could be made either large or small. Now, some character generators in the $500 price range have 50 or more fonts that can be resized for maximum effect.

Background Colors

A character generator should be able to produce at least two types of backgrounds: a single solid color and the blank background, which allows video to be played through the character generator. Most character generators have at least eight solid background colors. The blank background choice allows the user to superimpose a graphic over another video source, like a camcorder or videotaped footage. The video source is connected to the input of the character generator. The graphics message is typed, and the blank background is selected. The graphic is then superimposed over the video source. The most common application of this feature is the name of your news anchor superimposed over the anchor's close-up.

Some character-generator companies have added background patterns to their equipment. Although this is not a necessary feature, it does liven up ordinary graphic messages. A program with several graphics pages could benefit from these extra background choices.

Character Colors

Just as a number of background colors should be available, the same colors should also be available for the letters. Many character generators can also add shadows and borders to their character-generator letters. Shadows and borders help the letters stand out from the background, making the graphics page easier to read.

Character Movements and Transitions

Look for examples of character movements and screen transitions as you evaluate character generators. A character generator should be able to scroll graphics (bottom to top, like movie credits) and crawl graphics (right to left, like a special weather bulletin). Some character generators also allow the user to fade in and out of graphics pages and perform other transitions described earlier in the "Video Mixer" section. Don't be satisfied with simple screen-on/screen-off character-generator functions.

Memory

Because it is really a single-function computer, a character generator will have computer memory. This memory takes two forms: the number of pages that can be stored and changed in working memory while the character generator is on and the character generator's ability to save pages when the machine is turned off.

Pages in Working Memory

Some character generators will offer only 10 or 12 blank pages on which you can create your graphics. This may not be a problem if most of your programs are short and simple. But more-complex programs may require more graphics pages. Be very skeptical of purchasing a character generator that allows access to only a few pages during one working session.

Long-Term Page Storage

When your character generator is turned off or unplugged, is all of your information erased? Most modern character generators feature some type of long-term memory storage. In some systems, the storage is automatic; as soon as a page is created, it is saved until the user erases it. This feature is especially useful in schools, where equipment is frequently unplugged or turned off by accident. The character generator uses a long-term (five-year) battery to save these pages.

Other systems save the pages on a computer floppy diskette or a computer hard drive. In these systems, the pages are not stored automatically; they must be saved or updated each time the user completes composition. Even though this method adds an extra step to the process, it is advantageous in schools where many students will be using the character generator. Students can save their graphics pages on their own diskettes or on a designated section of the hard drive. This practice reduces the chance that one student will inadvertently erase another student's graphics pages.

Make sure that your character generator can store many pages of graphics when the machine is without power. This is an invaluable feature for school-based production.

Passing Lines of Resolution

Earlier in this chapter, we referred to the number of passing lines of resolution that a video mixer can handle. The emphasis there was to make sure that your video mixer can pass just as many lines as your camcorders and VCRs can produce and record. The same point can be made for the character generator, especially if you plan to use the character generator's blank background page to superimpose graphics over another video source. Your character generator should be able to accommodate at least 240 lines of resolution if you are working with an entry-level format like VHS or at least 400 lines if you are working with an advanced format like S-VHS. If you use a character generator that can pass an acceptable number of lines of resolution, your video picture quality will not suffer just because you decide to superimpose graphics.

Types of Inputs and Outputs

Closely related to passing lines of resolution is the type of input and output jacks available on the character generator. Look for S-VHS inputs and outputs, especially if you are already using that format for production and recording. Some higher-end character generators offer IEEE-1394 inputs and outputs, allowing the character generator to pass a digital-quality signal and create graphics with outstanding picture quality.

Ease of Operation

As you can gather by reading the previous sections, character generators can get quite complex. As educators, we must select equipment that can be used for teaching, as well as production. Most (if not all) of your students should be able to learn to use your character generator in a reasonable amount of time. Do not accept only one or two of your brightest students learning to use the character generator. The model that you select should allow the user to create a graphics page in a few minutes. Whether you are working at the elementary, middle, or high school level, make sure that your character generator has a steady and appropriate learning curve for all of your students.

Using Computers as Character Generators

Long before complex character generators were affordable to schools, teachers and media specialists used computer programs such as Slide Shop, VCR Companion, and even the preview output of The Print Shop to create computer graphics for video productions. Now, screens from PowerPoint and HyperStudio are making their way into school news shows, via the computer's video output jack. This topic is fully addressed in chapter 5, "Creating Your Video Production Studio." In that chapter, look for details on how to configure your computer to contribute graphics to your news show. As you read chapter 5, you can decide for yourself whether you should use a computer or a character generator to create graphics, or—as many schools are doing—whether you should use both! Some schools, for example, are using character generators to create simple graphics like birthday lists and lunch menus while using computer graphics programs and a digital camera to feature the "Student of the Week" and art show winners. Ultimately, the choice is up to the media production teacher. That decision may hinge on the availability of a $500 character generator versus a $1,200 computer. Whatever you decide, don't let your familiarity with computers be an excuse for not educating yourself about stand-alone character generators.

Evaluating video production equipment for use in the school setting requires a good information base about the equipment and a firm grasp of the school's actual video production needs. By applying the criteria discussed in this chapter, you can be well on your way to building a video production program that will be a valuable asset to your school.

Helpful Internet Links

Professional Resources

SCHOOLTV.com (The authors' Web site features helpful information to educators working with television production.): http://www.schooltv.com

Video Equipment

Bogen Manfrotto (Tripods): http://www.bogenphoto.com

Davis-Sanford (Tripods): http://www.tiffen.com/tripod_page.htm

Focus Enhancements (Video mixers, character generators; company that owns Videonics): http://www.focusinfo.com

JVC (Camcorders, VCRs): http://www.jvc.com

Panasonic (Camcorders, VCRs): http://www.panasonic.com

Sony Electronics (Camcorders, VCRs): http://www.sonystyle.com

Videonics (brand from Focus Enhancements; Video mixers, character generators, and more): http://www.videonics.com/products/productsv.html

Chapter 2

~~~~~~

Audio Equipment
DESCRIPTION AND SELECTION CRITERIA

I s audio as important as video? You bet it is. Can you imagine watching a school news show, an orientation tape, or a student project without sound? In fact, most of the television that we watch on a daily basis would be meaningless without good audio. Some of the highest-paid television professionals produce or record the audio aspect of the broadcast.

Then why is audio so often overlooked and underemphasized at the school level? Perhaps it all began when the camcorder manufacturers decided to mount microphones on the front of all of their products. Did we think that was enough to record interviews and musical performances? Or perhaps the whiz-bang impact of video made us forget about the importance of music in our productions. Whatever the reason, let's get back to the basics and give audio its due respect. A great deal of technology has been dedicated to developing and improving the tools that record great-sounding audio. Learning about these tools and learning how to select them can only improve your school's television production program. In this chapter, we'll examine four areas of audio: microphones, wireless microphone systems, audio mixers, and audio sources. Then, we'll take a careful look at the legal use of music in your school television production program.

Evaluating Microphones

Correct selection of microphones depends not only on the merit of individual models but also on intended use. A high-quality microphone that performs perfectly in one setting may be completely useless in another. For this reason, first select the right *type* of microphone and then look at evaluative criteria that apply to all microphones.

Selecting the Right Type of Microphone

All microphones are *not* created equal, nor were they meant to be. Some microphones are designed for loud pep rallies, whereas others are best suited for quiet piano solos. Microphones can be designed for group or individual recordings. And some microphones just won't work at all with certain audio mixers or camcorders. The following paragraphs explore some basic features that set microphones apart.

Microphone Elements

The element is the part of a microphone that gathers the sound of the real world and converts it into electrical audio signal that can be processed by audio mixers and camcorders. There are two types of elements used by microphones found in most schools: the dynamic element and the condenser element. Each element has distinctive characteristics that make it useful in particular situations.

The dynamic element is very good with moderate-to-loud sounds but only moderately successful with soft sounds. This makes a dynamic microphone perfect for the news report or school pep rally but probably not for the flute solo. Dynamic microphones handle physical shock reasonably well—one or two drops will likely not destroy the microphone. Dynamic microphones are the least expensive, well within the scope of many schools. They range in price from $25 to $100.

The condenser element is perfect for recording high-quality moderate-to-soft sounds. Condenser microphones are often used to record voice, music, and special news reports. Using a condenser microphone requires care because the condenser element is more fragile than its dynamic counterpart. Condenser microphones are also more expensive, beginning at about $40 and proceeding up to the very expensive microphones used in recording studios. Unlike microphones that use the dynamic element, condenser microphones require a power source. That power source may be a battery installed in the microphone handle or in a separate battery pack. Other condenser microphones require phantom power, which is power that must be provided by the audio mixer.

Microphone Directionality

Microphones also differ in the direction from which they pick up sounds (see fig. 2.1). Some microphones pick up sounds from the entire physical environment—front, back, and all sides. These are called omnidirectional. Other microphones pick up most of their sounds from the front or top of the microphone and very little from the sides or back. These are called unidirectional. They are also referred to as cardioid microphones because a diagram of the directional pattern is heart shaped. Some microphones have a stronger directional pattern. These may be called super-, hyper-, or ultra-cardioid microphones. These highly directional mi-

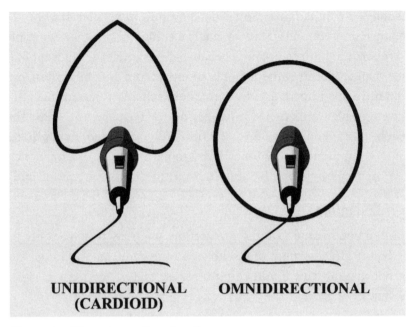

UNIDIRECTIONAL   OMNIDIRECTIONAL
(CARDIOID)

Figure 2.1 Microphone directionality

crophones can be used to record specific sources from a great distance or to block out unwanted sounds in a noisy environment (such as a rock concert or airport where an interview is being recorded).

Microphone Impedance

Impedance is resistance to signal flow. As the microphone signal travels down the microphone cord into the audio mixer or camcorder, it resists the flow and tries to "escape" the cord. Microphones create a high-impedance signal or a low-impedance signal, depending on their design. High impedance (also known as Hi-Z or unbalanced) is used in most consumer and industrial/professional microphones. The quality of the high-impedance signal is not quite as good as the low-impedance signal, and high-impedance signal can only run in microphone cable lengths of about 30 or 40 feet. After that distance, it begins to fade and deteriorate.

Low impedance (lo-Z, balanced) is used in broadcast and upper-level industrial/professional productions. The low-impedance signal produces somewhat better sound quality and can travel through hundreds of feet of cable. For this reason, low-impedance systems are usually installed in concert halls and large television production studios.

Microphone and input impedance must match, so determine the impedance rating (high or low) of your audio mixer and camcorder. Almost all camcorders used in school are high impedance and require a high-impedance microphone. Lower-level audio mixers are usually high impedance, whereas more expensive audio mixers are usually low impedance. Some newer audio mixers accept both high- and low-impedance microphones. Many schools use high-impedance microphones for their field reporting (interviews, etc.) because their camcorders accept only a high-impedance signal. Those same schools often feature full television production studios that use a low-impedance system. These schools must carefully select a variety of low- and high-impedance microphones. Make sure you know the impedance of each microphone in your collection and the impedance requirement of each item of equipment that will use a microphone signal. If impedance doesn't match, the microphone won't be able to "talk" to the camcorder or audio mixer.

Building a Collection

At this point, if you're new to audio production, you may be a bit confused. Given the three factors already mentioned, how can the right microphone be selected? It's really not that difficult if you combine these factors to create all possible microphone types:

> Dynamic, omnidirectional, high impedance
> Dynamic, omnidirectional, low impedance
> Dynamic, unidirectional, high impedance
> Dynamic, unidirectional, low impedance
> Condenser, omnidirectional, high impedance
> Condenser, omnidirectional, low impedance
> Condenser, unidirectional, high impedance
> Condenser, unidirectional, low impedance

Using what you've learned, try to imagine the correct use for each microphone. For example, the dynamic, unidirectional, high-impedance microphone would be used when a reporter conducts an interview using a camcorder that requires a high-impedance microphone. A condenser, omnidirectional, low-impedance microphone could be used to record a string quartet in a concert hall. Have your students imagine these situations as a class exercise.

So which microphone should you buy? It is important to build a *collection* of microphones based on your previous and anticipated needs. Examine your recording situations, and buy microphones as funding becomes available. The best microphone wish list is the list created by you and your students.

Microphone Format

Selecting the correct microphone format is also an important consideration for collecting good sound. The paragraphs that follow look at five microphone formats: handheld, lavaliere, shotgun, pressure zone (PZM), and surface mount. Wireless microphones deserve special consideration; they are discussed at length later in this chapter.

Handheld Microphone

The handheld microphone, as the name indicates, is held by the talent or mounted on a microphone stand (see fig. 2.2). Handheld microphones are available in every configuration imaginable—high and low impedance, omni- and unidirectional, dynamic and condenser. Handheld microphones are often the least expensive, with prices beginning at about $20.

Lavaliere Microphone

The lavaliere microphone is often called a tie-pin microphone because the talent affixes the microphone to his or her clothing with a tie-tack pin or alligator clip (see fig. 2.3). Lavaliere microphones are almost always condenser microphones, and because of the way they are positioned on the body, they are almost always omnidirectional. Using lavaliere microphones on your news show gives your anchors a professional look and also frees your reporter's hands to manipulate objects.

Shotgun Microphone

The shotgun microphone is a *highly* directional microphone (see fig. 2.4). It can be used to capture sound from a small area at a great distance. A person using a shotgun microphone can capture a conversation from across a noisy room. There are other uses for a shotgun microphone as well. Students creating dramatic videos often use a shotgun microphone on a boom (a pole) to capture dialogue while keeping the microphone out of the shot. Reporters in noisy surroundings (such as an

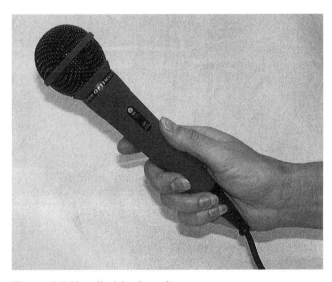

Figure 2.2 Handheld microphone

Figure 2.3 Lavaliere microphone

Figure 2.4 Shotgun microphone

airport or a gymnasium during a basketball game) use shotgun microphones to eliminate unwanted environmental sounds during interviews.

Because shotgun microphones are so directional, someone associated with the production—the audio technician, the talent, or the producer—wears headphones to make sure the shotgun microphone is pointed in precisely the right direction. A variance of only a few degrees can result in capturing the wrong sound or no sound at all.

Shotgun microphones are, of course, unidirectional. Some shotgun microphones even have adjustable directionalities, controlled by a three-way on-off switch (off-unidirectional-shotgun). Shotgun microphones are usually condenser and available in both high and low impedance. Expect to spend at least $65 for an entry-level shotgun microphone. The shotgun microphones used by professionals are more sensitive and therefore more expensive. (Note: When evaluating a shotgun microphone, make sure that the microphone actually has an extremely directional pick-up pattern. Some microphones look like shotgun microphones but are really just regular unidirectional microphones in the shape of a shotgun microphone.)

Pressure Zone Microphone (PZM)

A pressure zone microphone (PZM) is a flat microphone that resembles a fly swatter without the handle! The PZM lies flat on a table (or any other flat surface), and the entire surface becomes a conductor for the sound (see fig. 2.5). This is a great microphone for recording group discussions. It is also a great hidden microphone for dramatic or fictional videos. Most PZMs are condenser microphones. Expect to pay about $70 for an entry-level PZM.

Surface-Mount Microphone

Have you ever needed to place a microphone on a tabletop or any other flat surface? A surface-mount microphone is a great microphone for that application. Imagine a microphone that is a little larger than average, flat on one side, and with no handle. That's a surface-mount microphone (see fig. 2.6). Surface mount microphones are great for recording group discussions and conversations around a boardroom table. A surface-mount microphone is omnidirectional so that it can capture sounds from all 360 degrees of the environment. Surface-mount microphones

Figure 2.5 PZM microphone

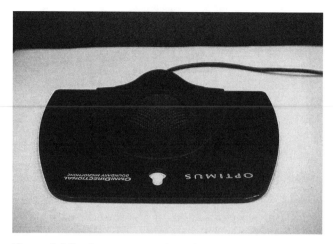

Figure 2.6 Surface-mount microphone

may be either dynamic or condenser and are available in high-impedance and low-impedance models. Expect to pay about $60.

Microphone Selection Criteria

Once you have determined what type of microphone to buy based on your analysis of element, directionality, impedance, and format, consider the following additional microphone features.

Frequency Response

The pitch of sound is measured in hertz (Hz). The lower the pitch (like a low note on a tuba), the smaller the hertz value. The higher the pitch (like the highest note on a piccolo), the greater the hertz value. The human ear can hear from 20 Hz to 20,000 Hz. Unfortunately, not all microphones can pick up this entire audio spectrum. Read the specifications of each microphone that you plan to purchase and note how their frequency responses compare to the range of human hearing. Poor-quality microphones may seem like a bargain, but don't use them to record a duet between a tuba and a piccolo.

Cable Length

Determine the cable length needed for your microphones and use that as a criterion for purchase. Some microphones do not include a cable in the purchase price. Be ready to ask what seems like an obvious question: "Does this microphone include a cable?" A 6-foot cable may not be long enough to accommodate an on-camera interview, requiring you to purchase an expensive microphone extension cable. Unpacking your new microphone purchase to find that the cable is either too short or nonexistent is an unpleasant surprise. Know the cable details before you buy.

Microphone Casing

A good microphone has a casing made of metal (usually an aluminum alloy). A plastic casing can indicate a substandard microphone that may crack if dropped.

Switchable Impedance

Many microphones allow the user to select high or low impedance with the flip of a switch. The feature is quite useful and may save you from having to purchase several microphones with different impedance ratings.

On-Off Switch

An on-off switch can be a valuable feature on a microphone, especially if it is to be used in a public-address situation.

Field Service

Before your buy, ask the vendor if the microphone is field serviceable. In other words, can a qualified technician repair the microphone? Microphones that are not field serviceable must be trashed when they break. Field-serviceable microphones are usually more expensive, but they will seem like a bargain when the microphone becomes inoperable and can be repaired for a few dollars.

Type of Connector

There are three major connectors used with microphones: 1/4-inch phone, 1/8-inch mini, and XLR. Determine the types of connectors on your camcorders and audio mixer, and try to buy microphones that fit those jacks. Some microphones include adapters that will perform connector conversions.

Shock Mounts, Pop Filters, and Windscreens

Shock mounts, pop filters, and windscreens all reduce undesirable external noise that microphones can inadvertently record. Some microphone elements are padded or shock mounted inside the microphone housing to decrease vibration and potential damage. A pop filter is a strip of synthetic material (usually foam) that is placed inside the microphone directly in front of the element. The pop filter helps reduce the explosive sounds of the consonants *p, d, b,* and *t* as they occur in speech. A foam windscreen can be placed over the surface of the microphone to further dampen sounds and reduce microphone rumbling sounds on a windy day. Some microphones include windscreens; others do not. Look for shock mounting, pop filters, and windscreens in microphones that you are considering for purchase.

Phantom Power

Condenser microphones require a power source, and some specifically require phantom power. Phantom power is electricity drawn from the audio mixer, used to power the condenser microphone. A microphone that requires a battery is a minor inconvenience. A condenser microphone requiring phantom power may represent a real problem. For schools, this means that the microphone probably can't be used with your camcorder and may not be usable with your existing audio mixer. Not all audio mixers are configured to provide this microphone power supply, so find out if your mixer is configured that way before buying a microphone that requires phantom power.

Microphone Case or Pouch

Many microphones come with their own hard-shell cases or zippered pouches. Although not a required feature, a case or pouch generally indicates a professional-quality microphone. Travel shaving kits make great microphone pouches.

Swivel Adapter

Will your handheld microphone be mounted on a microphone stand? If so, the microphone needs a swivel adapter. If not included with the microphone, it may require an additional purchase.

Remember, the audio portion of a television program carries a significant part of the message. Your microphone will probably be the primary resource for recording that information. Make sure that you have provided your students with a useful collection of microphones.

Evaluating Wireless Microphone Systems

Wireless microphone systems consist of a handheld or lavaliere microphone, a transmitting unit, and a receiving station (see fig. 2.7). The microphone is used just as any other microphone—for interviews, music recording, and so on—and connects to the transmitting unit. (Many handheld wireless microphones feature the transmitting unit built into the microphone handle.) The signal produced by the transmitting unit is received by the receiving station, which is a radio receiver tuned exclusively to the frequency at which the microphone transmits. The receiving station is connected to a recording device, such as a camcorder, audio mixer, or VCR.

Many schools want to add wireless microphone systems to their collections. Wireless microphones are best used when stringing microphone cable between the sound

Figure 2.7 Wireless microphone system includes
microphone, transmitter (left), and receiving station.

source and the camcorder or audio mixer is impossible, impractical, or unsafe. For
example, a wireless microphone can be used by any of the following people:

- A guest speaker so that audience members do not trip over the microphone
  cable.
- A student news team that interviews the winning football coach as he and
  his players run into the locker room.
- A student reporter, standing in the middle of a crowded hallway, describing
  school overcrowding problems.

Wireless microphones are available from a wide variety of vendors, from professional microphone distributors to electronic hobby shops. Wireless microphone
system prices begin at about $50 for the systems used by video hobbyists to hun-
dreds of dollars for the systems used for audience-participation talk shows and professional sporting events. As you can imagine, these microphones also vary greatly
in performance and features. Use the criteria outlined in the previous section to
evaluate the microphone. Don't buy a substandard microphone just because it hap-

pens to be wireless. Make sure that the directionality, impedance, element type, and format all meet the needs of your microphone collection. Also consider the following criteria when evaluating wireless microphone systems.

Range

Anticipate all possible uses for the wireless microphone in your school. Estimate the distance, or range, of the longest use, and begin shopping with that measurement as the minimum range that you will accept. For example, if the longest distance for which you will use your wireless microphone is 300 feet (about 100 meters), your system should at least cover that distance. Some wireless microphone systems have ranges of a quarter mile (about 410 meters) or more. Others have ranges of less than 30 feet (10 meters). Make sure that your wireless microphone will send a high-quality signal to a distance that meets all your needs.

Signal Frequency

Check the wireless microphone's specification sheet to determine the frequency at which the microphone signal is transmitted. You will find that wireless microphones send signals in two frequency ranges: around 49 megahertz (MHz) and around 180 MHz. (These frequencies are designated for use by the Federal Communications Commission.) Select a microphone that broadcasts close to 180 MHz. (This may, in fact, range from about 175 to 195 MHz.) Signals broadcast in the 49 MHz range are generally of low quality, sounding hollow and tinny. The 49 MHz range represents a lower-quality transmitting unit, like those used in children's toy walkie-talkies. Remember, higher frequency equals higher quality. Do not sacrifice on this feature.

Ask the vendor if the microphone is available at different transmitting frequencies. Although we just described ballpark frequencies for wireless microphones, a wireless microphone system actually broadcasts on a specific radio frequency, such as 187.5 MHz. Determine if, in the future, you can purchase microphones that broadcast on the same frequency (in this case, 187.5 MHz) and on different frequencies (such as 186.3 MHz). Here's why the first criterion is important: Imagine that you are planning to use your camcorder to videotape a segment for your school news show in the school commons area. You would like your student anchors to each have their own microphone, and wireless microphones are a great choice because your anchors will be walking and talking while on camera. However, if your camcorder has only one microphone jack, how will you use both wireless microphones? You must have two wireless microphones transmitting on the same frequency. The single receiving station connected to your camcorder's microphone jack will then receive signals from both microphones.

For an example of when different frequencies would be required, imagine that your advanced production class creates a weekly panel discussion program for your local cable TV company. Because program guests are usually students and community members who have no experience in handling microphones, you decide to use wireless lavaliere microphones. The host and guests each have their own wireless microphones. Each microphone has its own receiving station in the control room, and all the receiving stations are plugged into individual microphone jacks in the audio mixer. With this arrangement, the audio technician can select and mix the speakers' voices and compensate for guests who speak loudly or softly. In this case, each wireless microphone would have to transmit on a separate frequency.

This multifrequency capability may not be necessary for all wireless-microphone purchasers. But if you run an advanced program that gives students a chance to develop and use creative new techniques, you should consider your potential needs in this area.

Power Supply

All wireless microphone systems need two power supplies, one for the transmitting unit and another for the receiving station. Determine if this power demand is alternating current (AC; electrical wall outlet) or direct current (DC; battery), and select a microphone that fills that need. Will you be using the wireless microphone system primarily for conducting interviews around campus? Then you definitely want a DC-powered system. If you anticipate AC access in most of your recording situations, then you may prefer an AC-powered system to save on batteries. Some systems allow both AC and DC power. Note: Wireless microphone systems drain batteries quickly and require full battery power to function. A system can drain a 9-volt battery in 45 minutes or less. A rechargeable battery system should be purchased for use with a battery-powered wireless microphone system.

System Design

Because of their physical design, some wireless microphone systems are best suited for the production studio or some other controlled environment. A receiving station the size of a shoe box and powered by AC is obviously a studio system. Portable systems will be battery powered and have receiving stations the size of a cigarette pack. Some smaller receiving stations even come with Velcro for attachment to the camcorder body.

As you decide which wireless microphone system best suits the needs of your school television production program, consider the following issues. First, configuring and using a wireless microphone system is a skill that requires instruction and practice. Regular (nonwireless) microphones can simply be plugged into the camcorder. Operation of a wireless system is more difficult. If you expect each student to operate the wireless system successfully, plan at least one class session for instruction and practice.

Second, try before you buy. The performance of wireless microphone systems depends greatly on the physical environment in which they will be used. The presence of high-voltage electrical lines and fluorescent lights can reduce a wireless microphone system's range dramatically. A good wireless microphone system represents a substantial investment for most schools. Select a vendor who will allow you to return the system if it does not meet your expectations.

Evaluating Audio Mixers

An audio mixer is an electronic component that facilitates selection and combination of various audio signals (see fig. 2.8). Microphones, music sources (cassette, minidisc, MP3, and compact disc players), and VCR audio outputs can all be connected to audio mixers. Using slide controls called fader bars, an audio technician can increase or decrease volume, fade in and out, and combine voice and music. The use of an audio mixer can greatly improve school-based video production. As with most of the items described in this chapter, audio mixers are available in a wide range of features, functions, and prices. Simple audio mixers that may only allow combination of one music source and one microphone can be purchased for

Figure 2.8 Audio mixer suitable for schools. Photo courtesy of RadioShack Corporation.

less than $50. Complex audio mixers such as those used for broadcast television programs and live concerts can cost $10,000 or more. School production needs fall somewhere in between. Anticipate your audio needs, and use the following criteria to select an audio mixer for your school.

Microphone Inputs

When examining the microphone inputs of the audio mixer, consider three things. First, determine the number of microphone inputs, or channels. Most schools require a minimum of three microphone input channels. Schools operating complex programs may need as many as seven or eight microphone inputs. How many microphone inputs will you need?

Second, consider the impedance of the inputs. Is this audio mixer designed for high-impedance or low-impedance microphones? If you already own several high-impedance microphones, and you would like to use them with your audio mixer, plan to purchase a high-impedance mixer. Some audio mixers offer a high-low impedance selection for each microphone input channel. This feature certainly has merit in the school setting.

Finally, examine the accessibility of the microphone inputs. You may frequently need to add or unplug microphones from your audio mixer. Does the mixer facilitate easy microphone connection and disconnection?

Line Inputs

All nonmicrophone inputs on an audio mixer are considered "line" inputs. As with microphone inputs, consider the number of line inputs on the audio mixer. Sources that will use line inputs include compact disc (CD) player, audiocassette player, MP3 player, minidisc player, and sound from a source VCR. Other inputs may include older formats such as turntables and reel-to-reel tape decks. A minimum of three or four line inputs is recommended for schools just starting video production. Schools with established television production studios will need more line inputs to accommodate multiple-source VCR audio and satellite feeds.

Outputs

Once the audio mixer has processed the signal, it is sent to a recording VCR to be recorded simultaneously with the video signal from the video switcher. Audio mixers have an output marked "main out" or "line output" that sends this signal. Some audio mixers also have a separate "record out," which can be connected to another recording source if a second copy of the program is required.

Volume Unit Meters

A volume unit (VU) meter is used to measure the intensity of an audio signal. All audio mixers used in schools should have VU meters. Traditional analog VU meters resemble car speedometers (see fig. 2.9). As volume increases, the VU meter's needle climbs. LED VU meters use colored LED (light-emitting diode) lights in place of the needle (see fig. 2.10). In both types of VU meters, a line is marked to

Figure 2.9 Analog VU meter

Figure 2.10 LED VU meter

indicate 100 percent VU. The audio inputs should be adjusted so that the VU meter approaches that 100 percent mark but doesn't go past it. Audio that never approaches 100 percent VU sounds empty and hollow. Audio that is frequently above 100 percent VU is distorted. On an analog VU meter, the area above 100 percent VU is marked in red. LED VU meters usually use green lights for intensity below 100 percent VU and red lights for the area above 100 percent VU. Both types of VU meters are useful, and all students should be taught to use VU meters to properly adjust audio signal. The authors prefer the traditional analog VU meter because the bouncing needle is easier for the beginner to read and adjust than the flashing LED lights, and because some students are color-blind and have difficulty distinguishing red from green. Unfortunately, analog VU meters are disappearing in all but the most professional audio mixers.

Stereo/Mono Capability

Most audio mixers currently feature two-channel stereo processing, making it possible to send different sounds to the right and left channels. This stereo feature is essential for audio mixers used in professional stage shows and professional music recordings but has little use in the school television production program. Playback of your programs will most likely be on mono (single-channel) VCRs and mono television sets. For this reason, it is important that your audio mixer have a stereo/mono switch that allows you to record all sounds on each channel.

Headphone Jack with Volume Control

The audio mixer should have a headphone jack for the audio technician to use. This headphone jack should have its own volume control that operates independently of the recording VCR.

Cue Function

At times during program production, it may be necessary for an audio technician to listen to audio sources that are not being sent to the recording VCR. For example, imagine your students are producing their weekly cable TV talk show. The group has selected a theme song from a music audiocassette. The song is played on the cassette player as the show begins. The audio technician wants to use the same song at the end of the show for a closing theme. How does the technician recue the audiocassette to the beginning of the song? By using the audio mixer's cue function. When the cue function is engaged, the audio technician can send a sound to the headphones different than the sound sent to the recording VCR. Different audio mixers accomplish this task in different ways. Some audio mixers feature a multiposition dial near the headphone jack. When the audio technician selects "mix" or "line-out," the sound going to the recording VCR is also sent to the headphone jack. But when the audio technician selects "CD" on that same dial, the sound from the CD player alone is sent to the headphones. Some audio mixers accomplish the cue function with a button marked "cue" above each audio input. (Some audio mixers use the terms "preview" or "solo" instead.) When that button is pressed, the sound from that input is sent only to the mixer's headphone jack. Pressing the cue button again takes the input out of the cue function.

Cross-Fader

A cross-fader is a fader bar placed between two other fader bars. By operating the cross-fader, the audio technician can fade in one audio source while fading out another. This feature has limited use in television production situations, but you can imagine its value to a disc jockey who likes to make a smooth transition from one song to another.

Evaluating Audio Sources

Most school news shows would seem incomplete without music. Music introduces our programs, provides content and continuity, and serves as a great ending. Because music is so important, careful consideration should be given to the purchase of audio source components. This purchase will probably take place in the domain of consumer audio at your local electronic stores. Because those stores offer equipment with a wide variety of features and prices, you should go shopping armed with a list of important features to look for. Audio sources used in school TV production include CD players, audiocassette players, minidisc players, and MP3 players.

Before discussing each audio source, let's differentiate between an audio component and a self-contained stereo, also known as a boom box. Audio components, the correct purchase for school TV production, are usually single-function devices and must be connected to an audio mixer or stereo amplifier to be used. Each audio component will be connected to the audio mixer. Do not buy a self-contained stereo system. These units, which often contain several components, such as CD players and audiocassette players, are meant to be stand-alone units and often do not facilitate connection to other TV production equipment. These stand-alone systems may seem like bargains, but they are not very useful in the school production setting.

Compact Disc Players

CD players use optical technology to read digitally recorded audio. CD players produce crystal-clear sounds and are quite useful in the television production setting. A CD player suitable for school use should cost about $100. Many features described here are standard on all CD players. Look for these features as a sign of quality.

Instant Track Access

The main benefit of the CD player in the production setting is the quick, direct access to specific locations on the compact disc. Cueing the CD player to the eighth song on the CD requires pressing only one or two buttons. The same task on an audiocassette deck would require several minutes of listening and searching. Theme songs can be quickly recued when mistakes are made that require restarting a television program at the beginning. Hundreds of sound effects can be recorded onto a CD, adding further value to the instant track access.

Headphone Jack

A built-in headphone jack with volume control is a nice feature for CD players. Students can privately preview songs before selecting them for their video projects.

Time/Counter Functions

Because the CD player uses digital technology, real-time information is easy to access. Users can determine the length of each song as it plays. Other time/counter functions include time remaining in the song and time remaining on the CD, which make it easy for students to access a point midway through a selected song.

Audiocassette Recording/Playback Decks

An audiocassette recording/playback deck plays and records on audiocassette tapes. The audiocassette deck becomes a music source when connected to your audio mixer. When shopping for an audiocassette deck, look for the features discussed in the following paragraphs. A deck that contains these features will cost about $100.

Logic Controls

A logic-controlled audiocassette deck accesses the different functions (rewind, play, etc.) electronically rather than manually. Audiocassette decks that are not logic controlled give a "clunk" sound when any button is pressed. This sound can be inadvertently recorded on your programs through a microphone. The "clunk" also indicates a lower-end machine. Long after the buttons on manually controlled decks break, logic controls will continue to offer smooth, silent service.

CrO₂, High-Bias, and Dolby Controls

High-quality blank tapes are created with chromium dioxide (CrO_2). Select the CrO_2 button on the audiocassette deck when recording or playing CrO_2 tapes. High-bias tapes are manufactured to emphasize the highest pitches in the musical spectrum. When using a high-bias tape, select the corresponding button on the audiocassette deck. Dolby is not a special kind of tape but a modification of the recording process that decreases tape noise often found on audiocassettes. Pressing the Dolby button on the audiocassette deck before recording and playback activates this noise-reduction function. The presence of buttons that control CrO_2, high bias, and Dolby indicates a higher-end consumer audiocassette deck suitable for schools.

Adjustable Recording Level

A student or teacher using an audiocassette deck to record a program should be able to adjust the recording level. This function facilitates fade-ins and fade-outs.

Volume Unit Meters

To properly control the recording level, the audio technician must be able to see the strength of the signal. Look for a VU meter on the audiocassette deck as an indication of this capability.

Microphone Jack

If you plan to use the audiocassette deck as a stand-alone recording component, you will need a microphone jack. Students can practice scripts on audiocassette and evaluate their performances.

Headphone Jack

A high-level audiocassette deck has its own headphone jack. This jack facilitates recording and playback.

Counter

High-quality audiocassette decks will have a tape counter that can be reset. This can be a valuable tool in video production, especially when specific locations on an audiocassette must be found quickly.

Minidisc Player/Recorder

A relatively recent arrival on the audio component scene is the minidisc player/recorder (see fig. 2.11). A minidisc is a recordable compact disc permanently encased in a square plastic shell. A minidisc is smaller than a standard CD—

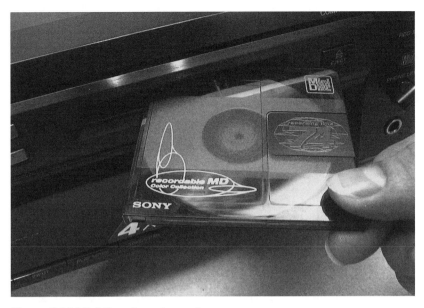

Figure 2.11 Minidisc player/recorder

about 2.5 inches square—yet it holds 74 minutes of recorded CD-quality stereo music. Both portable and component minidisc player/recorders are available, priced around $150 and $250, respectively. Blank minidiscs sell for about $2 each. A minidisc can be recorded, erased, and rerecorded without damage, and most minidiscs carry a lifetime guarantee from the manufacturer. Another interesting feature is that the minidisc format allows the user to enter a name for the disc, as well as the name of each song. These titles are recorded onto the minidisc's table of contents and displayed on the player when the minidisc is played. This feature can be quite useful to an audio technician looking for a specific song. Like a good CD player, a minidisc player also displays the length of each song, as well as time remaining, and so on.

Although the minidisc is recorded in a digital format, the recording process is done in real time. The minidisc player/recorder is not a computer component, although the audio output of the computer can be connected easily to the input of the minidisc player for real-time recording of computer-music compositions. Think of a minidisc player/recorder as a digital, updated audiocassette deck.

In addition to the standard audio inputs, minidisc players also have optical inputs. Many newer audio components, most notably CD players, have optical outputs. When these optically equipped CD players are connected to minidisc recorders, the result is a pure digital recording of outstanding quality.

Many of the portable minidisc players have microphone jacks. Students can narrate scripts onto a minidisc and later incorporate those recordings into their video projects.

Currently, less than a handful of companies manufacture minidisc player/recorders, with Sony dominating the market. Most player/recorders will have the advanced features discussed here, but double-checking is never a bad thing. The minidisc player has the potential to be a useful tool in the school TV studio. If you're not familiar with this format, ask a sales clerk the next time you visit an electronics store.

MP3 Players

Unless you've been totally isolated for the past few years, you've heard or read about the MP3 digital audio format, as well as the controversy surrounding MP3s and copyright. Songs from standard CDs can be converted to the MP3 format using widely available computer software. Even at its highest-quality setting, an MP3 file is 10 times smaller than other comparable audio formats. This small size means that entire music collections can be saved on portable media formats. It also means that these files can be traded over the Internet, violating copyright and sullying the reputation of the MP3 format.

Another recent software development—music creation software—makes a portable MP3 player a consideration in the school TV setting. (This software is discussed in the next section.) Students who create original music using this software can save their compositions in the MP3 format. The MP3 player can be connected to the audio mixer and used as a resource for school TV productions. Although this application may seem a bit contrived, one thing is certain—the MP3 format is not going away anytime soon. Students are quite knowledgeable about this format, and teachers would be wise to learn about its positive uses.

The selection of good-quality audio equipment is critical to the success of your school television production program. By maintaining the standards outlined here, you should be able to purchase equipment that will provide excellent educational opportunities for your students for many years.

Music in the School Production Setting

Up to this point, our discussion of audio has focused on the equipment, or the "hardware," of audio production. Now it's time to look at some of the music resources available and appropriate for the school setting.

When discussing the use of music in the school setting, the conversation almost always turns to the issue of copyright. Most media specialists are aware of copyright law. School districts have recently become quite concerned with following national copyright guidelines, and many are writing or adopting specific copyright directives. As a result, media specialists are aware that popular music cannot be duplicated without permission from the music publisher, record company, songwriter, and performers. Simply stated, you are violating copyright law if you use recorded music on a videotape or multimedia presentation that you will play for an audience, duplicate, or sell unless you receive the proper permission. Sometimes, we hear about certain percentages of a song that can be played; these nebulous rules are usually phrased as "no more than … " expressions. Someone will say, "no more than 10% or no more than 30 seconds," and it gets real confusing, real fast. A media educator with a law degree and a slide rule might be able to calculate the amount of a popular song allowed for use on a school orientation tape. But that practice is unnecessary when the educator learns about the legal alternative: production music—either ready made and purchased on CDs or created with the assistance of computer programs. The following sections take a look at both of these options.

Production Music

Production music is composed specifically for use in audio and video productions. It sounds quite similar to the pop and jazz tunes that we hear on the radio, but it is designed to be purchased by video producers (including schools) for use in programs that will be broadcast or duplicated. When video producers buy the production music, they are buying not only the right to listen to the music (as with commercial CDs) but also the right to duplicate it in their video productions.

By purchasing production music, the school sidesteps this copyright problem by buying the duplication and broadcast rights to the production music. In other words, the music is now *your* music. You have paid the producer for the rights to broadcast, duplicate, and sell the video program on which the music occurs.

Before we describe each aspect of production music in detail, we should mention some other important reasons for using production music and original music in the school setting.

Production music is anonymous. Unlike current popular songs and classic standards, production music tunes bring no meanings or connotations to your video production. Because production music is unknown, it allows your audience to focus on the video program, not the song. Audiences have diverse personal experiences, and a well-known song used in your video may elicit unwanted emotions. A popular tune used as music for your orientation video may remind some parents of a romantic dinner, others of an exciting vacation, and still others of a departed loved one. Needless to say, none of these parents will be focusing on the message of your video program.

Production music is designed to accommodate and complement narration. Most production music songs are instrumentals, with no dominant solo instruments in the foreground. Students can match their script's pacing to the musical style. Also, they can select a song that perfectly matches their narration. Students will appreciate the availability of so many instrumental songs. The variety of production music provides selections appropriate to almost any production situation.

The content of much popular music is also simply not appropriate in the school setting. Production music, on the other hand, contains no sexual references or violent themes. When you hand a student a CD of production music, you can be sure that the music is appropriate for your school news program or any other school production activity.

Production music helps to create a professional atmosphere in your TV studio. Sure, a few students will be disappointed when they learn that they can't use their favorite songs in their video projects. But most will be thrilled to use "real TV music." Gone is the distraction of trying to decide among best-selling songs. One high school student expressed relief that his friends could no longer pressure him to play their favorite songs on the school news show every day. A middle schooler declared, "Hey, this is just like a real TV studio." "No," replied the teacher. "This *is* a real TV studio."

Production music allows you to create theme songs. Now, your news show can have its own theme song—a song that is uniquely yours because no one has heard it before. "Hey, that's the *Falcon News Show* song." You can also create themes for regular show segments, such as "The Sports Calendar," "Today in History," or "African-Americans of Achievement." Your audio technician will love the responsibility of selecting theme songs for your show.

Still not convinced that your school should purchase production music or the software to create it? Remember: Anytime that 1) a nonstudent produces a program or 2) a student produces a program to be viewed by a nonstudent audience, duplicated, or sold, copyright-cleared music should be used. The following are some productions for which production music would probably be required:

- A school orientation tape that will be viewed by parents or duplicated
- A highlights tape for the sports banquet
- A video yearbook or any other program that will be duplicated or sold
- A video contest
- A program about the school aired on a television station that does not make routine royalty payments
- A school awards assembly tape

Once you and your students begin to use copyright-cleared production music, you will find that it offers greater reward than just obeying copyright guidelines.

Buying Production Music

Dozens of companies are in the business of creating, marketing, and selling professional-sounding production music (also called buy-out music). Most of this music is sold in the CD format. A CD of such music (often called a collection or a volume of production music) usually contains 10 to 12 songs. Depending on the production music company, the songs may be similar in mood and style or they may be quite different from one another. Some production music companies will put all fast jazz on a CD, for example, whereas other companies strive for diversity in each volume.

Most production music companies record several different versions of each song on the CD. The CD shown in figure 2.12 lists 14 different songs. But a closer inspection reveals that the CD has 48 tracks: there are three or four versions of each song on the disc. The first song is called "Back Roads." By consulting the CD's booklet, you would find that track 1 is the full version (2 minutes, 37 seconds) of "Back Roads." Track 2 is an alternate full version: the same melody, but with a little different instrumentation. Track 3 is the underscore for "Back Roads"—the song's accompaniment, without the melody or dominant instruments. This track would be

Figure 2.12 Example of a production music CD. Image courtesy of Music2Hues.

great as a soundtrack for narration. And track 4 is a 30-second version of "Back Roads"—perfect for commercials, program openings, and other brief productions. All 14 songs on this disc are presented in a similar way.

As already noted, most production music is sold on CD. Those who have used CDs in video production know their outstanding features—quick cueing of songs and instant recueing if mistakes are made. This feature is especially important with production music because of the large number of tracks available on each CD and the fact that the several versions of each song sound similar.

A single CD volume of production music will cost from $45 to $100, depending on the production company. "Ouch," you say. Can't you buy several popular compact discs for the same price? Yes. But remember, when you pay $12 for a CD at the music store, you are *not* buying the right to use it in your own video production and distribute the results. Compared to the cost of finding a new job or paying a hefty fine or out-of-court settlement, production music is quite cheap. Have you ever heard a popular "golden oldie" played in a movie or television commercial? The songwriter, artists, and music publisher were paid thousands of dollars for the use of that song. You are paying less than $100 to use several songs. In the world of music, that's a bargain. Plan to buy one or two CDs of production music each year that your school is active in video production. With 10 or 12 songs on each disc, you will find more than enough music to serve your program.

When buying production music for your school, there is a very important concept to consider: *Listen before you buy!* That's right—it is critical that you listen to a sampling of the specific production music before you buy it. Fortunately, this is easy to do, and all serious production music companies will give you this opportunity. The two prevalent ways of sampling a company's production music are with demo CD and through the company Web site. Many of the more-established production music companies have a sample CD that features a few seconds of each of their songs. This is a great tool for educators, who need to spend their money wisely. Just pop the CD in the car on the way to work, or listen on your lunch break, and take notes when a song piques your interest. You can obtain a demo CD by calling the production music company's toll-free number or requesting one on their Web site. (A list of several production music companies, their phone numbers, and their Web sites is included at the end of this chapter.)

The company's Web site can also be a great way to listen to production music before you buy. You are usually just a mouse click away from hearing a sampling when you log on to these Web sites. Because their business *is* audio, most production music companies host Web sites that make full use of the Internet's audio capabilities. Compare the samples of several different companies. You will find great diversity in the production music marketplace. Most production music sounds quite professional, but some companies offer weaker collections. Don't purchase until you have heard music that you like. Keep looking and listening. It's out there.

And don't overlook other ways to hear production music before you buy. The next time you are visiting colleagues, for example, ask them what kind of production music they use. They will probably be happy to let you listen to their collection. Also, production music companies, recognizing the buying power of schools, are starting to exhibit at media conferences. Look for them the next time you are in the exhibit hall. Production music topics are frequently listed on the agendas of technology conferences. (In fact, one of the authors' most popular presentations is about production music.)

Before buying a volume of production music, read the company's literature or call the sales representative to make sure that you know exactly what you're buying. In most cases, you will be buying the rights to the use of the music in audio and video productions, as well as the right to show, duplicate, and sell those productions without further payment for as long as the studio (the school) is in business. Generally, you are *not* buying the right to duplicate the music for use as production music at another school. Each location must buy its own music. (Some school districts, purchase, for a reduced rate, the rights for all schools in the district to use the music.) Determine if you are allowed to sell the music as a video service. In other words, can you charge other schools for using your music in their video productions? (Some companies frown on this practice, whereas others encourage it.) Some companies will also stipulate that their name must appear in a written credit at the end of your video production. This condition is easily appeased, but the exercise seems somewhat superfluous in the school setting. In any case, make sure that you know exactly what rights you are buying when you buy production music.

Some music companies require payment with each order, others request a purchase order, and a few will send the CD with a bill. Whatever the billing arrangement, make sure to keep copies of all invoices and payments. These will be valuable if your ownership of the music is ever questioned. When you receive your production music disc, listen to each track. If you find defects, contact the music company immediately and plan to return the disc quickly. Any delay in return will arouse suspicions that the music has been recorded for later use.

Finally, when buying production music, make sure to "shop the sales." Many companies offer discounts for purchasing several CDs at once. Others have special educational discounts. Make sure to ask. And don't pass up the chance to let your school administration or PTA buy your production music for you. After all, you are buying the music to meet legal guidelines. Following the law should not result in the punishment of a shrinking media budget. Explain the legal ramifications of using production music, and see if your principal will help with this "administrative" cause.

Alternatives to Buying Production Music

Although buying the rights to music is the most popular way to satisfy music copy-right laws, there are two other ways to obtain production music: the music lease and the needle-drop fee. In the music-lease program, each song is leased, not pur-chased. Television stations that need theme songs for local news shows but don't intend to duplicate or sell the music often use this approach. At the end of a cer-tain period, the lease is discontinued, and the television station must find a new theme song. For most schools, the lease program is not practical because schools frequently make duplicates of their video programs.

The second alternative, the needle-drop fee, may seem attractive to some schools. Instead of buying a production music collection, the production facility receives several CDs free of charge. The school is required to keep a log of its use of production music and send payment monthly. This way, an entire music library is accessible to a small production company that may just use one or two songs a year. For the busy school, the chore of keeping a log outweighs any savings, though. Furthermore, few production music companies offer the needle-drop option any-more. Most companies focus on selling CD collections and working with individu-al television stations that need to lease music. For the school, the buy-out option represents the best value.

Creating Production Music with Your Computer

Several software programs are available that will let you custom create production music for use in your school. You will be surprised at the quality of music that you and your students can create—even with little or no musical experience. And all the music that you create is royalty free! That's right—just like purchased produc-tion music, you won't have to pay any additional fees to use this music in your video productions. There are two types of programs—loops-based creation, and Smartsound software.

Loops-Based Music Creation Software

Loops-based creation software involves combining "loops"—brief segments of prere-corded music—in a sequence. Music loops made from keyboards, guitars, and drums, as well as sound effects, are commonly available. The program that you buy will prob-ably contain hundreds of loops. Your finished song can be saved as a WAV file, and recorded onto videotape, audiotape, or minidisc (via your computer's sound card out-put), or recorded onto a compact disc, using your computer's CD-R "burner" drive.

Creating a song with loops-based software involves importing audio loops from a menu located on the screen. The user drags the mouse to "paint" the sounds onto this work screen (see fig. 2.13). For example, you might start by selecting a drumbeat, then adding a bass guitar, and continuing with other musical instruments until you get the sound you want.

After reading the previous paragraphs, you may be excited about creating your own music—or you may be hesitant to undertake such a task. Loops-based software is exciting but also complex. Chances are that you have a few students who would love to try this process. The two most common loops-based software companies are Sonic Foundry and Cakewalk. Both companies sell a wide range of products; the entry-level software is the best place for the inexperienced user to start. Sonic Foundry's Acid 3.0 is a great beginning program and sells for less than $100. Sonic Foundry also sells a version designed especially for children 6 to 10 years old, called Super Duper Music Looper (see fig. 2.14). Cakewalk's Music Creator and Club Tracks products are also inexpensive starting points.

SmartSound Software

If you're interested in making your own custom, royalty-free music, but you don't have the time for the loops-based products, you should try a more-automated approach. SmartSound Software markets revolutionary software programs that rep-

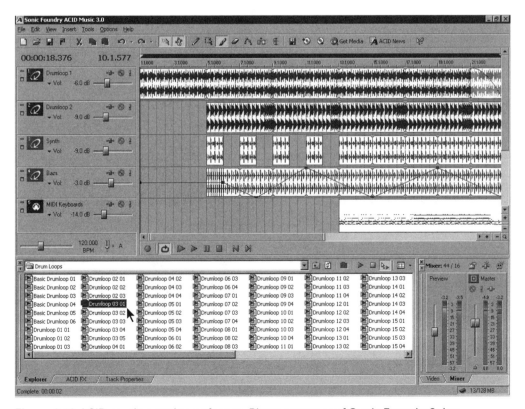

Figure 2.13 ACID music creation software. Photo courtesy of Sonic Foundry®, Inc.

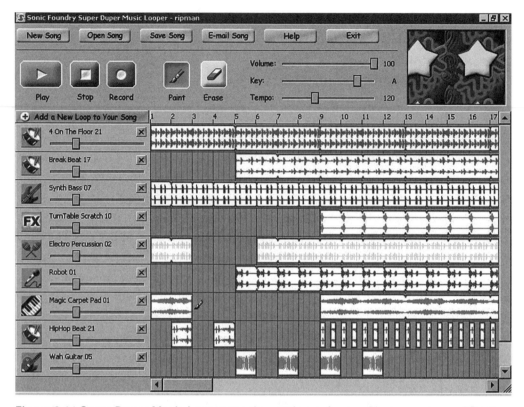

Figure 2.14 Super Duper Music Looper music creation software. Photo courtesy of Sonic Foundry®, Inc.

resent real value to schools. These programs include Movie Maestro and Sonicfire Pro. Each program allows users to select from a menu of musical styles to create royalty-free production music that will meet their needs. With Movie Maestro, you make a series of selections based on the soundtrack needs of the video production. The user chooses from a menu of musical styles—action, background, drama, and so on—and then enters the desired length of the song (fig. 2.15). Movie Maestro then offers the user samples of the various songs available. After making a few more choices, the user is presented with a custom-made production music song. Movie Maestro even offers quick exporting to popular nonlinear editing and presentation programs.

Sonicfire Pro is an advanced music creation tool for serious video editors who need numerous audio editing options.

The music for all SmartSound Software music creation programs is based on "audio palettes." SmartSound Software has purchased the rights to some of the best production music available, and their engineers have broken each song into short

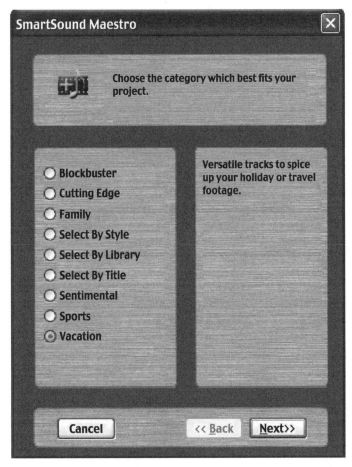

Figure 2.15 Movie Maestro music creation software. Photo
courtesy of SmartSound Software.

segments of various lengths, ranging from a couple of beats to two or three full
measures of music. The SmartSound software combines these segments into a
seemingly infinite number of combinations to give the user a myriad of production music choices. Each SmartSound program comes with an audio palette of
songs, and additional audio palettes are available for purchase, multiplying the musical styles and choices. These programs are user friendly and well within the price
range of the education market. You can log on to the company's Web site and request a free demonstration CD-ROM.

Production music is a valuable asset to schools engaged in video production.
Whether purchased from professional sources or created by your students, all
schools should own and use an adequate collection.

Helpful Internet Links

Audio Equipment

Audio-Technica (Microphones): http://www.audiotechnica.com

Mackie (Audio mixers): http://www.Mackie.com

Panasonic (Audio mixers): http://www.Panasonic.com

RadioShack (Microphones, audio mixers, headphones): http://www.radioshack.com

Shure (Microphones): http://www.shure.com

Sony Electronics (Audio source components): http://www.sonystyle.com

Music Creation Software

Cakewalk Music and Software (Loops-based music creation software): http://www.cakewalk.com

SmartSound Software (Audio palette–based music creation software): http://www.smartsound.com

Sonic Foundry Media Software (Loops-based music creation software): http://www.sonicfoundry.com/products/home.asp

Production Music

The Canary Collection: http://www.canarymusic.com

Davenport Music: http://www.davenportmusic.com

Geoffrey Wilson Buyout Music: http://gwilsonbuyoutmusic.com

Mokal Music:http://www.productionmusicmall.com

Music2Hues: http://www.music2hues.com

PBTM/QCCS Music Library: http://www.pbtm.com

Signature Music: http://www.sigmusic.com

Soundzabound Music Library: http://www.soundzabound.com

Professional Resources

SCHOOLTV.com (The authors' Web site features helpful information to educators working with television production.): http://www.schooltv.com

Chapter 3

Nonlinear Digital Video Editing

N o phase of audio or video production has changed as much in recent years as video editing. Camcorders are basically the same—point the camera and push the record button. Sure, the videotape format might be different, but the process hasn't changed. Ditto for the VCR—"play" still plays the videocassette, and "rewind" still rewinds it. Your video mixer has taken a giant step forward, with dozens of effects and even digital chroma key. However, the concept of switching from camera 1 to camera 2 hasn't changed. But video editing has made a fundamental change in the past few years. The entire process of arranging, adding, and deleting scenes to create a video program is nothing like it was a few years ago.

In this chapter, we'll examine nonlinear digital video editing (called nonlinear editing for short). We'll explore some of the advantages and disadvantages of nonlinear editing and offer some selection criteria for purchasing a nonlinear editing system. Finally, we'll look at the nonlinear editing marketplace and recommend some additional purchases to complement your nonlinear editing system.

Explanation of Nonlinear Digital Video Editing

If you think about it, the term *nonlinear* is an odd way to describe an editing process. Most processes are not described in negative terms, using the prefix *non*. Nonlinear editing gets its name from the fact that video editing need no longer be accomplished in a straight line, from point A to point B. Now, we can start in the middle of our video projects. We can start at the end and work our way forward. We can even start at the beginning. So the name *nonlinear editing* describes the freedom from the rigid editing process that dominated the first 60 years of television production.

Before continuing, it is helpful to recognize that you readers form two distinct groups—those who have edited in the traditional linear method and those who have not. Have you ever connected two VCRs together and copied a videotaped program? That is editing in its simplest form. Did you pause the "record" VCR to eliminate part of the program from your duplicate tape? Then you were performing a basic edit. Maybe you used an editing control unit to set pinpoint edits. Or maybe you took it a step further, combining assemble editing and video insert editing to make complex programs. All of these processes, from the simple to the complex, are examples of traditional video editing. This type of editing seems peculiar to some of our readers—those whose editing experience consists only of nonlinear editing. But since the inception of videotape until very recently, all video editing was done that way.

The process just described, in which two VCRs are connected to edit videotape, can be called linear, or traditional, video editing. Most people realize that videotape cannot be physically cut and pasted back together. That technique, which works great for film and motion picture editing, is not supported using magnetic videotape. The two-VCR method was really the only way to combine scenes to make a video program. And although decades of great programming was created in this era—from complex TV episodes, movies, and documentaries to projects created by students and hobbyists—the system was not without problems, inconveniences, and limitations. Probably the most frustrating aspect was the linear restriction, which dictated that editing began with the opening title graphic and ended with the ending credits. What if, after finishing your program, you found a great video clip that would be perfect for the opening sequence? Forget it. The opening was done. You could make a new opening and then re-edit the remaining program. Or you could tack the completed program on the end of your new opening, but the audience would probably notice a drop in the picture quality. This limitation was especially frustrating to TV production educators, who would make recommendations for improving student-produced videos, knowing full well that those changes would never be implemented.

With that historical information on the record, we can now focus on the concept of nonlinear digital video editing. Simply stated, nonlinear editing involves four steps:

1. **Importing audio and video elements into a computer, saving them in a digital format.** This is accomplished by connecting the source equipment to your nonlinear editing system (see fig. 3.1). VCRs, camcorders, DVD players, CD players, microphones, and audio mixers are examples of source equipment. The nonlinear editing computer has a process for capturing these elements and saving them as files for use in the next step.

2. **Arrange, delete, and trim audio and video segments.** This is the actual editing process. The imported segments are then arranged in the desired order—lined up on a storyboard. Segments can be trimmed to begin and end at exact points. Longer segments can be split into shorter segments.

3. **Add effects, graphics, transitions, and sound.** Effects such as slow motion and color adjustments can be added to segments. Graphics screens can be added—with solid backgrounds or superimposed over video. Transitions, such as

Figure 3.1 Camcorder to editing computer connection, using IEEE-1394

wipes, fades, and dissolves, can be placed between segments. Music and narration can be inserted and combined.

4. **Record the finished program onto videotape or DVD, or save in a digital format for future use.** The finished project is then recorded into a desired format. Most commonly, this involves connecting a VCR to the nonlinear editing system and recording the project onto videotape. Many nonlinear editing systems offer the ability to create (burn) a DVD. The program can also be saved to a storage media (a hard drive, an external drive) or saved on a computer network to be shared with other users.

Several brands offer various features, but the process remains the same. Import the elements, arrange the elements, add to the elements, and export (record) the program.

Advantages of Nonlinear Editing

Of course, the biggest advantage to nonlinear editing is the nonlinear aspect—being able to edit and rearrange segments as easily as moving paragraphs in a word processor. But the nonlinear editing process has additional advantages.

Cost

Perhaps surprisingly, nonlinear editing systems are less expensive than traditional editing systems, and they offer a real value in the school setting. An entry-level system, complete with transitions, graphics, effects, and music-editing capabilities, can be purchased for less than $1,500. That's about half the price of an entry-level traditional editing system. And that traditional system would provide cuts-only editing—no graphics, no transitions, no effects.

Smaller Size

A high-powered laptop computer can serve as a nonlinear editing system. (Apple's iBook is advertised this way—with a young man editing his vacation movies on the plane ride home.) Other systems are about the size of a desktop computer. Traditional editing systems required large tabletop space or expensive editing cabinets. Nonlinear systems fit comfortably on existing library or classroom tables and countertops.

Cross-Format Capabilities

Sometimes when editing a project, you will find that your video sources exist on a variety of formats: VHS, S-VHS, 8mm, MiniDV, DVD, and so on. With a traditional editing system, all of these sources would have to be converted onto your system's format (probably VHS) before editing. Because most video equipment has standard video outputs, the nonlinear editing system can import them all. For example, imagine you are making a video project about the school softball team. You have some game video that you shot on MiniDV. A parent has provided additional footage, shot on 8mm videotape. And you also want to include some footage from last year's softball tournament that you have on VHS. Simply connect each component—your MiniDV camcorder, the parent's 8mm camcorder, and a VHS VCR—to your nonlinear editing system, and import the video segments. Once imported, the nonlinear editing system can work with all segments equally well.

Image Quality

One of the biggest drawbacks to traditional editing is the loss of image quality during the editing process. Because the resulting traditionally edited program is a copy, the picture quality is degraded. That degradation continues if "a copy of a copy" is made. Editors call this "generational loss," and it was common knowledge that fourth-generation video was embarrassing and fifth-generation was unwatchable. Students entering video contests were previously constantly faced with this challenge—should they send their master tape (second generation) or a copy (third generation) to the contest? Or what if the master tape is damaged, and the third generation is the best copy that exists? You can see the problem (literally).

Nonlinear editing erases this problem. The edited version looks as professional as the original footage—maybe even more so, if image enhancement features have been used in the editing process. In other words, the copy can look better than the original! And subsequent copies made from the program stored on the nonlinear editing system's hard drive look as crisp as the first.

Quick Learning

Most students can learn nonlinear editing basics in just a few minutes. The computer platform for nonlinear editing has allowed programmers to include intuitive aspects into the editing process. The "click-and-drag" process that students already use in presentation software and file management is also used in nonlinear editing. Nonlinear system customers frequently report a positive "straight-out-of-the-box" experience when they first use their machines.

Easy to Learn

The nonlinear system is basically easy to learn. "Help" menus and graphics-based menus provide support. Certainly, some students will become more adept at nonlinear editing, and others will be more creative than their peers. But most, if not all, students will be able to skillfully edit their programs after a few minutes of instruction. Advanced functions can be added as the students advance at their own pace.

Integrated Graphics, Effects, and Transitions

Nonlinear editing systems can be thought of as all-in-one machines. Students can add graphics, effects, and transitions without going to a different "station" in the studio or reconfiguring the equipment. Those who have edited on a traditional system can fully appreciate this advantage. In the past, schools spent thousands of dollars for two high-quality editing VCRs, two monitors, and an editing control unit, and the result was simple cuts-only editing—no effects, no graphics, no transitions. Mechanically inclined teachers would reconfigure equipment, adding expensive character generators and video mixers in between the "source" and "record" VCRs to achieve basic effects. With a nonlinear editing system, those effects are taken to the next level at a fraction of the cost.

Correcting Mistakes, Making Updates

Mistakes made during the editing process are easily corrected using a nonlinear editing system. Segments anywhere in the program can quickly be trimmed or replaced. Also, existing programs can be updated with ease, as segments that no longer apply are replaced with appropriate segments. For example, imagine a student at your school wins the city science fair, and your video production students create a segment based on that accomplishment. After seeing the segment on your school news channel, the principal encourages you to submit the program to your local cable TV station for broadcast on their "Student Accomplishments" program.

In the meantime, the junior scientist wins the state science fair! Do you have to totally reedit your program? No—just update the necessary elements with the nonlinear editing system.

Creating Various Versions of the Same Program

Because the individual audio and video elements in the nonlinear editing process are easily interchangeable, it is easy to create various versions of the same program. For example, imagine you are a high school media specialist, and you have created a five-minute orientation video for the incoming freshman class—the standard "Welcome to Our School" video. Because your audience consists of 14-year-olds, you have selected production music that fits their tastes and have included several brief student interviews in the program. As your first open house approaches, your principal asks you to show the video to parents and community members. But you're not sure how they will respond to the hip-hop soundtrack, and you'd like to feature parent and teacher interviews in addition to the student interviews. If you edited your original orientation program on a nonlinear system, you can simply replace the soundtrack and add the additional interviews. Creating the adult-friendly version would only take a few minutes.

Audio and Video File Sharing and Transporting

Digital audio and video files can easily be transferred to network servers for sharing among many users in a TV studio. Raw footage can be loaded onto the computer server (shared hard drive), and editors working at various stations around the school can access those files. Okay—you're probably not going to do that anytime soon. But networks like CNN and ESPN are doing that now, as editors for different newscasts access raw footage to incorporate into their programs. And imagine how easily highlights from previous ballgames can be accessed when they are stored on a hard drive and downloaded like word-processing documents. This sure beats searching an entire videotape for that one clip. And as high-speed online access becomes commonplace, news reporters and videographers in distant lands can log on to their company's computer network and upload their raw footage, giving instant access to editors at the studio. Digitized media is certainly the preferred production format of the future.

Excellent Teaching Tool

Because of its ability to correct mistakes, update existing projects, and create various versions of the same project, a nonlinear editing system is a wonderful tool for teaching the video production process. Teachers can take an active roll in their students' projects by recommending changes, and the students can instantly see the results. The editing station becomes a learning lab, in which students can experiment with various transitions and effects before committing them to videotape. Video segments can be rearranged to maximize the program's impact. Different soundtracks can be added, and different students can provide narration. Teachers can also use the nonlinear editor to create simple video projects that teach the emotional impact of music, the result of using too many effects, or the appropriate use of transitions. Teachers who incorporate nonlinear editing into their curriculum will see the educational value of their classes enhanced exponentially.

Disadvantages of Nonlinear Editing

With all of those advantages, it might seem like you've found the perfect solution to your editing needs. Nonlinear editing is great, but not without a few problems. The following sections take a good look at the disadvantages.

Cost—Not Free!

Sure, nonlinear editors are a lot less expensive than the earlier linear versions, but they aren't free. In fact, your nonlinear editing system could be the most expensive item in your TV production studio. That's why it's important to make the best decision about a nonlinear editor for your school.

Hardware and Software Considerations

Sometimes, nonlinear editing systems involve both hardware *and* software considerations. This is especially true when the PC platform is chosen. Did the company that makes the hardware also write the software? If not, you could run into some real problems. Imagine your computer is made by company A. You install an IEEE-1394 port made by company B and an analog video card made by company C. Company D makes the software. In this scenario, hardware and software from four different manufacturers must all be configured properly and work together. Fortunately, the one-manufacturer option, or stand-alone system, exists and is discussed later in this chapter.

Memory, Storage

As already mentioned, one of the biggest advantages of nonlinear editing is that, because the raw footage is "active" in the computer memory, different versions can be created and mistakes can easily be corrected. But the question arises: How long do we keep that footage on the nonlinear editing system's hard drive? At some point, that footage will have to be deleted because of space considerations. Most nonlinear editing systems are sold with hard drives that hold less than 20 hours of storage space (although this number is sure to improve over the years). That might seem like a lot, but in an active video production program, with beginning students editing simple documentaries, intermediate students creating news shows and instructional videos, and advanced students working on contest entries and video yearbooks, that hard drive space will quickly fill. This situation leads to a tendency to erase projects as soon as they are recorded onto videotape. When you are shopping for a nonlinear editing system, make sure to ask about your options for upgrading the hard drive, as well as the system's ability to accommodate external drives, such as an external IEEE-1394 hard drive, or an ORB drive that stores 2.2 gigabytes of memory on oversized disks.

Need for Additional Upgrades

Often, advertisements and vendors will tell you the *base price* of a nonlinear editing system, which may not include the hard drive space or the features that you really want. In other words, there's a difference between what the system *can* do (with upgrades) and what the system *will* do, configured the way you bought it. Also, those upgrades may not even be available. You may have to "graduate" to the advanced system, spending thousands of dollars for a completely new nonlinear editing system.

Need for Additional Purchases

Realize that most nonlinear editing systems do not make videotape! Huh? That's right; you'll have to buy at least one VCR, a TV, and perhaps a computer monitor as well. With traditional linear editing, the VCR *was* the editing system, but not anymore. Be prepared to open the wallet a little wider to buy everything you need. Those purchases are discussed later in this chapter.

Techno Crashes

Computers crash. That's probably not news to any readers. Don't forget—your nonlinear editing system is a computer. "Save as you go" is an important rule with nonlinear editing. Fortunately, the one-manufacturer (proprietary) systems are more stable because all problems are corrected as the product is tested. Usually.

Simple Projects Are Easier Using Traditional Editing Methods

"Okay, Sally, go out in the hallways during class changes and record some video that we can show with the ending credits." We make these requests several times a week. Or maybe, "Go down to the science room and make some tape. They built bridges out of matchsticks, and they're trying to make them collapse. Get some footage." Editing these projects with traditional linear editing systems was a snap. Editors who have experience with traditional systems will be used to doing this type of "crunch editing." Of course, this is not possible with nonlinear editing systems. No matter how simple the project, the footage must be imported, trimmed, arranged, rendered, and recorded. The old way is quicker for those simple, no-frills projects.

Lack of Training Opportunities

Lack of training opportunities speaks for itself. There really aren't many workshops on nonlinear editing. And because there are several options on the marketplace and each system has its own process, the local workshop might not help at all. Buyers of nonlinear editing systems need to be content with the instructional manual, the toll-free "help line," and instructional videos produced by third-party companies.

Don't misinterpret the last few paragraphs. Nonlinear editing is leaps and bounds ahead of its linear predecessor. Even the most hardened traditional editors will remember with fondness the day that they started editing on a nonlinear editing system. Just remember—it's not all roses!

Nonlinear Digital Video Editing Selection Criteria

Now that we've examined the advantages and disadvantage to nonlinear editing systems, it's time to describe the selection criteria for nonlinear editing systems. The objective is to make sure that you buy the editing system that is the best purchase for your school. Because schools have different needs, those selections will certainly be different as well. By carefully examining the needs of your program and the features of several editing systems, you can buy a nonlinear editing system that will serve your school for years to come.

Stand-Alone Systems versus Hardware-Software Systems

As you survey the marketplace, you will find stand-alone nonlinear editing systems, and you will find hardware and software products that you can add to an existing computer to convert it to a nonlinear editing system. As you read about the selection criteria in the following paragraphs, you will see that we find that the stand-alone system best meets the needs of most schools (see fig. 3.2). Certainly, some

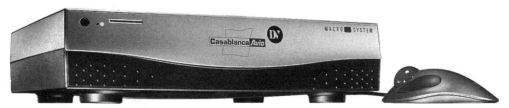

Figure 3.2 AVIO stand-alone nonlinear editing appliance. Image courtesy of MacroSystem US, Inc.

readers will disagree; that is why we use the word *most*. As you read the following paragraphs, you can examine your needs and abilities and proceed from that point. Yes, there are some media educators who have the time and the aptitude to upgrade desktop computers, add new video cards, download drivers, and work through an endless list of set-up menus. Some actually *enjoy* it! But from our experiences, most media educators never have enough time, feel more comfortable with the outside of the computer than the inside, and could really use a system that works perfectly the first time they turn it on. This brings us to our first selection criteria.

First-Time Setup: Out of the Box

Most of us want our computers, our camcorders, and yes, our nonlinear editing systems to work "out of the box." We want to turn them on and see a menu screen. We want a "quick-start" guide printed on cardboard that will show us how to import footage, recombine clips, and export the finished program onto videotape. Ask the salesperson and talk to other educators who use the same nonlinear system: "How long before I'm editing my first project?" Ask another customer to describe his or her *first* experience with the system. "Well, it took us a while to get it configured correctly, but once we did, it worked okay." If that's the description of their first experience, then you may want to look elsewhere for a system.

Importing Video

Most nonlinear editing systems have a similar procedure for importing video segments: the user connects a camcorder or VCR to the system and clicks an on-screen button similar to a "record" button on a VCR (see fig. 3.3). When the desired segment is recorded, the user presses the "stop" button. Look for a system that lets you name clips when you import them; if you are importing several clips, it could otherwise become confusing. Also, look for systems that allow importing at several different quality levels. Importing at a higher level gives a better-quality picture; importing at a lower level saves hard-drive space.

Importing Audio

Importing video is pretty straightforward. Importing audio varies from model to model. First, determine how you can import narration. Is there a microphone jack on the unit? Importing narration on a nonlinear system without a microphone jack means that you will have to attach an audio mixer to the system and plug the microphone into the audio mixer. Or you could narrate your script onto a videotape and import it via the VCR. Both solutions are easily avoided with a microphone jack!

Figure 3.3 Importing audio and video. Image courtesy of Applied Magic.

Next, determine how music will be imported into your program. Does the non-linear editing system have a built-in CD player? With some systems, a menu listing of audio tracks appears once the CD is inserted. Just click to import. If the CD player is not installed, can your portable CD player (a Walkman-style) be used? How about a cassette deck or an audio mixer? Find out before you buy.

Finally, how many audio tracks are available? One? Two? Three? Most nonlinear editing systems have at least two audio tracks—presumably one for narration and the other for music. But what if you want to add sound effects? Can you combine audio tracks on your prospective purchase?

Inputs and Outputs

Think about the outputs and inputs of your video and audio equipment: standard phono (RCA) connectors, S-VHS, IEEE-1394, microphone jack. Now, how many of these connectors can your prospective purchase accommodate? A system with multiple connection options—both input and output—is a great convenience.

Options do exist for systems that don't support multiple connections. For example, iMovie3, a software program on Apple computers, is a great entry-level editing program. But educators are often frustrated by the system's input and out-puts—IEEE-1394 (FireWire®) only for video, and a mini-jack for a microphone, along with the CD-ROM drive for music. Not a lot of choices. In other words, if you want to import video, it's FireWire® or nothing. You can add to your options by purchasing an analog/digital media converter, also known as a "codec" (for coder/decoder). A codec accepts the audio and video signal from your VCR or analog camcorder and converts it into IEEE-1394 signal. In essence, it is encoding your signal for use by the Apple iMovie software. The codec also decodes the digital signal, converting it to standard audio and video signal for recording onto a VHS VCR. A codec costs about $300, and a decoder-only unit (for converting finished projects to audio/video signal) sells for about half that. Sure, it would be great if the codec hardware was installed in the Apple computer, but it isn't. So we adapt.

In summary, look for a variety of input and output options on your prospective nonlinear editing purchase, or be prepared to buy an expensive media converter.

Trimming Clips

You will probably want to "trim" the audio and video clips that you import into your nonlinear editing system. To "trim" a clip means to adjust the starting point and the ending point of the clip (see fig. 3.4). Do you have to change screens to trim a clip? If so, is it easy to find your way back to the editing screen? Can you hear the audio while trimming a clip? This is important, especially when the audio information is important to the production. Finally, when you trim a clip, is there a way to restore it if you accidentally trim too much? All of these are important considerations.

Figure 3.4 Trimming clips stored in digital format. Image courtesy of Applied Magic.

Transitions

Remember those traditional linear editing systems we told you about? Well, most of those systems were "cuts only." In other words, you could only perform editing cuts—no dissolves, no fades, no wipes, no swirls. Some nonlinear editing systems perform only a handful of transitions. Others perform dozens, with additional transitions available for purchase. Certainly, it is easy to have too many transitions in a video project, but it is nice to have a full menu from which to choose.

Image Adjustment

What happens if an image is too bright or too dark? Does your nonlinear editor allow you to adjust the image? Some systems allow you to correct the color, or even eliminate it altogether, creating black-and-white segments. Image adjustments will help your editors correct those less-than-perfect shots.

Effects

A generous effects menu is a nice feature of a nonlinear editing system. Slow motion, fast motion, strobe, and reverse image are just a few of the most common effects. Sure, it is easy to overuse effects, but one or two effects well placed within a video project can enhance its creative content and make it more watchable.

Graphics

Most nonlinear editing systems have built-in character generators that allow the editor to add text to video projects. When evaluating this aspect of a nonlinear editing system, use the same criteria as discussed for character generators in chapter 1. Look at the quality of the graphic screens. How many fonts are included? Can additional fonts be added? Can the graphics fade in and fade out? Is there a scrolling function? Your nonlinear system's graphics function should meet or exceed the quality of your stand-alone character generator.

Image Processing Speed (Rendering)

As we composed this chapter, science fiction enthusiasts were celebrating the twentieth anniversary of the motion picture *Tron*. *Tron* was the first movie to make extensive use of computer graphics, and it is considered a breakthrough in computer effects. Graphics for *Tron* were rendered at 10 minutes per frame. It took about

9,000 hours of computer time to make *Tron*'s 30 minutes of on-screen computer graphics.[1]

It is with this knowledge in hand that we consider the rendering time of the nonlinear editing systems on the market today. Compared with 1982 standards, even the slowest nonlinear editor is light-years ahead. Compared with the attention span of the average middle schooler, today's rendering speeds are either "adequate" or "eternal."

When a transition (a dissolve, a wipe, etc.) is selected, an effect applied, or text added, most nonlinear editing systems will need to render that effect. New digital footage is created by the editing system, frame by frame, to accomplish the transition, effect, or graphic. This takes time. In some editing systems, the editor can continue working on other phases of the production—importing audio, trimming clips, and so on—while this rendering takes place. With other systems, the editor must patiently wait while the machine does its work. Some rendering sessions last only a few seconds. Others (like applying a slow-motion effect to a three-minute clip) can take 10 minutes or more. Time to read the newspaper or watch TV (*Tron*, anyone?).

Before buying a nonlinear editing system, find out how long typical rendering sessions last. Create scenarios you might encounter, and ask a salesperson to estimate. "If I want to add a transition between two segments, how long will it take to render?" Or, "If I need to brighten a 15-second segment, how long will that take?" "If I need to add a title to my program, how long will that graphic need to render?" If they can't provide accurate estimates, call the manufacturer or better yet, interview a fellow educator who uses the same system. A notable exception to the rendering rule is Applied Magic's Screenplay system, which needs rendering time for only the most complex functions (such as combining slow motion and a dissolve with a graphic), and those rendering times are quick. Of course, Screenplay is one of the most expensive models in its class—two or three times the price of nonlinear editors with longer rendering times. But if your time is limited (as with most educators), and you need to have several students use the nonlinear editing system within a certain time frame, then this could be a wise choice for you.

As you can imagine, rendering time decreases as computer processing speed increases. Nonlinear editing systems use components identical or similar to those used in computers. As newer nonlinear systems become available, rendering speed may become a marginal issue. For now, however, it is a characteristic worthy of careful investigation and evaluation.

Memory Storage

Because a nonlinear editing system is a computer, memory is always an issue. There are three memory-related criteria for a nonlinear editing system: 1) How

l drive that comes with the system? ? and 3) Are there external storage

etter. Think about the total time for g" at the same time. For the second system uses and if you can upgrade rd drive in the future and install it hard drive that must be installed at tion, find out about external mem- er hard drive via a USB, IEEE-1394, iose external drives? Also, does the ing projects on a disk-based system DR? Make sure to buy a system that

Upgrades

Just as you will probably want to add to your hard-drive space, you will probably also want to upgrade the nonlinear editing system at some point. (Typical upgrades could include adding more effects, more fonts, a digital video IEEE-1394 interface, or newer releases of the software that runs the editor.) Determine if the system you are considering is upgradable. Will you be able to upgrade your system, or must you buy an entirely new system? Also, determine if the upgrades are easily available, if they are affordable, and if more upgrades are continually developed.

Finally, make sure you know exactly what you are buying. Models on the exhibit hall floor or in the equipment showroom often feature every hardware and software option available. Ask for a demonstration of the system that you are going to purchase. A selling point for you might actually be an upgrade that you hadn't decided to buy.

Number of Projects, Passwords Protection

Some nonlinear editing systems limit the user to the number of projects that can be stored at once. Most manufacturers sell special "school editions" that increase that number to accommodate more ongoing student productions. Make sure that your nonlinear editing system will accommodate an adequate number of continuing video projects. In addition, some systems offer project password protection, so that one student cannot open another student's project. (A master password for the teacher is usually part of the package.) This is a nice added feature, especially if several students will be using the same nonlinear editing system throughout the day.

Value and Price

Of course, all of these criteria lead to the issues of value and price. For most of us, price is a primary consideration. We have a certain amount of money that we can spend and a certain number of students that we would like to serve. With a budget of $8,000, we could buy two Applied Magic Screenplay systems, but we could buy 6 AVIOs by Macrovision or 10 entry-level iMacs with iMovie3. Which is the better decision? That is up to you. Consider how many students are enrolled in your production class, how many projects they will be editing, and the possibility of future funding. Learn all you can about each system by applying the above criteria. Determine which systems represent the best value for your school.

Added Purchases

As mentioned earlier in this chapter, you will need to buy additional audio and video equipment to make full use of your nonlinear editing system.

Videocassette Recorder

Because nonlinear editing is tapeless editing, a VCR will not be included in a nonlinear system that you buy. All nonlinear editing systems are capable of producing excellent-quality video, so it makes sense to invest in a higher-quality video format, such as S-VHS or MiniDV. (A complete discussion of video formats appears in chapter 1.) The S-VHS format is extremely appealing to educators these days. Recently, the price of S-VHS VCRs has dropped dramatically, from about $600 just a few years ago to about $150. Accordingly, S-VHS videotape—necessary for recording a true S-VHS signal—has dropped in price as well, from about $10 per tape to less than $4 per tape. The next format to follow this price-dropping trend will probably be MiniDV. A dual-deck VCR that accommodates both MiniDV and S-VHS formats is available for about $1,000, thousands less than previous editions.

Can you connect a household-quality VHS VCR to a nonlinear editing system, providing the correct jacks are available, and record your programs onto VHS videotape? Sure, but it seems a shame to record a potentially high-quality video signal (not to mention CD-quality sound) onto VHS, which is capable of recording only 240 lines of resolution. S-VHS records at least 400 lines of video resolution, and MiniDV records at least 500 lines. Consider investing in a higher-quality format, and investigate the lower-priced S-VHS units.

Camcorder

Of course, you will need a camcorder to record the raw footage that you edit. The same argument for a high-quality format also applies to camcorders. If you're using VHS or VHS-C camcorders, consider upgrading to S-VHS or MiniDV. Prices of higher-end format camcorders have dropped dramatically in recent years, making them affordable to schools.

TV/Monitors

You will need at least one TV/monitor as a work screen for your projects. Some systems seem more comfortable with two monitors—one for the editing menu screen, and another to display the output of the VCR. Consumer-level TV/monitors will be appropriate for beginners. Advanced students will notice the higher-quality picture of industrial-level monitors, which sell for about $300 for the 13-inch size.

Computer Monitor

Some nonlinear editing systems require a computer monitor. A 17-inch monitor provides a better on-screen workspace than a smaller monitor. With these systems, it is appropriate to connect both a computer monitor and a TV to the system; the images will look slightly different. (Of course, the TV should be the benchmark because that will be the viewing medium for the final program.)

Audio Components

Depending on the system, you may need to buy additional audio components. Of course, this need is based on the type of video production you will be performing. Simple editing of videotaped segment will require no additional audio components. However, a microphone will be necessary for additional narration. Some nonlinear editing systems have built-in CD players; others do not. You may need to buy a CD player or cassette deck, or both, to import your music. (Fortunately, Walkman-type portable players can usually connect to nonlinear editing systems via the audio input jacks.) The need for additional audio equipment varies greatly between nonlinear editing systems. Remember to determine this need before you buy, and factor the cost of these elements into your purchasing decisions.

Music

Your students will want to add music to their productions. If you haven't already, this is a great time to start a production (buy-out) music collection. A complete discussion of production music appears in chapter 2, and we've relisted some useful production music Web sites at the end of this chapter.

Animated Backgrounds

Have you ever noticed those cool animated backgrounds in TV programs and commercials? You know—the rolling clouds, the starry skies, the swirling geometric figures, and the science fiction scenes, just to name a few. Those animations are available for your nonlinear editing systems, and your students will love using them as backgrounds for titles, for chroma key, and as transitional video segments. Three companies that offer animated backgrounds are Digital Hotcakes, Digital Juice, and Elite Video. Animated backgrounds are usually available on high-quality formats—S-VHS and MiniDV. Some companies also produce animations on CD-ROM for use in nonlinear editing systems that can import those formats as well. Make sure you know which format to buy before ordering. Pricing for a volume of animated backgrounds—from 10 to 25 animations—begins at about $100. Check the Web sites listed at the end of the chapter for more details.

Buying a System

Now that you know the selection criteria for nonlinear editing systems, where do you look? The local electronics stores don't sell editing systems (yet), and it really doesn't make sense to conduct such an expensive purchase via catalog or the Internet based simply on advertising material. No, you need more information than that!

Try before You Buy

Nowhere is the concept of a "test-drive" more important than in the purchase of a nonlinear editing system. There is simply no substitute for using the equipment before you buy. And just as you probably conducted two or three test-drives before buying your automobile, you need to test-drive more than one editing system so that you will have a good basis for comparison.

Visit Other Schools

Make a few phone calls to other schools in your area and determine which non-linear editing systems are available. Call your fellow educator (bring some snacks!), and plan to spend an hour or more on their nonlinear editing system. Ask your colleague about his or her impressions of the system. Does it do what they want it to do? Do students enjoy using it? How about rendering time? Did it work "out of the box?" What additional purchases were necessary? Ask to see some video projects made with the nonlinear editing system. Use the criteria discussed here and take lots of notes.

Technology Conferences

If you have the opportunity, attend an educational technology conference. Many nonlinear editing systems are on display at these conferences, and it's a great time to talk to the manufacturer directly. In the exhibit hall, you'll get the chance to work with the system and learn how it works with other audio and video components (see fig. 3.5). Most technology conferences post their list of vendors on the Internet a few weeks before the conference.

In addition, one-hour sessions and extended workshops that address non-linear video editing are becoming more frequent at these conferences. (The au-

Figure 3.5 Screenplay nonlinear editing system with additional purchases—camcorder and monitor. Image courtesy of Applied Magic.

thors frequently present on this topic.) When you hear about a technology conference in your area, visit the conference's Web site and make a few phone calls. With a little luck, you'll be able to participate in sessions and talk to vendors in the exhibit hall.

Host a Workshop

If several educators in your area are interested in buying nonlinear editing systems, consider hiring a consultant who can bring each system to your school district for an extended hands-on audition. This might seem excessive, but do the math. Fifteen educators in your district plan to spend about $4,000 each on nonlinear editing systems. Can your district afford a $60,000 mistake? (The authors are among several consultants who will provide this service. For details, see www .SCHOOLTV.com.)

Magazines

As nonlinear editing becomes more popular, a few magazines have emerged to meet the desire for more information. *Videomaker* magazine is head and shoulders above the rest, and every school that is interested in nonlinear editing should subscribe. Pick up an issue at your local newsstand, or visit the company's Web site, listed at the end of the chapter. Although a magazine can't substitute for a hands-on demonstration, *Videomaker* frequently offers evaluations of current systems and informs readers about new developments in the industry.

Walk through a Project

All nonlinear editing systems operate just a little bit differently—different enough to be compared but similar enough to generalize a description of the process. To make sure you understand the role that each nonlinear editing system feature plays in the process, this section will walk you through the creation of a complex video project. The goal is to show you the importance of each criterion and to let you assign your own value to the criteria so that you can select a nonlinear editing system that best meets your needs.

Several of your students have recently become interested in the preservation of a local river. The river has long been a source of recreation and enjoyment for members of your community, and almost everyone can point to a time when they swam, canoed, or picnicked at one of the river's many public parks. Recently, the owners of the privately held riverfront property have shown an interest in building homes and condominiums along the river, and the local residents are concerned about the development's impact on their treasured resource. Several students in your TV production class are also members of the school's Science Club, and their sponsor, Ms. Earle, is supportive of their video production efforts. The students would like to create a video documenting the history of the river, the enjoyment that local residents experience on the river, and the potential change to the riverfront property. Ms. Earle sees this project as a way to enhance the students' understanding of the ecosystem, and you see it as an excellent vehicle to explore the capabilities of your nonlinear editing system.

After a brainstorming session, and the creation of a list of necessary elements, the students begin collecting the raw footage for the project. One group of students travels to the river on a Sunday afternoon and uses a MiniDV camcorder to videotape several groups enjoying their leisure activities. The parent of one of your students rents a canoe and paddles along the river as his daughter, seated in the front of the canoe, records a 10-minute trip segment using another MiniDV camcorder. Another pair of students uses a MiniDV camcorder to conduct on-camera interviews with local parties who have a stake in the river: the chairperson of the local planning commission, lifelong community members, riverfront property owners who wish to develop their property, and the president of the local conservation society opposing the development. Finally, another student is researching the history of the river. He uses a digital still camera to take snapshots of historic photos that he cannot borrow because they are too rare and too valuable—in essence, he is taking "a picture of a picture." While conducting this research, the student meets a local resident who lets him borrow an old VHS videotape, made in the 1980s, of their family reunion held along the river.

Students are also working on music for the program. They have reviewed the school's collection of production music and selected an appropriate song for the introduction. They have also used Smartsound software to create a custom-made musical selection to play during the video. The Smartsound song is burned onto a CD for use at the school.

When all of the raw footage and music is collected, students begin to import those elements into the nonlinear editing system. The MiniDV camcorder is connected to the nonlinear editing system via the IEEE-1394 jack, and the video and audio signals are recorded onto the system's hard drive. This recording, or "importing," includes the Sunday-afternoon footage, the river-trip footage, and the on-camera interviews.

A VHS VCR is then connected to the nonlinear editing system via the composite (RCA-phono) jacks, and the video from the 1980s family reunion videotape is captured onto the hard drive. Then the digital still camera is connected to the nonlinear editing system via the digital camera's video out jack. Each digital photo is recorded for several seconds (remember, you used the digital photos to capture the historic photos).

Now, the two musical selections—both on CD—must be imported. Fortunately, this nonlinear editing system has a built-in CD player, so importing the songs is a snap. (In the absence of a built-in CD player, a portable CD player could be connected to the audio inputs of the nonlinear editing system.)

The students now begin the task of assembling their video segments into a finished project. Most clips will be trimmed—an easy task using the nonlinear editing system. The historic photos are all converted to black and white for consistency, and color correction is used to adjust the videotape from the 1980s. Clips are selected from the "bin," an on-screen list that features thumbnail frames to help you identify each clip. Then, the clips are dragged onto a storyboard line in the desired order (see fig. 3.6). Transitions (mostly dissolves) are placed between each shot and rendered by the nonlinear editor. Music is added at appropriate points.

Graphics are created and superimposed over the appropriate shots. The name of each on-camera guest is placed near the bottom of those screens, and the date of each historic photo is superimposed over those shots as well. "We need to make a credits page for the end," says one of your students. "Yes," says another, "and we need to list the community members who provided information for this project." A few graphics screens are created to meet these needs and placed at the end of the program.

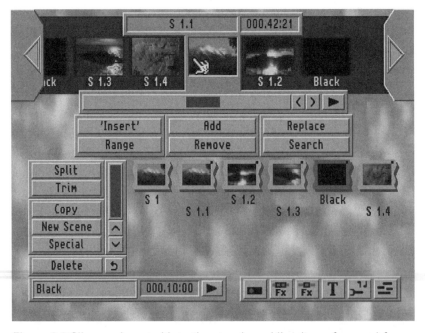

Figure 3.6 Clips are inserted into the storyboard line (top of screen) from the clip bin (center). Image courtesy of MacroSystem US, Inc.

Just when the editing process is almost finished, you ask your students, "Has anybody thought about a title for this project?" They quickly realize that they need to not only decide on a title but insert a graphic screen at the beginning of the program as well. If you were using a traditional editing system, this late realization would have been a catastrophe. The students would have had to begin all over again, this time starting with the graphic. But with a nonlinear editing system, the students can quickly create a graphic with their title—"Our River—Profit or Promise?"—and place it at the beginning of the program.

Your students decide that the title screen needs to be something special—not just a graphic over a background color. They want a beautiful sunrise to serve as the background. The students recall that all of their videotape was recorded well after sunrise, and they're sure no one has a sunrise on videotape. Instead of fretting, or planning a predawn trip back to the river, they use an animated background from "Animated Skydrops" by Digital Hotcakes, which the school owns on S-VHS videotape. An S-VHS VCR is connected to the nonlinear editing system's S-VHS input, and that portion of the videotape is imported. The graphic is superimposed to create the title.

One of the students now presses the "play" button, and you all watch the finished program for the first time. It's wonderful (of course!), but you have a couple of suggestions to make—rearrange a couple of the interviews, and fade out the music when it gets a little too loud. As you probably realize, these changes would be impossible using a traditional linear editing system. But with a nonlinear system, the changes are made quickly. The students view the result and agree that the changes improve the program.

Now, it's time to record the program. Because the S-VHS VCR is already connected, the students record the program onto S-VHS videotape using the S-VHS and audio outputs of the nonlinear editing system. Then a standard VHS VCR is connected, and several VHS copies are made—one for each crewmember and a couple to save for contest entries. (Because the music and animated backdrop that you used are royalty free, you can make copies without worry.) Finally, the MiniDV camcorder is connected, and a copy is made in that format as well. Why? Because MiniDV is the highest-quality format that you own. This videotape will serve as your archive copy in the likely event that the original project will one day be erased from the nonlinear editing system's hard drive.

In recent years, nonlinear editing systems have improved exponentially, dropped dramatically in price, and represent the only reasonable option for schools that want to buy editing equipment. As with most audio and video equipment, the marketplace is diverse, ranging from million-dollar systems designed for network television to featureless cut-and-paste systems that offer no more than a digital chopping block. Armed with the selection criteria discussed in this chapter, and willing to spend the time required for hands-on evaluations of affordable nonlinear editing systems, educators can make a wise decision and purchase a system that best meets the needs of their school.

Helpful Internet Links

Animated Backgrounds

Digital Hotcakes/Tri-Lab Productions: http://www.animationsforvideo.com

Digital Juice: http://www.digitaljuice.com

Elite Video: http://www.elitevideo.com

Audio and Video Production Equipment

Audio-Technica (Microphones): http://www.audiotechnica.com

JVC (Camcorders, VCRs): http://www.jvc.com

Mackie (Audio mixers): http://www.Mackie.com

Panasonic (Camcorders, VCRs, monitors, audio mixers): http://www.panasonic.com

RadioShack (Audio mixers, microphones, VCRs, headphones): http://www.radioshack.com

Shure (Microphones): http://www.shure.com

Production (Buy-Out) Music Libraries

The Canary Collection: http://www.canarymusic.com

Davenport Music: http://www.davenportmusic.com

Geoffrey Wilson Buyout Music: http://gwilsonbuyoutmusic.com

Mokal Music: http://www.productionmusicmall.com

Music2Hues: http://www.music2hues.com

PBTM/QCCS Music Library: http://www.pbtm.com

Signature Music: http://www.sigmusic.com

Soundzabound Music Library: http://www.soundzabound.com

Professional Resources

SCHOOLTV.com (The authors' Web site features helpful information to educators working with television production.): http://www.schooltv.com

Videomaker Magazine: http://www.videomaker.com

Royalty-Free Music Creation Software

Smartsound Software (Movie Maestro and Sonicfire Pro): http://www.smartsound.com

Stand-Alone Editing Systems

Apple I-Movie: http://www.apple.com/imovie

Applied Magic (Screenplay and Sequel): http://www.applied-magic.com

MacroSystem (AVIO and Kron): http://www.casablanca.tv

Note

1. David Hutchins, "'Tron' Turns 20," *Tech Live,* January 15, 2002. Available: http://www.techtv.com/screensavers/print/0,23102,3368378,00.html. Accessed February 14, 2002.

Chapter 4

~~~

Buying Television Production Equipment and Services for Schools

In the previous chapters, we described audio, video, and nonlinear digital video editing equipment. We told you exactly what to look for in your prospective purchases. Now, you need to buy the equipment. But where? The choice of vendor is every bit as important as the equipment choice itself. A substandard vendor can ruin even the wisest purchasing decisions. And an excellent vendor can make the purchasing experience rewarding for everyone. By carefully spending your allotted budget with the right vendors and augmenting those funds using resourceful techniques, you can help your school develop a functional television production studio.

Although many teachers and media specialists are unfamiliar with purchasing large-ticket items for schools, the interaction between educator and vendor can be mutually beneficial. Whether you are buying editing equipment, blank tape, or duplication services, you should enter each transaction aware of what to expect from a vendor. In this chapter, we'll focus on the business relationships you'll need to run a successful school television production program. They include equipment purchases, equipment rental, equipment repair, purchase of blank videotape, and video duplication service.

But before you start spending money, or even looking for the best vendor, you need to establish some criteria for deciding that it's time to make a purchase for your program.

Assessment of Existing Equipment

"Do you have any television production equipment in your school?" This is a silly question to ask most teachers and media specialists. Although television production is relatively new in educational applications, most schools do have at least a few pieces of equipment. Whether the equipment collection contains up-to-date camcorders, audio mixers, and editing suites or just a 10-year-old VCR and a TV, very few schools will be starting from scratch when establishing a television production program. However, the amount of use that this equipment has received usually depends on the media specialist's attitude toward video production. It is typical for a teacher or media specialist who decides to undertake television production to find a cache of equipment in the media center that is old, outdated, or in disrepair. He or she must assess this equipment and its value to the school. This task becomes especially important as tough funding decisions come up. Is it finally time to replace that camcorder? Should I spend my equipment budget on a new character generator? As you try to determine the usefulness of the equipment that your school presently owns, ask yourself the following questions.

Can Students Create Good Programming with the Equipment?

Most video production equipment has improved greatly over the past few years, and audience expectations have followed suit. The equipment on hand may not be able to produce the shows that your administration, faculty, and students expect.

Although sincere in effort, a video program produced with outdated equipment may draw more attention to the outdated technology than to the intended message. If your program of instruction is to develop, faculty and students must be able to make video projects of which they will be proud.

One of the most profound equipment improvements has been in the development of inexpensive, professional-looking character generation. Fifteen years ago, most schools were happy with the built-in character generators available on video cameras, even though typing a title was similar to setting a digital watch, and cameras offered no choice of fonts or letter size. Most schools fumbled through these operations because sophisticated character generators cost thousands of dollars. Now, character generators offering multiple fonts and dazzling effects can be purchased for less than $500.

Another example of inexpensive technological advances has been the development new videotape formats that have emerged in recent years. In the early 1990s, there were really only two videotape format options for schools—regular VHS and S-VHS. Regular VHS was affordable and offered only average picture quality. S-VHS had superior picture quality but was expensive. Now, formats such as MiniDV and Digital 8mm are superior in quality and much less expensive than VHS was 10 years ago. Audiences are accustomed to seeing bright, sharp video and will probably notice when a video program is made with older VHS equipment.

Is the Equipment Dependable for Daily Use?

Nothing can destroy enthusiasm for television production more quickly than equipment that breaks frequently or performs only part of the time. Imagine a battery charger that doesn't work consistently. Each morning your students dutifully connect the camcorder battery to the charger, and in the afternoon it's still dead as a doornail. Or imagine recording an interview, only to discover later that the microphone cut in and out. If your older equipment is not dependable, send it to surplus and begin evaluating the newer models.

Does the Equipment Need Frequent Repair?

Equipment that is frequently in the repair shop may cost more to maintain than the purchase price of a new item. Perform a quick cost-benefit analysis on each item of equipment that is sent for repair. What will be the value of the equipment *after* it is repaired? A five-year-old camcorder that has performed considerable service is probably worth less than you expect. Repair service can cost more than $50 per hour and often involves losing the use of the equipment for several days or even weeks. Make sure that your equipment budget isn't spent just on keeping obsolete equipment in working order.

Does the Equipment's Size and Weight Make It Difficult to Operate?

Like cellular phones and personal stereos, television production equipment has gotten smaller and lighter over the past few years. This is especially evident in camcorders and camera-deck systems. Schools that purchased video equipment in the early to mid-1980s probably selected separate camera and recording deck systems. Such systems are probably too large and heavy for smaller students to successfully operate. Many older systems even required a media cart to store the "portable" system. Smaller, lightweight camcorders that can be handled by all children should be made available.

Does the Equipment Require Extreme Operating Conditions?

Once again, video cameras and camcorders provide the best example for improved operating under extreme conditions. Older video cameras and camcorders require a great deal of light—so much that lighting instruments are required. Classroom shooting without these extra lights is impossible. Newer camcorders can produce an excellent signal with normal classroom lighting.

Microphones provide another example. In past years, microphones were hidden in flower arrangements or mounted on fish poles held by robust technicians. Now, advanced lavaliere, shotgun, and PZMs provide unobtrusive audio recording in difficult situations. Equipment available today can operate in the normal school environment.

Does Continued Use of Equipment Impede Production Goals?

Students and school personnel, as well as the general public, have become quite sophisticated in their knowledge of the capabilities of video production. Are students who use the equipment continuously frustrated by its limitations? Here are some features that are considered basic in newer school video production equipment:

Chroma key. The ability to make people appear to be in a different setting by placing them in front of a green screen. (The weather reporter uses this technology to appear standing in front of a giant weather map.)

Digital effects. Strobe, paint, positive-negative, freeze-frame, and image reversal are available on most advanced camcorders and video mixers. Split-screen and that little graphics box over the news anchor's shoulder are also commonplace.

Graphics. Character generators offer dozens of type styles and background colors. Drop-shadows and graphic superimposition are also common features. Titles and credits now roll and crawl smoothly on most systems.

Digital video editing. Students can import their raw footage into a computer, trim and rearrange segments, add graphics and audio, and export the finished project to a videotape.

Do you dream of chroma key, digital video editing, multiple fonts, and digital effects (all of which are now available economically)? If your equipment becomes a source of frustration instead of an outlet for inspiration, then start shopping.

Is Updated, Reasonably Priced Equipment Available?

You will probably be able to find equipment that meets both your needs and your budget. In many cases, prices are falling as production power increases. Here are some examples.

In 1997 a VHS camcorder recording at home-video quality cost about $1,200. In 2003, a MiniDV camcorder that shoots broadcast quality video sells for half that much.

In 1997 digital video editing was not affordable to most schools (in fact, in our 1998 book, we discouraged such a purchase). Now, outstanding digital video editing systems are priced in the $1,300 price range—less than half the cost of the previous two-VCR editing configuration.

If you haven't opened a video equipment catalog or visited your equipment dealer recently, you should. Amazing developments have been made in the past few years that may allow your students to create programs that they dream of making.

Does the Equipment Facilitate Teaching Valuable Skills?

This question is probably more important to teachers working in high school than in middle or elementary school. Enlightened television production instructors realize that television production class is the present-day shop class. Students in auto-repair shop get to use tools that are also used in professional situations. Serious television production students should be given the same opportunity. Ideally, students who complete two or three years of high school video production class have learned enough to help them in a vocational or college program or in the workforce as entry-level video workers. Strive to obtain production equipment that will help prepare students to meet their future goals.

Learning about audio and video equipment and staying informed about new developments represent significant challenges for media professionals. Do not let these tasks prevent or delay your involvement in television production activities. Begin with a small group of dedicated students and the rudimentary tools of the trade. Relax. Create. Have fun. Learn and grow with your students as you build your school production facility.

In the rest of this chapter, we examine five ways in which school television production programs work with vendors: equipment purchases, equipment rental, equipment repair, purchase of blank videotape, and videotape duplication service.

Equipment Purchases

Video equipment is expensive. Schools that are developing television production departments will find that a stand-alone digital editing system costs more than a multimedia computer, a dozen overhead projectors, or a class set of history books. Signing the check for the equipment purchase is only the final step in a complex selection process. First, the purchaser must become aware of the equipment that is on the market.

Discovering the Marketplace

There are several ways to learn about audio and video equipment currently available for purchase. Probably the best way is to talk with other teachers and media specialists who are working in television production. Call or visit and ask for specific model numbers of the equipment that they are using. Ask questions such as the following:

"What is your favorite feature on this component?"
"What is the greatest difficulty in using the equipment?"
"What features would make the equipment more useful?"

Consult your district-level media supervisor for a list of recommended video production equipment. Many school-district offices have small television production studios. Visit this facility and ask the same questions. After several phone calls and visits, you will have a good idea of the equipment available for purchase.

Another way to learn about equipment is to read articles in mass-market and educational periodicals. Several newsstand magazines about videography have emerged in recent years. Although they target the consumer or hobbyist, these magazines can provide a bridge to the marketplace. Pay special attention to the equipment advertisements. Several professional educational technology periodicals are also available. Reading a few issues should bring you up to date on recent equipment developments. Your district-level media supervisor should be an excellent source for these periodicals.

You may find that some periodicals are published by national and state professional educational-technology organizations. All teachers and media specialists who work with television production should become members of these organizations. Your access to information about equipment will greatly increase once this professional connection is made.

Your next state media conference should also be an excellent resource for learning about equipment. Such conferences usually offer several workshops about production techniques. A few hours spent in the vendor exhibit hall will undoubtedly be educational. Local and national vendors frequently display their latest equipment models at these shows. Conferences are especially important to teachers and media specialists working in rural areas or in areas that are not already involved in production activities.

Of course, the World Wide Web is a great place to learn about the different equipment models and their features. Almost all of the equipment manufacturers have their own Web sites filled with details about their products. You can also use company Web sites to make sure that the most recent model is being purchased. Imagine the heartbreak of learning that a newer camcorder or audio mixer—with a lower price—was available for purchase! Speaking of price, manufacturers' Web sites usually list the suggested retail price for their equipment. The company price is usually a bit high, leaving room for vendors to compete for your sale. Learn the suggested retail price before the shopping process begins.

Finally, visit local vendors who sell audio and video production equipment. Talk to the salesperson and describe your interests and needs. A good salesperson will be happy to demonstrate the latest models. This first contact can be very important when evaluating vendors. Visit your vendor monthly to stay informed about television production equipment.

Funding Equipment Purchases

Once you become familiar with audio and video equipment and select a specific model based on the criteria discussed earlier in this book, you are ready to find funding for your purchase. Money to purchase equipment may be available from several sources at your school, at the school district level, and outside the school system.

Donations

Many smaller items that would otherwise deplete school funds can be obtained through donations. School parent-teacher groups such as the PTA have long supported schools by providing funding for purchases that exceed the school budget. Make a presentation at your next PTA meeting. Play any videotape programs that your students have created in class and describe equipment that would enhance the students' educational experience. For example, tell the PTA about the importance of a tripod. You could include a humorous demonstration, asking a parent to videotape briefly without using a tripod. Then explain that a new tripod can be purchased for $150. This equipment-based approach will probably work better than asking for a flat $150 donation.

Businesses have also been known to make donations to schools. Perhaps a parent is the manager of a local discount store and can arrange for the donation of a dozen blank videotapes. Local merchants might also donate headphones, audio equipment, and office supplies that your program needs. Write a letter to store managers to request a small donation. You may only receive a few positive responses, but you will never know until you ask.

Is there a television station near your school? This may be another source of donations. Most television stations use videotape only once or twice and then discard it. Instead, the stations could donate their slightly used videotape to your program. Used equipment or discarded sets, including backdrops, props, and furniture, may also be available. Station employees are often quite interested to know that their trade is being taught in schools. A phone call or visit to a television station can result in a rewarding partnership.

Television stations and video production facilities can also make another kind of donation—a donation of service. Until they can raise the money to buy their own editing systems and character generators, many schools receive help in those areas from television stations. An added benefit to this relationship is that you are providing your students with industry role models. A student who visits a television station to create graphics for the video yearbook may soon find him- or herself working part-time at the station.

School Funding

In most school districts, the school principal receives discretionary money to spend on school projects. In fact, with school site-based management gaining popularity, this amount of money should be increasing. More than ever, school administrators have the power to make financial and curriculum decisions at their schools. Certainly, the school principal is an important ally in the attempt to gain funding for television production equipment. A good way to gain that support is to produce a short orientation tape for the next open house or back-to-school night. The program doesn't have to be complex—just a few camera shots with script audio dubbed. Perhaps your district-level media specialist or the media specialist at a neighboring school can help. A complete discussion appears in *Television Production for Elementary and Middle Schools* (Keith Kyker and Christopher Curchy [Englewood, Colorado: Libraries Unlimited, 1994]).

Most principals are thrilled with even the simplest programs. After the applause has subsided, make an appointment with your principal to talk about all the equipment you need to make even better videos. This approach always works better than complaining about the lack of equipment. A note of caution, however: Don't make unreasonable promises to produce video programs for the school as a condition for obtaining equipment. Many people are not aware of the time involved in school productions. A promise to produce a weekly 10-minute program for the local cable TV station is probably not realistic for most media specialists. Instead, emphasize the educational aspects of video production. Use books like our *Video Projects for Elementary and Middle Schools* (Keith Kyker and Christopher Curchy [Englewood, Colorado: Libraries Unlimited, 1995]) to suggest projects that students can create with the new equipment.

Most elementary and middle schools host one or two book fairs each year. Even a modestly successful book fair can raise $1,000 for the school. If you put on such an event, plan to reserve at least a portion of the profit for future equipment purchases. A book fair could easily buy an audio mixer, cassette deck, CD player, and several microphones. And certainly, your administration would applaud this earnest attempt to provide funding for your studio.

Finally, many states have earmarked special funding for technology. Ask your school administration and your district media specialist about the availability of special technology funds.

Grants

Many teachers and media specialists have become proficient grant writers. School districts have established grants offices to assist schools in obtaining private funding. Grant writing involves hours of work and may not result in a payoff, but many schools have built production studios and technology labs using grant awards.

Video Sales and Services

Funding from video sales and services is used by schools that already have established television production programs. (Obviously, one cannot produce video for profit unless equipment is already on hand.) Many schools make a profit on graduation tapes, fashion-show tapes, and video yearbooks. See our *Television Production: A Classroom Approach* for complete details on video yearbook production. Also, nonprofit groups may make a donation to your school in exchange for video services. Once a program is established, new fund-raising opportunities in video production become available.

Be aware that none of these ideas is designed to stand alone as a source of funding for a television production department. In a single year, an aggressive media specialist could obtain donations from a parent-teacher organization, local businesses, and a local television station. The specialist could also receive school funding to buy a new camcorder and buy audio equipment with book-fair profits. A high school may even record graduations and sell the tapes for profit. Once the program has the necessary equipment, funding efforts can instead focus on equipment maintenance and adding new items of interest.

Selecting a Vendor

Once the decision to buy equipment is made and the funding is obtained, the media specialist must select a vendor from whom to purchase the equipment. Unfortunately, this process is quite different from the purchasing that most teachers are familiar with, such as ordering books, periodicals, and supplies. Television equipment prices can vary greatly from vendor to vendor, depending on the vendor's source of the equipment. Vendors who purchase directly from the factory and in quantity can offer better prices. With television equipment, you may also need the vendor to answer technical questions and provide service if the equipment breaks. For this reason, we present a critical list: the 10 ways to spot a good vendor.

1. **The vendor is factory authorized to sell the brand name and product line.** If you have decided to purchase a MacroSystem AVIO nonlinear editing system, you should be buying from a MacroSystem factory-authorized dealer. Manufacturers carefully investigate the integrity of these vendors. They have planned a long-term relationship and have established bookkeeping, warranty, and return policies with these vendors. Think of factory authorization as a "Good Housekeeping Seal of Approval."

2. **Professionally produced literature is available in quantity.** The vendor should be able to provide a printed pamphlet about each piece of equipment. This literature should include photographs, a complete description, and technical specifications and should address most of the criteria discussed in previous chapters. Don't be satisfied with poor-quality photocopies.

3. **Equipment is available for demonstration in a showroom.** The vendor should have a well-stocked showroom in which a salesperson can demonstrate each item of equipment for sale. Do not buy from a catalog unless you are already familiar with the equipment.

4. **The vendor can answer general questions from memory and technical questions within minutes.** This knowledge indicates daily involvement with the equipment. Select another vendor if you find yourself educating the salesperson.

5. **The vendor can give quick price quotes and is willing to meet competitors' prices.** Vendors should have a working knowledge of the price of their equipment. Need for a return telephone call may indicate that the vendor is check-

ing his or her source, which may also be retail. Good businesses have established prices and should be willing to meet other quotes to keep your long-term business.

6. **Professional support and instruction are available if required.** A good vendor should be willing to provide brief instruction on substantial purchases. Unscrupulous vendors will quote a low price and then demand an "instruction fee" of $25 per hour or more to assist with the technical aspects of the purchase. The vendor should also provide information about using the item with your existing system. For example, if you purchase a character generator, the vendor should provide instructions for connecting the component to your VCR and monitor. Don't be subjected to vendor "dump and run." Ask about this service *before* you buy from a vendor.

7. **The vendor follows professional bookkeeping practices.** Your vendor should accept a school purchase order, provide all necessary paperwork at no ad-

ditional charge, follow a 30-day billing cycle, and understand that schools are generally slow in payment. If you find that your vendor is making harassing telephone calls to your school or district bookkeeper, discontinue all business with that vendor and voice your dissatisfaction to that vendor and to the district purchasing supervisor.

8. **References are available on request.** Ask about other customers and speak with them about their satisfaction with the vendor. Good vendors are proud to tell you about their happy customers.

9. **The vendor is attentive.** A good vendor likes to answer your questions. The staff wants to sell you equipment that will help your school, not equipment that is overstocked. Share your long-range plans with your vendor.

10. **The vendor acts as part of your educational team.** Good vendors want to know about your school. They want to see programs that your students have produced with the equipment that they have sold to you. This knowledge will help the vendor recommend future purchases. A good vendor knows that a strong school makes for a strong business community.

Are we looking for Super Vendor? Absolutely. Spending tax dollars is a huge responsibility and should be done carefully. Most experienced television production teachers and media specialists can relate instances when bad vendors have cost their program. Talk with colleagues and learn from their mistakes. Use these 10 criteria as a yardstick by which to measure all equipment vendors.

Needless to say, equipment mail-order companies and Internet-based vendors do not meet many of these criteria. Sometimes educators who are experienced with video production and know exactly what they want to buy can obtain better prices from a mail-order or Internet outlet. However, schools are usually better off forming a relationship with an established vendor who will work with the school and share responsibility for the program's success.

Total System versus Piecing Out

Imagine that your principal has budgeted $10,000 for the establishment of a small TV studio in your school. Your shopping list includes two camcorders, a VCR, a video mixer, a character generator, and some other pieces. Should you try to obtain the best price for each item, or should you request a system price that includes all components in one package? If you have little experience with connecting and operating the equipment, your best bet is to request the total-system price from several vendors and then buy all items from one vendor. The vendor who gets the sale should be willing to help connect the equipment and provide a brief demonstration. The opposite approach, "piecing out" the equipment, may save a few dollars but can backfire on you. A vendor who is selling only the VCR will probably not be too interested in helping you connect your video mixer. To give a real-life example, one school ordered $20,000 in video equipment and pieced out *every single item.* Can you imagine the expression on a vendor's face when he learned that he had been awarded the sale of one 6-foot cable? Eight different vendors were involved in the project, none of whom felt any particular responsibility to the school. If not for some aggressive self-education by the media specialist, the equipment may have never been used. Six months after the order was placed, the last item of equipment arrived, and the media specialist painstakingly installed the equipment herself. Perhaps a few dollars were saved, but the students that year gained very little experience with the equipment. Unless the teacher or media specialist has an above-average understanding of production equipment, we recommend that system pricing be used when possible.

Equipment Rental

Sometimes renting television production equipment is a desirable alternative to purchasing equipment. Renting may sound like a luxury, but in certain instances it makes real economic sense. Here are some of those situations:

Infrequent use. Certain items are needed only once or twice each school year, and their price makes purchase prohibitive. One example is a professional-quality portable video light, which sells for more than $300. A school that wants to shoot footage of the prom and homecoming dances will probably need the light to videotape on the relatively dark dance floor. Another example is an expensive wireless microphone system or a professional-quality shotgun microphone to be used in producing a dramatic video.

Special projects requiring sophisticated effects. When producing special projects, such as video yearbooks and orientation tapes, schools may want to add sophisticated editing techniques, digital video effects, and graphics. Video production businesses found in most medium and large cities offer suites in which the general public can use advanced equipment. These suites usually rent on an hourly basis and may include instruction. Many video businesses will give lower prices to schools.

Extended demonstrations and evaluations. Most vendors allow single-day evaluations of video equipment, but some media specialists may desire extended demonstrations. Extending the evaluation period to several days could require a rental fee. For example, a school contemplating purchase of a digital video mixer may want to rent the mixer for a few days to allow several students the opportunity to evaluate the equipment. Also, high schools preparing students for college or vocational video work can rent the latest equipment for a few days to allow students to gain experience on components that the school cannot afford to purchase.

Equipment failure. Equipment rental can be a lifesaver when the school's equipment breaks as a deadline approaches. One school's editing system broke the day before the video yearbook master tape was to be sent for duplication. A local vendor provided a low-cost rental so that the school could complete this important fund-raiser.

When to Rent, When to Buy

When deciding whether to rent or purchase video production equipment, consider the following questions:

How often will the equipment be used? If the item will be used only once or twice each year, then renting is a real option.

What is the status of the current equipment collection? Is your school making the most of an understocked production studio? A second or third camcorder that would receive daily use is a wiser investment than a wireless microphone that would be used once a month.

Is the video production department financially healthy? A department that survives on a meager budget should not spend the entire amount on a rarely used prestige item, such as an animation computer. Avoid persuasive sales pitches and focus on your program's real needs.

Alternatives to Renting

There are two viable alternatives to renting rarely used equipment: equipment co-operatives and the district media center equipment. With the cooperative approach to equipment purchasing, two or more schools each contribute to the purchase of infrequently used equipment. The equipment can be housed at one school and scheduled for use by the other schools. The schools can share the repair and maintenance costs of the equipment.

Many school media centers are serviced by a district media center. Production equipment can be made available for check-out from the center. The center can also establish a small editing and graphics facility that teachers and students can visit to produce complex programs. Both cooperative equipment sharing and a district media center's involvement take planning and coordination among schools. However, the ownership of equipment and increased availability makes these options attractive when compared with rental costs.

Liability

Make sure to notify your school administration about your intention to rent video production equipment. School systems may require additional liability insurance to cover risk of loss or damage. Some school systems may not allow such rental. In any case, it is always better to inform your school administration about all business dealings that involve your video production program.

Equipment Repair

Video equipment that is used regularly will need repair and service. In fact, most schools active in video production can expect at least one repair each year. Whether the repair is as simple as fixing a broken microphone jack or as complex as replacing a video head, the repair must be done by someone qualified to perform the service.

Most instructors maintain a log of repairs performed on each item of equipment. If the same item needs frequent repair, it may be time to consider replacing it with a new purchase.

Before beginning any repair procedure, check the warranty on the equipment. Warranty periods and conditions vary greatly by vendor and manufacturer. Some schools even require an extended warranty period for their purchases. Also, be aware of impending warranty expiration dates. Make sure that the equipment is functioning at the time the warranty expires. The worst time to recognize a problem is the day after the warranty expires.

Repairs at the School Level

Some minor repairs may be conducted at the school level. Many high schools offer electronics classes that specialize in simple repairs. Instructors and students in these departments can solder loose cords and fix broken connectors. Some video production teachers take simple electronics classes and keep a soldering iron in the file cabinet. As always, make safety a prime concern, and leave major repairs to the professionals.

Professional Repairs

Most equipment repairs will be made by professionals. Most medium to large cities have repair shops that specialize in the repair of audio and video equipment. Here are some things to look for when selecting a repair company.

▣ **Reputation.** Ask fellow educators which businesses they use for repairs. The repair company should measure up to all the applicable criteria in the list that appears earlier in this chapter under "Selecting a Vendor."

▣ **Certification.** Select a repair business that has been authorized by the manufacturer to make repairs on the equipment. Call the telephone number listed in the manual, or check the manufacturer's Web site for a nearby repair facility. Such a listing or authorization generally indicates some level of professional training—either through a correspondence course or local workshop—in the repair of the specific equipment and a positive evaluation of the repair business. Businesses proudly display plaques, certificates, and professional signs that denote this factory endorsement. Audio and video components are quite complex and probably cannot be properly serviced by someone who also repairs vacuum cleaners and toaster ovens. Even if it means traveling to a nearby city or shipping your equipment via a parcel service, deal only with a factory-authorized repair facility.

▣ **On-site repair.** Beware of repair businesses that only fill out paperwork. Make sure that the repair will be performed on site at the repair shop. Some less-than-reputable repair facilities will send the equipment to another repair shop and increase your bill to make a profit. Also, if the actual repair facility loses or damages your equipment, you may not be able to fully recover your loss. Ask to meet the repair technician and see the repair bench.

▣ **Length of repair time.** Deal with a repair facility that can promise service within a few days. Beware of businesses that must continuously order parts and wait for delivery. They may not be factory authorized. Most factory-authorized repair shops keep replacement parts on hand or can obtain them within a day or two. Do not settle for extended time in the repair shop.

▣ **Pricing.** If you are fortunate enough to be able to choose between several facilities that meet the above criteria, comparison shop for the best repair prices. Equipment repair shops charge an hourly rate, and most repairs are preassigned a minimum charge time. Be aware of this minimum charge and the increments of time for additional charges (hour, half-hour, quarter-hour, etc.). For example, a camcorder repair that takes 45 minutes may be billed at two hours by a company with a two-hour minimum. Another repair that takes 75 minutes may be billed at two hours by a company that bills only in one-hour increments. Remember, prices for replacement parts can vary greatly, from just a few dollars for a microphone jack to hundreds of dollars for a new circuit board or zoom lens. Consider the big picture when comparing repair rates.

The following is an illustration of a reputable repair shop. The repair facility charges an hourly labor rate of $75 for service to audio and video equipment. Repairs are billed at half-hour increments with a one-hour minimum. Repair estimates are billed at regular billing rates, but the cost of the estimate (labor) is ap-

plied as a credit to the repair bill. (In other words, if a school brings in a broken camcorder, the facility charges $75 to estimate the cost of repair. That $75 is considered a prepayment on the final bill.) The repair technician has more than 20 years' experience in repair of audio and video equipment and is factory authorized to repair industrial/professional and broadcast equipment for several major brands, including Sony and Panasonic. Almost all service is done on site and is usually completed within a few days.

Keep in mind that diagnosing a repair is almost impossible without a complete evaluation of the equipment. A seemingly simple problem (e.g., "The camcorder won't come on") can indicate any number of repairs needed, from repairing a connection on the on-off switch to replacing the main circuit board. Selecting a repair facility is an important task for the television production teacher. Make sure that the repair business you deal with provides fast, professional, and economical service to your school.

Purchase of Blank Videotape

After the major expense of purchasing and maintaining equipment, you may be inclined to treat the purchase of blank videotape as an afterthought. However, the videotape on which you record your programs is an important element in the video equipment chain. Using poor-quality videotape will result in a dull picture and poor sound reproduction.

No item in the video production chain has dropped so drastically in price as videotape. When VHS tape first appeared in the 1970s, a two-hour blank tape cost at least $15. Now, a much higher quality tape costs as little as $2. Amid the abundance of cheap blank videotape are many brands of tape that are substandard. Videotapes that perform adequately at home do not do as well in the production arena. Although you may not notice color or picture degradation on a recording of your favorite situation comedy, you will likely be disappointed if the colors and textures of the school play are badly reproduced on a poor-quality videotape.

With tape quality as our yardstick and price as an additional consideration, we explore in this section two ways of buying blank videotape: at the retail store and through a blank-videotape dealer.

Retail Purchase of Blank Videotape

Blank tape is readily available in many markets. Most schools purchase the blank videotape they use from retail stores—discount chains, drug stores, and grocery stores. If a school program buys less than 50 blank tapes a year, retail is probably the best way to buy tape. By checking weekly sales flyers, schools can get remarkably good prices on high-quality videotape. Stores often treat videotape as a loss leader to lure customers into the store. The store sells the tapes at or below wholesale and often receives incentives from the videotape manufacturers, who want to foster brand loyalty. Teachers and media specialists should definitely take advantage of such marketing efforts.

But as we stated earlier, quality should be the first priority. Two indicators of high-quality blank videotape are brand name and tape grade.

Here is why brand name is important. Most blank tape sold in retail stores is marketed by about a dozen international companies. These company names are household brand names that most consumers have known for years. Some market only magnetic products, such as audiotape, videotape, and computer discs, whereas others also sell film, audio and video components, and office machines. These brands are available at many different stores and are not unique to one retail chain. Remember, a major company will protect its reputation as its most valuable asset. The company knows that if you buy a poor-quality videotape with its brand name, you are likely to associate poor quality with all of its products. Therefore, videotape that bears a major brand name should be purchased for use in schools.

In addition, buy the highest grade of blank videotape available. Most major manufacturers offer two or three different grades of videotape. The lowest grade is generally for recording television programs on a home VCR. The midgrade is designed for recording on a home VCR special programs that are to be kept for several years. The highest grade is designed for camcorder use. Will the lower grade work in the camcorder? Sure. But for the highest-quality picture and sound and the most durable videotape, buy the highest grade available.

Blank-Videotape Purchase from a Tape Dealer

Usually, a company dealing in blank videotape actually assembles the tape by buying huge reels of blank videotape stock and loading it onto empty cassettes. These companies usually sell videotapes in bulk, with 40 tapes a standard minimum order. There are many advantages and a few disadvantages to buying videotape through a tape dealer.

Advantages

ASSURANCE OF A QUALITY PRODUCT Because videotape sales are their main, if not only, business, blank-tape dealers take the issue of tape quality very seriously. Most salespeople from these companies stress that their tapes surpass all industry standards. Often their cassettes are loaded with the highest-quality blank tape, the type reserved for television stations and production companies. As with any transaction, make sure to ask a lot of questions. But chances are that the blank tape provided by a tape dealer will be at least as good, if not better, than the highest grade for sale on the retail market.

AVAILABILITY OF "SHORT LOADS" Most blank VHS videotapes available from a retail store are T-120, meaning that they accommodate 120 minutes of recording on the SP (fastest) speed. However, because tape dealers load their own videotapes, they can provide "short loads"—videotapes of various shorter lengths. For example, a T-30 is a 30-minute tape, a T-10 a 10-minute tape, and so on. There are many advantages to purchasing short loads for use in school-based video production. Very rarely is a two-hour tape needed for school video production. With the exception of the occasional school play or holiday program, most school videotaping opportunities can be recorded on a T-60 or shorter. The interview with the softball coach, the Spanish class singing "Feliz Navidad," and the documentary about the school lunch program could each be recorded on separate 10-minute videotapes. If the principal needs a copy of the most recent school news program to show at the PTA meeting, copy it onto a T-10. If a science teacher needs an experiment recorded, it will probably fit on a T-20.

One of the main advantages of buying short loads is the price. A high-quality T-30 costs less than $2. Another advantage is the relief of the obligation that all thrifty educators feel when they open a new T-120—"How can I fill this tape if I just need to record a five-minute interview?" Most media educators also know the inconvenience of finding one segment on a T-120 tape. And if that tape is lost or stolen, all programs on that tape are gone. Better to buy economical short loads and store one segment on each tape. Longer tapes can be used for archival purposes (storing all of your news shows, for example) and recording longer school events.

BUSINESS ACCOUNTING Unlike most retail stores, blank-tape dealers provide accounting services, including shipping with a purchase order, tax exemption, and billing to the school. In many schools, it is much easier to get permission to buy a product and receive a purchase-order number than it is to get reimbursed for a direct purchase made at a retail store. Most tape dealers will process and ship your tape order if the school provides a purchase-order number or faxes a copy of the purchase order. This practice helps provide speedy service. Tape dealers are also familiar with the tax-exempt status of schools. Finally, tape dealers provide an invoice that the school can pay just as it pays for other large purchases, such as paper and supplies. Most school bookkeepers prefer this type of transaction over a reimbursement.

FAST SERVICE Because tape is their number-one business, blank-tape dealers can make a mail-order tape purchase almost as quickly as a trip to the store. Dealers frequently ship your tape order the same day that you call or fax the purchase order. It is not unusual to call in an order on Monday morning and receive it Wednesday afternoon.

Disadvantages

There are a few disadvantages to using a blank-tape dealer. Probably the biggest is the minimum-order requirement. Most dealers sell in lots of 40 or 50 tapes for each length. In other words, the minimum order for T-60 is 40 tapes, the minimum for T-10 is 40 tapes, and so on. Many schools use fewer tapes than this in a school year. (To alleviate this problem, perhaps district leadership could arrange to compile school orders into one large order.) Another disadvantage is that when you buy a tape from a tape dealer, you get only the blank tape—you must purchase the label and case separately. Fortunately, the dealer also sells these supplies for a very reasonable price. In fact, this could even work to your advantage if you have a supply of labels or tape boxes left over from previous years. Still, it is an extra consideration. Finally, the shipping-and-handling dragon rears its ugly head. Make sure to ask the dealer about shipping and handling costs and factor them into the purchase price.

Locating Blank-Tape Dealers

Most schools or school districts have already been contacted by a blank-tape dealer looking for business. If not, or if you want to contact another company, there are several ways to do this. Contact your district media services or instructional services office to ask about vendors. Call a local high school, college, or business that is active in video production. Check the advertisements in the consumer video magazines found at newsstands and grocery stores. Perform an Internet search for "Blank Videotape." Whether your school needs 50 or 500 blank videotapes each year, it is worthwhile to investigate buying videotape from a blank-tape dealer. The advantages gained from such a contact far outweigh any disadvantages presented and will likely result in a more-professional video production program at your school.

Video Duplication Service

This section does not refer to duplication of copyrighted materials, nor is it meant to supersede any school-district policies or directives. Examples used in this section are school produced with respect to copyright law.

Most media specialists have been asked to duplicate videotapes. Perhaps the guidance department would like its own copy of the school orientation tape to show to new students. The football coach may request a copy of last week's game to send home with his starting quarterback. Several proud parents may request a copy of the tape made at the school awards ceremony. The orientation tape copy can be completed in a few minutes by connecting two VCRs. Duplicating the tape of the football game will take a bit longer but is quite simple and doesn't require constant attention. But what about duplicating the school awards assembly? Imagine that 50 parents have called your media center, each requesting a copy of the tape. Should you flatly refuse, stating that you don't have time to make copies of the 90-minute assembly? Should you take orders and finish them as time allows? And won't all that duplication time increase the wear and tear on your school's VCRs? Fortunately, there is a fast, economical solution to this problem: videotape duplication service.

What Is a Videotape Duplicator?

A videotape duplicator is a business specifically set up to make multiple copies of videotape programs. Typically, a customer meets with a salesperson from the duplication company and requests a certain number of duplicates to be made from the original master tape. The salesperson quotes a competitive rate for the duplicates, which includes the cost of the blank tape. The salesperson also offers other options such as labeling (preprinted or custom designed), packaging (plain paper sleeve, plastic case, custom-printed case, shrink-wrapping), and distribution (will the customer pick up the tapes or should the duplicator mail the tapes directly to the consumers?). These special options are added to the duplication fee, and a final price for the job is established.

Most professional duplicators can complete the process in a day or two, depending on their schedule. How can they copy so many tapes in such a short period of time? First, it is not unusual for a busy tape duplication company to operate 24 hours a day. Second, the duplicator makes many copies at once. A technician connects the source VCR that contains your master tape to a series of distribution amplifiers. The signal is then sent to several recording VCRs. High-volume tape duplicators can record hundreds of duplicates at a time. (Most videotape is copied in real time, unlike audiotape, which is copied at high speeds.) With hundreds of recording VCRs, even the biggest orders can be completed in the time that it takes to play the master tape.

Let's return to our school-based example. Fifty parents have requested copies of the school awards assembly. The media specialist dutifully records the names and phone numbers of the parents and promises to notify them when a price is established. The media specialist visits the tape duplicator with the master tape in hand. The salesperson agrees to provide the copies for $6 each. (The program will be recorded on a T-90 tape, which the duplicator has purchased from a blank-tape dealer.) The media specialist decides on a simple face label printed with the school name, the title "Awards Assembly," and the year, at a cost of 5 cents each. Knowing that most families will keep the tapes for a number of years, the media specialist selects a durable plastic tape case in blue for an additional 40 cents. This brings the cost per duplicate to $6.45. No shipping charge is added, because our media specialist will pick up the tapes when they are completed. The tapes are promised for the next afternoon. Twenty-four hours later, the media specialist returns to the duplicator, presents a school check for the 50 tapes, and then notifies students and parents that their tapes are ready and can be purchased at the school.

Readers who have sold pencils and hosted book fairs to raise money are probably thinking, "Why not charge $10 per tape and make a nice profit?" If you are pleased with the quality of the tape that you produced, and if you think the community can afford the added cost, then charging the extra amount is certainly an excellent way to raise funds for your program. In this case, if the 50 tapes are sold at $10 each instead of $6.45, the media center will net $177.50, which is enough to buy a new audio mixer or a CD player and a couple of nice microphones. Next year, the media specialist can anticipate the demand for copies, calculate the price, and insert an order form in the awards-assembly program. With the cooperation and service of the tape duplicator, the otherwise-tiresome task of duplicating 50 tapes becomes simple and profitable.

Finding a Tape Duplicator

The process for locating tape duplicators is identical to finding blank-tape vendors. The most obvious strategy is to contact schools and businesses that have used tape duplicators in the past. You can also locate companies by consulting video production magazines and searching the Internet.

Selecting a Tape Duplicator

Any video hobbyists with two VCRs to connect together can buy business cards and list themselves in the yellow pages as a videotape duplicator. Apply the following criteria to tape duplicators in your area.

Take the Tour

The best way to evaluate a tape duplicator is to visit the facility. A professional tape-duplication facility is truly impressive, with dozens of VCRs lining the walls, all connected to a control room that seems to rival NASA. The storage room has thousands of blank videotapes waiting to be used. A professional art department is available to help customers design a tape label and cover. All of these factors indicate a business that is ready to meet your needs. A professional tape duplication business is a sophisticated, dynamic company. If the "tour" is a visit to a basement that contains a half-dozen VCRs connected with a web of cable, keep looking. (By the way, tape-duplication company tours are great field trips for television production classes.)

Professional-Quality Duplicates

Ask for a sample duplicate. Take it home and watch it on your home VCR (which is how your audience will view the program). Examine picture clarity and the vividness of the colors. Look for snowy spots, which may indicate the use of poor-quality blank tape. Test the tape shell by standing on it. It shouldn't pop or crack. Remember, your customers deserve a duplicate that looks almost as good as the original.

Single-Pass Capability

"Single-pass capability" refers to the number of "slave," or recording, VCRs that are available. Ideally, your program should be duplicated in a single pass. In other words, your master tape should be played only once to make the required duplicates. Returning to our awards-assembly example, imagine that the tape duplicator has only five recording VCRs. That means that the master tape will be played at least 10 times to make 50 copies. How does this affect the customer? There are three possible negative consequences: 1) each time a videotape is played, the picture quality may degrade, so the last five copies may look worse than the first five; 2) there is a greater likelihood of physical damage to the master tape, such as breakage, when a tape is played five or more times; and 3) playing the master tape several times results in a delay in delivery of the duplicates. Unless your duplication order runs into the hundreds, you should select a duplicator that can make your copies on a single pass.

Competitive Rates

You may have been surprised by the low cost of the duplicates in our example. Duplication rates are a function of several variables, including the length of the program, the number of copies ordered, the packaging requirements, and the competition level among tape duplicators in your area. Be sure to ask about school discounts—most duplicators are willing to work with schools on pricing. As with an equipment vendor, the relationship between a duplicator and a school can be mutually beneficial.

Duplication Is Their Business

Usually, the best service will be found at a business whose only enterprise is tape duplication. Hiring a duplicator that also produces commercial programs or sells video equipment may mean that your duplicates will have to wait until equipment becomes available.

Business Accounting

Select a tape duplicator that will work from a purchase order and bill or accept payment when the work is done. A duplicator that demands payment before the service may need your money to buy blank tape or rent VCRs, which is not a sign of a healthy duplication business. Also, payment in advance may indicate that the duplicator is just an agent and is planning to subcontract your business to a real tape duplicator. Expect professional business accounting.

Nonlocal Duplicators

Unfortunately, tape duplication services do not exist in all areas of the country; usually, they are found in medium and large cities. If your search does not turn up an acceptable tape duplicator in your area, consider traveling to a neighboring city. Contact the duplicator and plan a field trip. Perhaps the duplicates will be available by the time your group finishes lunch. (If not, the tapes can be shipped.)

Consider conducting your tape-duplication business through the mail if a duplicator is recommended by a trusted colleague. Here's an example. A district superintendent needed to advise all of the school district's employees about changes in several school policies. To enable employees to hear the information at a convenient time and review the material as the year progressed, the superintendent decided to use videotape as a medium. The district media personnel created a 45-minute videotape in which the superintendent described the new policies. However, with 75 schools in the district, tape duplication looked to be a tremendous task. Unfortunately, no tape duplicator was located in the area. The district media specialist called her counterpart in a neighboring district, who recommended a duplicator in a nearby large city. The district media specialist called the duplicator and spoke to a salesperson. Prices were established, a copy of the master tape was made, and the master was mailed to the duplicator later that day. By the end of the week, each school in the district received a videotape explaining the new district policies.

The moral of the story: Don't settle for poor quality just because you live in a small town. Like blank-tape sales, tape duplication can easily be handled by phone, fax, and mail.

The school-vendor relationship must be considered an important element of any school media program. Schools can greatly benefit from forming strong links with the business community. Although the task of establishing these relationships is formidable, the ability to access a reliable, professional network of vendors is critical to the success and survival of a school television production program.

Chapter 5

Creating Your Video Production Studio

This chapter will help you develop an understanding of how your video production equipment is designed to work in a typical school setting. Although some video components have slightly different configurations than the models pictured and described in this text, the basic underlying principles of connections and use remain the same.

Equipment Connections

Your television production equipment can easily be configured into a working production studio. Connecting video cameras, switchers, character generators, and audio components is not difficult when you have an explanation, a plan, and some simple diagrams.

Cords, Plugs, and Adapters

As you begin connecting your video and audio equipment, you will soon realize that the equipment you purchased did not come with all the necessary cords, plugs, and adapters to make it all work together. This is not a difficult problem. The easiest solution is to be prepared ahead of time and purchase some of the necessary items before you start connecting the equipment. It's frustrating to get excited about setting up your system only to find out you've reached a dead end because you do not have the right cords or cables. Although the following list is not all-inclusive, it will help you anticipate what you will need.

S-VHS or VHS?

Do you have an S-VHS camcorder? Are you planning on recording your show on an S-VHS VCR? Are your switcher and character generator configured for S-VHS? Will you be able to broadcast your show on an S-VHS tape? Are you planning on buying S-VHS videotapes to record your news shows? If the answer is "yes" to all these questions, then you need to purchase S-VHS video cords. You will need longer cords (20–50 feet) for connecting your video camera(s) to your recording equipment and shorter cables (3–6 feet) for connecting your switcher, VCR, and character generators together.

If you're planning to use the standard VHS signal, then you will need RCA cords to connect your camera(s), switcher, VCRs, and character generator together. Whether you're using S-VHS or VHS, you will probably have to order the longer cords (25–50 feet) from a video equipment supply company. Few local retail electronics stores carry these cables.

IEEE-1394 Connections (Digital Cameras and Equipment)

IEEE-1394 (trade names FireWire® and i.LINK®) is a high-speed serial input-output technology for connecting digital devices such as digital camcorders and cameras to desktop and portable computers, as well as today's newer models of switchers and VCRs. Widely adopted by digital peripheral companies such as Panasonic, Sony, Canon, JVC, and Kodak, IEEE-1394 has become the established industry standard for both consumers and professionals. Digital video cameras are now readily available for under $1,000 and can provide crisp, clear video images that make analog video pale in comparison. DV camcorders have IEEE-1394 ports and must use IEEE-1394 cords and connections. IEEE-1394 carries both the audio and video signals simultaneously. Currently, most of the DV camcorders available allow the transfer of video and audio signals through the use of S-VHS and analog ports as well, so they are conveniently integrated into existing analog systems. DV converters are also readily available to convert the DV signals into analog signals used by older equipment.

Audio Connections

For your audio connections, you will also need RCA cables. You will need a set (often called patch cords) for each audio component, such as a CD player, tape deck, and VCR. These cables can be purchased at an electronics store. Buy a few extra sets of cables to have on hand in case of broken cords or other emergencies.

TV or Monitor Connectors and Cables

Some monitors require a BNC connector to attach your equipment to the video inputs. Cords are available with an RCA plug on one end and a BNC on the other. If you can't find one of these in a video-supply catalog or store, you can purchase an adapter that will make your RCA cords work as a BNC connection. These adapters are found at most electronics stores and cost under $3.

Some schools may be using televisions rather than monitors in their production systems. A television requires an RF line (like the cable TV outlets in your home), which carries both the video and audio signals in one wire. A VCR can easily connect to a television because it has an RF output on the back. Switchers, video cameras, and character generators do not have an RF output, only a video output. To use a television with one of these components, you will have to purchase an RF modulator for each television you want to use in your system. The RF modulator will accept your separate video and audio signals (RCA inputs) and transmit them as an RF signal to your television. If you find yourself having to use televisions rather than monitors, you can find these modulators at any retail electronics store. In this situation, you will need both RCA cords and RF cords to complete your connections. (See fig. 5.1.)

Figure 5.1 A variety of cords and connectors are needed for television production: (left to right) S-VHS, phono (RCA), RF, and BNC.

Selecting a Site for Your Studio

If your school is currently being designed and built, you may be in a position to offer some insights concerning your television studio's site and layout. Most likely, though, you are in one of the following situations:

> You work at a school that has decided to purchase some television production equipment to start a school news show.

> You have been doing such a wonderful job with your school's news show that your principal has decided to let you buy more real equipment, allow you to move out of the book closet, and work with more students.

> You've written an award-winning grant, can now buy whatever you need, and are looking for the perfect place to set it up.

Whatever your situation, there are some important considerations for selecting the site for your television studio. You may not be able to find the perfect spot, but some places are definitely better than others. If you are broadcasting a live show, your location will be decided by access to your closed-circuit television system. The distance of your cameras and VCRs from this system will be limited by the length of the patch cords with which you will connect the equipment. The only way around this problem is to purchase a portable modulator and connect it to the RF outlet in the room where you are planning to locate your television studio. This is a viable alternative to setting up your studio in a small, dimly lit room just so it will be located near the broadcast system. Newer schools are being designed with broadcast systems similar to a television studio's control room, complete with two-way glass allowing an ample view of the studio and plenty of room for video equipment, cables, and monitors. We should all be so lucky, but of course we're not.

If you are in the process of selecting a studio site, the following are some major factors you should consider before making a decision.

Location

Is the site convenient for you and your students? You should be able to access the location easily without disturbing other classes and school workers. Make sure your students do not have to walk through offices or classrooms to get to the studio. A room located in the media center may offer a convenient location and easy access for you and your students.

Television production involves a lot of equipment. If you are working in a multistory facility, downstairs is the best place to start looking. Carrying monitors, cameras, and tripods up and down stairs each day can be tiring and dangerous. Even if you have an elevator, will the students be willing to wait for it every time they want to tape an event at school? Sets and backdrops will be nearly impossible to get upstairs, even with an elevator. Definitely think downstairs.

Space

How big should the room be? Of course, that depends on the amount of television equipment, number of students, and future goals of your program. If you have to ask one or two students to leave the room just so you can bend down and pick up a pencil or script, the room is too small. Television equipment and cables take up a lot of room. So do students and teachers working on the equipment. There must be ample space for students to move around and work equipment. (See fig. 5.2.)

Allow room for growth. You may only have five pieces of equipment now, but that does not mean you won't be adding more in the future. This is true for stu-

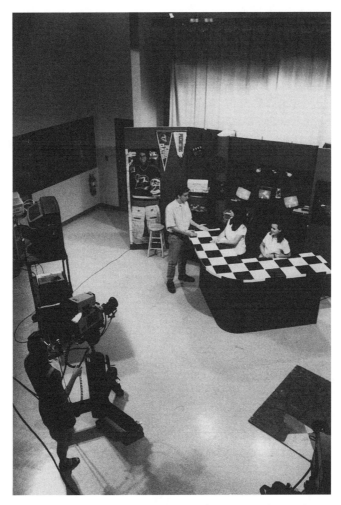

Figure 5.2 A television production facility needs ample room for equipment and sets.

dents, too. If it takes 7 students to run five pieces of equipment, it may take 10 to 14 to manipulate nine pieces of equipment.

Plan for the future. Once you take the little room, you may never get to move to the big room. If you are setting up a television studio at your school, why not invite classroom teachers and students in to produce and tape video projects, news stories, and interviews? The more use your studio has, the greater the likelihood your program will continue to grow. As your program grows, so will your equipment collection. An adequate room has enough space for all of the current equipment, cords, cables, and personnel. Each technical crew member should have enough space to operate his or her piece of equipment and not feel suffocated by other people. The teacher must have enough room to walk around to monitor each student's activity, give instruction, or demonstrate an operation on a video or audio component. Cords and cables need to be out of the way and not underfoot. Can the room be too large? Never.

Climate and Atmosphere Control

Electronic equipment should be kept cool (70–72°F) and protected from humidity. It operates better and longer at cooler temperatures and lower humidity. Dust and dirt are also big detriments to equipment life. Air conditioning is a must, and preferably, you should be able to control the temperature independently from the rest of the building. When all of the equipment is turned on, it will generate heat. So will your students. The room must be comfortably cool for both the personnel and the equipment.

In addition, the more temperature change the equipment has to deal with, the more likelihood of malfunctions and breakdowns. Therefore, a constant temperature, even over the weekends and holidays, is a requirement. Some school systems will shut off the air conditioning during noninstructional hours to save energy and money. Although this may be fine for most of the classrooms, television and computer equipment will suffer considerably. Air conditioning reduces humidity and keeps out the dust and dirt that will enter through open windows. Locating your studio in a room where the air conditioning can be controlled continuously is a good idea.

Lighting

Lighting (other than studio lighting) and sound characteristics are also important when considering a site for your studio. The production control area should have adequate lighting for the technical crew to see and operate their equipment. Sometimes overhead lighting can be too bright, making LED lights on switchers and audio equipment difficult to see. In a best-case scenario, you control the production-area lighting with some type of dimmer switch or panel. For instance, if your room is outfitted with florescent lights, perhaps a switch could be installed so you could dim the lights or even turn off some of them. Track lighting is also effective, especially when used with a dimmer panel. The track lights can be adjusted individually to light selected areas of the room. The dimmer panel gives you complete control over the brightness of the lighted areas. When initially setting up for taping or broadcast, you could turn all the lights up to full magnitude. As production begins, the lights could be turned down to a dimmer setting, enabling the production crew to adequately see and operate their equipment.

Furniture

Wooden tables and plastic chairs are fine in a library or media center setting but do not work well in a production studio setting. Because of the amount of cables and connectors needed for video production, as well as the shape and configuration of video equipment, it is best if you purchase furniture made specifically for video and computer equipment. Most school districts provide a list of furniture and equipment on a "bid list," which enables educators to purchase these materials at a low educational rate. Production furniture is often included on this list.

Furniture designed for production offers several advantages over basic school-type tables and chairs. First, it is usually made with rollers or casters on the legs so it can easily be moved to a location. This also makes it convenient to clean and dust under and around the cords and cables. Second, production furniture is designed to configure the most amount of equipment in the least amount of space. It usually has shelves and countertops that slide and move to accommodate all types of video components. In addition, the height and level of working space can be adjusted. This is especially important when smaller children are trying to see and operate controls on a switcher, audio mixer, or character generator. Finally, production furniture looks professional. Why spend thousands of dollars on nice equipment only to have it spread across some old lunchroom tables? A professional-looking facility inspires professionalism in your students and staff.

At conferences and school media centers, you'll find numerous catalogs filled with all sorts of production furniture. Visit other schools in your district or nearby facilities to see what kind of equipment and furniture they are using. Attend a local or state technology conference, and you'll find many furniture vendors glad to assist you in finding the right type of furniture for your studio site.

Power

Video production equipment requires a lot of electricity. All your equipment will require the standard 110-volt power from any wall outlet. The problem is that you will need numerous outlets to supply enough power to your monitors, switchers, mixers, and so on. If you are in the process of designing a studio site or reconfiguring a room for studio use, speak to a district representative who is knowledgeable about electronics. You should wire the site with several outlets with multiple jacks where you plan on placing your production equipment. This will eliminate the need to use several multiplug adapters and extension cords to create enough outlets for all your equipment.

Power surges are common and can be devastating to video production equipment. Lightning strikes and blackouts cause thousands of dollars damage to electronic equipment each year. Invest in one or two very good surge protectors for your studio. Make sure *all* your equipment is connected to surge protectors. They are inexpensive, and some of the better models even offer a guarantee to replace damaged equipment if the surge protector fails to safeguard connected components. Most retail electronics stores carry surge protectors in a variety of prices and configurations.

Room Layout

How you design and configure your studio and production area certainly depends on its size and location. Regardless of other factors, your studio will need two distinct areas: a production area, where the equipment resides and the technical crew produces and records the production, and a set area, where talent and backgrounds are located. Newer schools are being designed with production areas physically separated from the set area by a large glass window and wall. This provides a soundproof working area for technicians, and the teacher and crew can still visually monitor the crew members in the set area.

Many media specialists and television teachers are having to find creative ways to separate the production and set areas in their studios. Lack of space, poor planning and design, or just having to use older buildings for high-technology classrooms has forced teachers to find new ways of using old space. Portable walls, furniture, blackboards, and even theater flats covered with muslin have been used to separate production crews from talent and set areas.

Sound is an important factor in separating talent and crew. Open microphones on the talent can often pick up director cues and crew discussions during the course of the show taping and broadcast. Although whispering can work, it is not usually as effective as designing your site with this issue in mind. Hand signals, facial gestures, and mouthed directions are not usually the best way to communicate in a production facility, but it has been done. A location that can offer two distinct areas, one for production and one for on-camera talent, is best. A few holes drilled through a wall for microphone and camera cables can connect the areas for production purposes. A window in a wall can provide optimum visual supervision for talent and studio crew. A small "talk-back" system, a microphone in the production area and a speaker in the set area, can enable the producer or director to speak directly to the crew and talent without having to run back and forth between the two areas.

If you have input into the design and location, these are some factors you will want to consider. If you are simply given a location, make the best of it, adding what you feel you need to make the situation work for you.

Connecting the Video Components

Video Cameras, Camcorders

Whether your production facility has one, two, or even three video cameras, the connections are basically the same for each camera placed in the production system. The video camera is designed to record or transmit a video signal. First, you need to find the video output of your camera and connect it to one of three locations: 1) a VCR so that you can tape your show for later broadcast, 2) a video switcher so that you can switch from one video source (camera, graphics generator, or VCR for video segments) to another, or 3) your head-in (school broadcast) system so you can broadcast a live news show.

To connect your camera to one of these components, you need to locate the video output of your camera (see fig. 5.3). Of course, the easiest method of locating the video output is by reading your owner's manual. This is a good suggestion even if you know where the video output is located. If you don't have your owner's manual, look for an RCA or S-VHS jack labeled "video out." On some camcorders, this output is found on the AC adapter, not on the camera itself. On a few camcorders, this output is hidden by a small panel that is pulled open to reveal the video and audio outputs. Once you have found the video output, it's simply a matter of connecting that output to the video input of your recording VCR, the video input of the VCR connected to your broadcast system, or the video input of your switcher. This signal will carry the visual signal only, not audio. We will discuss the audio connections later in this chapter.

Figure 5.3 Video camera outputs

The Switcher

A switcher is designed to switch, or change, from one video signal to another. It can also produce transitions such as wipes, dissolves, or special effects while switching from one source to another. It is the component that controls which video signal is being recorded or broadcast, and its output is usually labeled "line out" or "main out." Many switchers require a preview monitor that enables the technical director (the person operating the switcher during production) to see what video source is on each input before switching to that source. A preview monitor can also enable you to access different effects and transitions. Connect your switcher's preview output to a monitor so that your technical director can easily see and preview the video sources and effects during production. You will also need a preview monitor for each one of your video sources. The preview monitors allow you to see what each camera shot is so you can eliminate mistakes made by switching to a bad camera shot or a miscued tape during production. Today's newer-model switchers create a digital preview screen for each input all on one preview monitor. This eliminates the need for purchasing preview monitors for each video source. Not only does this save money, but it also makes space (often a precious commodity) for other equipment. Those of us who have done production in the book closets of our schools know about that.

Connect your video camera to the switcher by locating the video input on your switcher and plugging the cord from the video output of your camera into it. Most switchers have several video inputs, and it doesn't really matter which input you use. It is easier to remember that camera 1 is source 1, and camera 2 is source 2, but this arrangement is just a recommendation. (See fig. 5.4.)

Once you have connected your video cameras to your switcher, turn the switcher on and check the preview monitor(s) to make sure you can see each video source. You should now connect your switcher's video output to your recording VCR or broadcast system. Once you have done this, you should be able to see the selected source on your switcher's line-out monitor (this shows what is being recorded or broadcast on the VCR). The switcher and its selected sources should be seen on both the preview and the line-out monitors. (See fig. 5.5.)

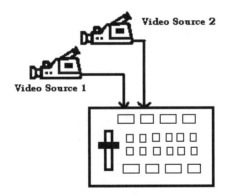

Figure 5.4 Camcorders connected to the video switcher

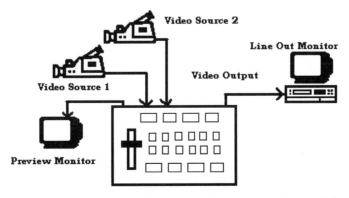

Figure 5.5 Camera and monitor connections to the video switcher

The Character Generator

A character generator is used to place graphics (e.g., titles, names, announcements) in your show (see fig. 5.6). Most media specialists and teachers like to place the names of their news shows and anchors over the images being recorded by the cameras. For example, as Anchor 1 reads the announcements, you place the anchor's name on the screen (see fig 5.7).

Figure 5.6 Videonics Titlemaker 3000. Picture courtesy of Focus Enhancements.

Figure 5.7 Use a character generator to add text over the images being recorded.

Or perhaps you would like to roll credits at the end of your news show over a camera shot or even a prerecorded video segment. For this reason, the character generator needs to be placed *between* the switcher and the recording VCR or broadcast system. That way, all the video signals are directed through the character generator and can have graphics added to them before being recorded or broadcast. The character generator (and its operator) will also need the use of a preview monitor to see and access the graphics prior to use in the video program. Connect the preview monitor to the character generator's preview out jack. If you turn on the power to both the preview monitor and the character generator, you should be able to see the preview screen from the CG on the preview monitor.

Now locate the video output jack on the back of your switcher and connect it to the video input on your character generator. "Video out" to "video in"—not that hard. After you have connected the switcher to the character generator, you will have to connect the character generator to your record VCR or to your broadcast system if you are producing a live show. Connect the video output of the character generator to the video input of your VCR: "video out" to "video in" again. (See fig. 5.8.) After you have made these connections, the line-out monitor should be displaying whatever video source is displayed by the switcher. Some VCRs will require you to switch to a "line" or "auxiliary" input mode to display the video inputs. If you do not see the switcher signal, check the VCR owner's manual to see if your VCR has such a requirement. If you are using a model that has two auxiliary inputs, you can select from auxiliary 1 or auxiliary 2.

Once you have correctly connected the video output of the character generator, you should now be able to switch from camera 1 to camera 2 and add graphics to any shot from camera 1 or camera 2. This can be done by producing a graphics page in which the background selected is "video" or "clear," depending on your character generator's make and model. Again, you should see this on your line monitor.

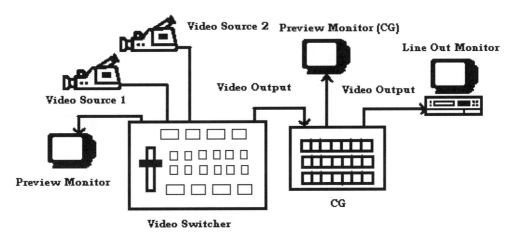

Figure 5.8 Integrating a character generator into the video system

If a solid-color background is selected, the page of graphics will block the camera video signals from appearing on the monitor screen.

Character Generator Options

Some teachers or media specialists decide to connect the character generator as a video source to the switcher rather than placing graphics over the video sources. In this configuration, graphics pages are self-contained pages used as visuals during the production of a show. This option becomes feasible if the switcher has enough inputs for the camera(s) and the character generator and if the mixer has transitions that make the graphics pages appear in a variety of special effects (wipes, "flying," and transitions). If you decide to use your character generator in this manner, simply connect the video output of the character generator to a video input on the switcher. The character generator is connected exactly like the video cameras. Now, connect the video output of the switcher to the video input of the VCR. (See fig. 5.9.)

Using this configuration, you will no longer be able to place graphics "over" your video sources. However, now the character generator can be used like any other video source and can be accessed via your switcher using the various wipes, fades, and other transitions available to the technical director. Creativity and experience using the switcher in this configuration can enhance your show's visual appeal.

Digital Cameras

The popularity of digital cameras, as well as their decreasing costs, has made them readily available in the school setting. They are easy for students, teachers, and media

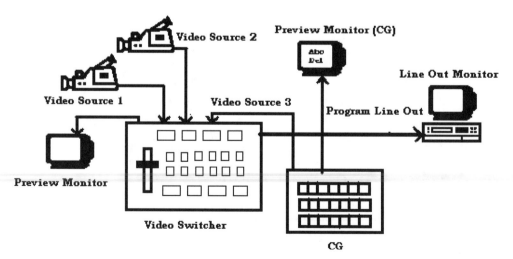

Figure 5.9 Integrating a character generator as a video source

specialists to use and cost effective for program and classroom applications. Although they can have many applications in the classroom, their use in the video production studio can truly be effective and appealing to program viewers. Assigning and training a news crew student to be the digital image operator can enhance your news program and provide images and information about student and faculty achievements. "A picture is worth a thousand words" was never truer than in this application. For years, media specialists have been asked to "parade" students into the newsroom to get them "on camera" for a variety of awards and student recognition programs. Often, these students, and teachers, were asked to step awkwardly in front of the camera for a quick nod or wave while their accolades were cited by the student news anchors. The trials and tribulations of arranging and accommodating groups of students in the cramped quarters of our school news show studios are numerous. Digital cameras offer a professional and courteous way of presenting this same information to the campus and faculty. Rather than parading the proud recipients in front of the video cameras, you can now provide a simple "snapshot" on the screen while the information regarding their achievement is read by the student news anchors.

To use a digital camera in your school's video production studio, you must be able to access the camera's image via the video switcher. Not all digital cameras' images are as readily accessible as a video input, however, so keep this in mind while comparing costs and availability. A key factor in purchasing your digital camera should be easy access to a "video out" signal. (See fig. 5.10.)

Figure 5.10 Make sure you can readily access your digital camera's video output.

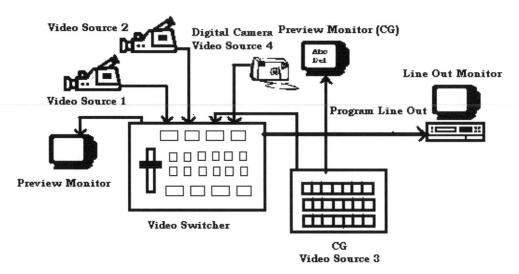

Figure 5.11 Integrating a digital camera in the video system.

The simpler the connection (no conversions needed), the better. Just connect the digital camera's video output to one of the switcher's video inputs (see fig. 5.11). Most of these connections will require the use of an RCA cord or plug, which generally comes with the camera during purchase. During production, the image can be "cued" on the camera and accessed by the technical director when needed.

Computers

Computers, and their ability to access the Internet, can provide an invaluable resource in the video production studio. Maps and weather satellite photos can be used in the morning news show weather segment, Internet sites and resources can be highlighted for faculty and student information to provide news show content, and computer programs such as Powerpoint can be used to provide graphics and photos for a variety of announcements and advertisements for school programs. Using a computer provides news crew students with skills and experiences using the latest technology in the production of their morning news program. It creates meaningful opportunities for more students to be involved in the news show staff. (See fig. 5.12.)

In order to access your computer during production, you must have a way to convert the computer's output to a video signal and input it into the video switcher. There are two main ways to do this:

1. **Video cards.** Simply stated, a video card is the best way to achieve results using your computer as a video source. If you are purchasing a new computer, be sure to have this feature installed on your computer as part of the purchase agreement. If you are using a computer already in your school or facility, video cards are

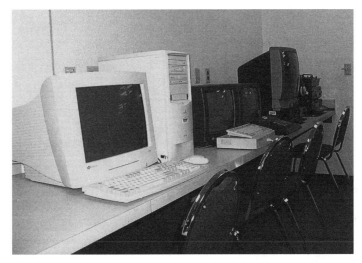

Figure 5.12 Computers can be easily integrated into a video system.

inexpensive and easy to install. Not only do video cards provide an easy way to access the computer's video signal, but many come complete with software that enables you to control features such as screen size, flicker, contrast, and brightness. Look for a video card that can provide a composite and an S-VHS signal, thereby giving you access to the best-quality image on your program. Video cards also provide access to a computer's sound system for connection to the audio mixer if needed. Video cards are available for both Macintosh and PC computers. (See fig. 5.13.)

2. **Conversion devices.** A computer's VGA or SVGA signal (the video display output from the computer's CPU to the computer monitor) is not compatible with inputs for VCRs, monitors/televisions, or other video components. Therefore, many schools have bought and used converters to change the computer's VGA signal to a composite or RF signal to use with classroom monitors or televisions and even older models of video projectors. These conversion units can now be easily used in the production studio to facilitate connecting a computer to the video switcher for access during production.

Once you have adapted the computer to have access to its video source, simply connect the video output of the computer to the video input on the switcher. The computer can now be accessed just like the other video sources connected to the switcher. (See fig. 5.14.)

Source VCR

A source VCR enables you to play a tape during your news show. This could be an opening for the show, an interview segment, or even some prerecorded footage of

Figure 5.13 Video card installed in a computer

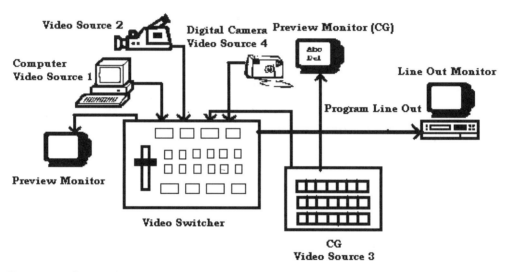

Figure 5.14 Connecting the computer as a video source in the video system. Note that the computer has replaced camera 1 as a video source in this diagram.

a school event over which you will roll ending credits at the end of your show. The source VCR is just another video input to your switcher. Once again, your switcher has several video inputs that you can use. A source VCR is connected to the switcher just like the cameras and the character generator. Connect the video output of the source VCR to the video input of the switcher: "video out" to "video in," just like before. (See fig. 5.15.) Now you should be able to play a tape in the source VCR, select the appropriate input on the switcher, and see the images on both the preview screen of the switcher and the line monitor. You cannot hear anything yet because you still have not connected any audio components. As your production

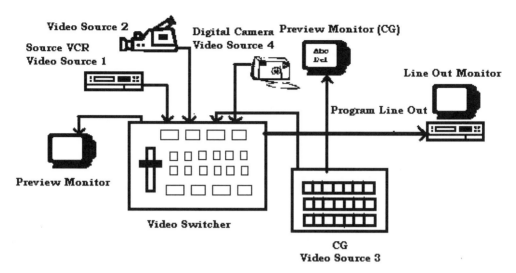

Figure 5.15 Connecting the VCR as a video source in the video system

crew gains experience, you will be able to use the source VCR to play a variety of news segments, openings, and other video clips that will make your show fun and interesting. For example, "Our basketball team has just won its fifth game in a row. Sports reporter Kelly Page stopped by practice to talk with Coach Lalone and some of the members of this rising team." After the topic is introduced, you simply press "play" on the source VCR, select the source VCR input on the switcher, and now everyone watches Kelly's interview. Just like *real* TV.

The amount and variety of video inputs will depend on the type of switcher currently used in the video system and the types of news information you want to present on the show's program. Once connected and in place, video components can be easily switched from one source to another. Simply leave the output cords connected and labeled, and vary your inputs to correspond to the show's content. Unplugging the computer and replacing it with another video source (camera, for example) is not very difficult. Several schools we have visited have even done this during the course of their productions.

Connecting the Audio Components

Audio Mixer

The audio mixer will mix, combine, and adjust all the sound in your production system. Microphones, CD player, tape cassette player, and VCR sound will be routed into the audio mixer and then out to the record VCR or broadcast system. The audio engineer (the student operating the mixer) will adjust the volume and output of each of these audio components.

Microphones

The audio mixer will have clearly labeled input jacks where each audio component is to be connected (see fig. 5.16). Look for the input jacks labeled "microphone" or "mic." Depending on the manufacturer and model, the inputs will either be 1/4-inch phone jacks or XLR jacks. It is important to match the microphone impedance level with the audio mixer. If the mixer has 1/4-inch phone jacks, it is high impedance and requires high-impedance microphones. When an audio mixer has XLR microphone input jacks, it generally calls for the use of low-impedance microphones. (See chapter 2 for more information on high- and low-impedance microphones.)

Matching the impedance levels of the mixer and the microphones is essential for obtaining the best sound levels. Most problems associated with poor microphone sound are related to incorrectly matching the audio mixer's impedance level with that of the microphone. Before you buy an adapter to change the microphone plug to fit the mixer, make sure you have correctly identified the impedance levels. (This information should be found in the owner's manual.) Simply changing the plug configuration so the connectors fit does not solve the problem; it only creates a bigger one.

Connect the microphones to the audio mixer. Move the fader bars up on the mixer while speaking into the microphone. You should see the VU meter move, which indicates you are receiving sound from the microphone. (See fig. 5.17.) At this point, you cannot hear the sound because the audio mixer is not connected to a monitor or speakers. Most mixers have a headphone jack, so you can plug in a set of headphones to hear the microphone sound. Repeat this procedure for each microphone connected to the audio mixer.

Sound Sources

If you are planning on playing music some time during your news show, you will need to connect a sound source to the audio mixer. If you look on the back of the

Figure 5.16 Microphone plug inputs on an audio mixer

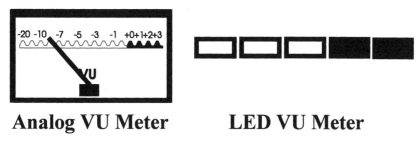

Figure 5.17 A moving VU meter indicates that the audio mixer is receiving a signal from an audio source.

CD player, you will see two RCA jacks labeled "output," or perhaps "left" and "right" output. Using patch cords, connect the CD player outputs to the audio mixer. The mixer input can be labeled "CD," but other models may have one labeled "aux" (auxiliary), which will also work as an input for a CD player. More-sophisticated mixers simply have a series of inputs that allow you to choose and adjust whichever input you wish. Place a CD in the player and push "play." Bring up the input from the CD player using the fader bars or knobs on the audio mixer that correspond to the CD or auxiliary input. The VU meter should indicate that sound from the CD player is entering the audio mixer. Once again, because the mixer's output is not yet connected to any other equipment, you can use a pair of headphones to listen to the CD player's sound.

A cassette tape deck is also used in many school television production systems. Because a tape deck is designed to both play and record sound, it is important that you identify the jacks labeled "audio out" or "output" for connecting the cassette deck to the audio mixer. There should be both a left and a right output on the cassette deck. Use an RCA patch cord to connect the cassette deck's outputs to the audio mixer's inputs. Most audio mixers have this input labeled "tape." After you have connected "audio out" to "audio in," play a tape in the cassette deck, bring up the fader bars for the corresponding inputs on the audio mixer, and make sure the VU meter is moving with the tape sound.

Source VCR

The source VCR will be used to play segments during the production of the news show. Because many of these news segments will have sound recorded (interviews, openings, student video projects), you need to connect the source VCR to the audio mixer. Locate the "audio output" or "audio out" jacks on the VCR. If it is a stereo VCR, there will be both a left and a right channel output. Mono (single-channel)

VCRs will only have one audio-out jack. Use another RCA patch cord to connect the audio output of the source VCR to the audio mixer. The source VCR can be plugged into any input not already in use: "tape in," "auxiliary," or even "CD." Put a prerecorded videotape in the VCR and push "play." Push up the fader bars on the mixer corresponding to the jacks you have used for the input of the source VCR. The moving VU meters will once again indicate that you have correctly connected the source.

At this point, all of your audio sources have been connected to the audio mixer. (See fig. 5.18.) There is sound coming into the mixer from the anchor's microphones, a CD player or tape deck, and a VCR. The audio engineer can now bring up sound from any source, blend or combine sound from two or more sources (mics, music), and control the level of sound during the production of the news show. If only one anchor is speaking, the audio engineer can bring up that anchor's individual microphone and keep the other mics silent. If you desire music playing during the ending credits, the audio engineer can play a CD and bring up the music on the mixer. If an interview is introduced on the show, the audio engineer can bring down the anchor's microphones and bring up the sound from the source VCR. The mixer offers total control of all sound sources.

Audio Mixer Outputs

Once all of the sound sources have been connected to the audio mixer, you need to route those sounds to the record VCR or broadcast system. On the back of the mixer

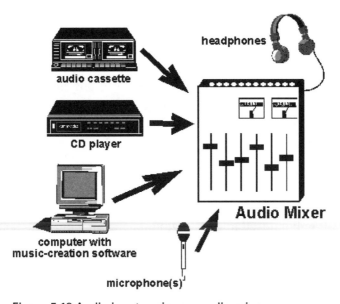

Figure 5.18 Audio inputs using an audio mixer

is a set of RCA jacks labeled "main output," "main out," or "tape out." Use patch cords to connect the mixer's output to the record VCR's inputs. If you are using a stereo VCR for recording, there will be both left and right channels labeled "audio in." A mono VCR will only use one input for "audio in." If you are connecting the mixer to a mono VCR, just use the "right" audio output of the mixer to connect to the VCR. Once you have connected the output of the audio mixer to the record VCR, you have completed both the video and audio connections of your system.

Outputs

Recording VCR

If you are planning on taping your show and broadcasting it later, you have connected the video outputs of the switcher and the audio outputs of the mixer to a recording VCR (see fig. 5.19). To see and hear the show during production, connect a monitor or television to the record VCR. If you are using a monitor that has separate video and audio inputs, connect the video output of the VCR to the video input of the monitor and the audio output of the VCR to the audio inputs on the monitor.

If you are using a television as a monitor for the record VCR, you can use an RF cord to carry both the video and the audio signals from the output of the VCR to the input of the television. Check if the VCR is set to broadcast on channel 3 or channel 4, and then switch the television to the appropriate channel.

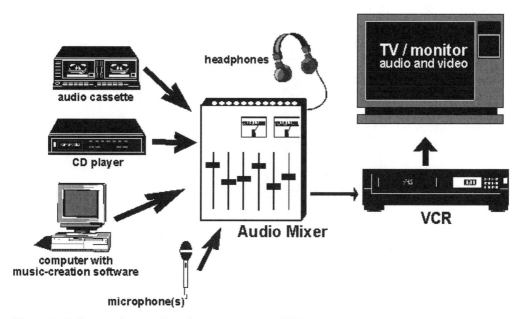

Figure 5.19 Connecting audio mixer outputs to a VCR

Broadcast System

If you are not taping the show but broadcasting it live, the video output of the switcher and the audio output of the mixer have to be connected to your broadcast system (see fig. 5.20). You can accomplish this by using one of the VCRs located in your broadcast system. Identify which channel you want to broadcast the news show on and find the audio and video inputs on the VCR connected to that channel. Using an RCA cord (probably a long one purchased for this purpose), attach the audio output of the audio mixer to the audio input of that VCR. Now, using another long RCA cord, attach the video output of the switcher to the video input of the VCR. At this point, once you turn on all the equipment, you should be able to see and hear the signals from your television production equipment in any classroom connected to the broadcast system. (See fig. 5.21.)

Essentially, most VCRs have their own internal switchers and have to be "told" to accept a signal from the line or auxiliary inputs. This is most often done with

Figure 5.20 A school broadcast system may include VCRs, laser disc players, DVD players, cable television tuners, amplifiers, and modulators.

the remote control or by tuning the VCR to channel 0. If you do not immediately see and hear the feed from your television production equipment on your broadcast system, make sure the VCR is set to accept the signal from the right input. Consult the owner's manual for the broadcast VCR if you have any trouble tuning into the video and audio signals from your television production system.

Testing the System

Once you have completed the video and audio connections, it is time to check the production system.

1. Place a new, blank tape in the record VCR.
2. Turn on the video cameras. Make sure each camera is set to a different shot.
3. Turn on the video switcher, audio mixer, CD player, and source VCR. Put a CD in the CD player and a prerecorded tape in the source VCR.
4. Have students turn on the microphones and sit on camera.
5. Type in one or two graphics pages to place on the screen during the test.
6. Press "record" on the record VCR.

At this point, have the anchors read some practice script that you have prepared for the taping. Have the technical director switch from camera 1 to camera 2 several

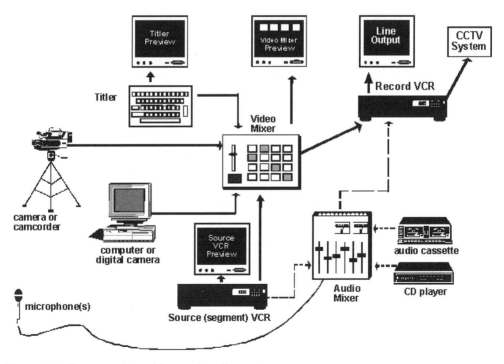

Figure 5.21 The complete video and audio system

times during the taping. Have the student operating the character generator super-impose graphics over a camera shot. Let the anchors introduce the video segment in the source VCR, and then roll in the segment by pushing "play" on the source VCR and accessing the video on the switcher and the audio on the audio mixer.

Try rolling the ending credits of the show while some music plays from the CD player. The idea here is to *test* the equipment, not produce an award-winning news show. Allow your students ample time to practice operating the equipment and figure out the controls on each video and audio component. This should be enjoyable, educational, stress free, and fun. There is plenty of time for hair-pulling, eyes-bulging, neck-tightening, fist-clenching, teeth-gnashing, real production later. When you are finished, rewind the tape in the record VCR. Watch the tape during playback. Were the sound levels loud enough, clear, and balanced for microphones, segment, and music sources? Did all the video switches get recorded? Did the graphics operate over the video source and as ending credits? Were your microphone levels set correctly? If your answers to these questions were in the affirmative, congratulations. If you noticed any problems with the production, review your equipment connections and instructions. Go back and individually retest any component not operating as it should. Now sit down, breathe deep, and relax.

Studio Communications

Communication between technical crew and talent is essential for television production. The producer/director also needs to be able to give directions and coordinate production activities during the taping. Mistakes can be reduced and even eliminated with good communication. There are two basic types of communication systems available for schools producing news shows: wired and wireless intercom systems.

Wired Intercom Systems

Wired intercom systems are costly but durable. Most professional cameras and switchers have built-in intercom systems. Intercom systems can be found in schools (usually high schools and colleges) that have a studio and television studio equipment as part of the architectural design. Broadcast-quality equipment installed when the television studio was built will likely have existing intercom systems and cables. This is the exception rather than the rule, however, in school news-show production.

Most schools will be purchasing a wired intercom system that operates independently from the video equipment. The headphones, jacks, cables, and connectors are purchased separately and do not connect directly to the school's video components. A benefit of such a system is that the intercom system can be moved to another taping location (stadium, auditorium, classroom) when needed. The crew's communications are transmitted via cables and headsets. Such a system includes the main station, belt packs, and headsets.

Main Station

The main station controls and supports the individual headsets and allows the crew to communicate with one another. Each individual's headset (earphone and microphone combined) is connected to the main station. Each crew member can speak with or listen to any other crew member. The main station usually requires AC or DC power and provides power to the individual headsets. More-expensive models allow control over individual channel volumes, selectable line/mic input level, and the capability to connect to stage and auditorium sound systems for announcing purposes.

Belt Packs

The belt pack is connected to the main station, generally with an XLR microphone cable. The length of the cables determines how far each crew member can travel from the main station.

Headsets

Each headset is complete with an ear piece to hear commands and instructions and a microphone to speak to other crew members (see fig. 5.22). The headset is attached to the belt pack. Most headsets can be activated with voice or manual controls. More-expensive models allow you greater control over volume (speaking and listening) and are generally more comfortable and durable.

How many headsets and belt packs do you need? Generally, the following crew members should be wearing a headset:

- **Producer.** Controls and directs all crew members.
- **Technical director.** Operates the switcher.
- **Camera operators.** Each videographer should be able to hear cues, adjust shots.
- **Floor director.** Relays producer's cues to talent, directs studio personnel.

Wired intercom systems are available at most professional audio/video dealers. Information can also be obtained directly from manufacturers. They will be more than happy to mail you literature and answer questions about their products. Many of these dealers and manufacturers can be found at educational technology conferences around the country.

Figure 5.22 Two-way communication systems are necessary for advanced production in a school television facility.

Wireless Intercom Systems

Wireless intercom systems use radio frequencies that actually broadcast the signals from one unit to another. The range and quality of these systems vary greatly along with manufacturer and price. They are very practical in situations where using intercom cable is impractical or difficult (e.g., stadiums, gymnasiums, across water). (See fig. 5.23.)

With this system, each technical crew member would have a headset and be able to communicate with all the other crew members. It is extremely important to purchase headsets that are all operating on the same channel. Radio Shack, for example, has two different channels for its headsets, A and B. Only headsets identified as channel A sets can communicate with any other channel A headset. Like-

Figure 5.23 A wireless intercom system is an inexpensive alternative to a wired system and can be used for production outside the television production facility.

wise, channel B headsets are designed to all work together. This system was designed so that two separate crews can use the headsets at the same time. For example, during a theater production, the theater crew can communicate by using headsets set to channel A, and the video crew can communicate using headsets on channel B. Their conversations and cues would not interrupt each other.

Although generally less expensive than wired intercom systems, wireless intercom systems have some distinct disadvantages:

- They are susceptible to interference from other communication devices and electronic interference from lighting and sound systems.
- They can have difficulty transmitting between walls and glass.
- Each headset requires its own power source (generally a 9-volt battery). Once the battery becomes weak, the headset's range and efficiency diminishes.
- Wireless intercom systems usually have antennas, which are very susceptible to bending and breaking.

When deciding on your communication needs, you should carefully examine the cost and effectiveness of each system. Visit other schools. Talk with teachers and students and see what type of systems they are using. Carefully weigh the advantages and disadvantages of each type of system, and purchase the one that you feel will fit best with your videotaping situations.

Studio Address Systems

The final step in meeting your studio communications needs may be a studio address system. This system enables the producer, director, or teacher to speak to every person in the room at the same time. Basically, it is like the school intercom system over which the principal can speak to every classroom and student at the same time. Do you need such a system? If your studio consists of one room or you're taping in a location such as the media center or hallway, you probably do not need a studio address system. You can raise your voice a little (or a lot, depending on the situation) and speak to everyone at once. However, if your studio consists of a production control room and a separate studio where the talent and camera operators are located, you will need a studio address system. It is too time consuming and tiring to run from the control room to the studio floor every time there is a problem. Studio address systems eliminate the need for yelling, and they are valuable during production for keeping all of the studio personnel and talent informed about production procedures. Cues such as "Rolling tape in one minute" and "Quit clowning around right now" command attention when the crew can hear your voice over a loud speaker in the studio. Studio address systems are not very expensive and can be purchased from most electronics dealers.

Chapter 6

Producing School News Shows

Producing a school news show is just one of the many jobs today's media specialists accomplish during the school day, but it is perhaps the one most visible to faculty, staff, administrators, and students. These daily or weekly programs contain announcements for the faculty and students, feature noteworthy accomplishments in the classrooms and programs at the school, and offer a great opportunity to showcase student video production efforts. The scope and size of the news show will depend on the availability of video equipment, training and practice with students, and some sophistication. Working with students to produce a school news show can truly be an exhilarating experience. It can also be a lot of other things we won't mention here! In this chapter, we provide some tips and techniques that can make this a positive experience for both you and your students.

Technical Skills

You need to become knowledgeable about the connections and features of the equipment you are using to create the news show. This book will certainly help, but gaining "hands-on" experience is essential to being successful. If you have single-handedly (or even with assistance and help) connected the video production equipment in the news room, and it works, you have gone a long way toward understanding how that equipment can be used to create good programming. If the equipment was already connected and in good working order, it is important that you can identify how it is connected and how it functions as a system. Why? Simply because when one of the students pushes a button, switches a wire, or rewires a piece of equipment (and they *will*), you can identify the problem and quickly find a solution. "Why isn't this working?" are four words you never want to hear in the news room, but if you can trace the problem to its source, you can quickly identify and solve the newest crisis. Use the diagrams in chapter 5, or even draw and label your own, to provide a working idea of how the video production system works. You don't have to be able to take apart each component with a screwdriver and soldering iron to be successful, but being able to identify how each video component (camera, character generator, switcher, VCR, etc.) is connected and relayed to the other is important. Even labeling wires ("Video In," "Video Out") can be helpful to problem solving in the future.

It is also important to know how to operate each piece of audio and video equipment so you can "teach" those technical skills to your students. It is amazing that students can operate and use video equipment when their supervising teacher has no idea of how they work. How did they learn in the first place? Mostly by trial and error, and chances are they will never get very good unless someone more knowledgeable steps in. As a teacher, take the time to learn to use all of the equipment, their features, and their many special effects and functions.

Teach the Skills

Spend time each day, or week, instructing the students how to use each piece of video or audio equipment in the studio. Show them the functions of each component and how to be more efficient in its use. Start simple and work up to more advanced features (such as chroma key, audio dubbing, etc.) as students become adept at using the equipment. For example, a student operating the video switcher should first be taught which inputs control access to each video source. Use simple switches, or even "cuts," to change from one source to another. Keep the amount of video switches to a minimum until the student gains ability and confidence. Then progress to using advanced transitions (wipes, fades, dissolves) and even later, using keys and other advanced features.

Allow students to rotate job positions. This gives them the experience they need to operate the equipment and also increases their interest and enthusiasm for participating on the news crew. Take the time to critique past news shows, pointing out positive aspects and analyzing mistakes to see what could have been done to correct them. Students will appreciate the instruction and rapidly improve their skills. You, the media specialist, will develop a role as a media teacher and instructor.

Teach a Class

Generally, there are two approaches to producing school news shows used in our schools today. The first, the "run-in-and-produce-it" approach, relies on a group of students showing up in the media center before or at the start of the school day. They literally "run in and produce" the school show, usually a live broadcast, and then run back to their classrooms to continue their school day. Although this method accomplishes the goal of producing a news show, it seldom if ever leaves time for real media instruction or the development of real media skills. Students seldom become proficient in the skills needed for more advanced and professional broadcasting skills. Producing the news show with this method can also be stressful for both students and the media specialist. There is little room for error, and none for growth.

The second method, teaching a media class, is preferable to both students and the media specialist. Whether this class meets two, three, or even five days a week, the skills of media production and news journalism can be taught and appreciated by both students and teachers. Scheduling a class positions the media specialist to be seen as a "real" teacher, an instructor of skills and knowledge. Students can gain valuable insights into the use and functions of the video equipment, and they can develop the skills to make their broadcasts professional and entertaining. In this venue, the news show becomes more than merely reading morning announcements on the television. Students have actual class time to produce meaningful video segments and provide a truly professional show for the school. Teachers and students will appreciate the benefits of having a morning news show that is fun to watch and features student activities and programs. The content of the show will improve, and so will its presentation. Administrators who support this type of instruction can easily view the results of their decisions on the video screen each day. Scheduling time and selecting students vary from school to school. High schools have little problems with scheduling and including television production classes. Most of them have more than one media specialist working in the media center, so finding a release time for the class is not too much of a concern. In fact, numerous high schools hire full-time television production teachers. Many middle schools have an exploratory period, and a media production class works well in this format. Others use a club format, and a video club is a welcome addition to the concept. Elementary schools and their media specialists usually have to be more creative in this capacity. Generally, there is not a time set aside for independent classes (media, photography, graphic arts, etc.), and the media specialist has to custom design a situation that works in the school.

Some successful media specialists have relied on the following methods of scheduling a production class:

▣ Schedule the production class two or three days a week. Select a time (e.g., the last 45 minutes of the school day) when it would be appropriate for teachers to allow a few students to come to the media center to participate in the class. Students can be recommended by their classroom teachers, and of course, the parents should be sent a letter explaining the program and asking for their approval.

▣ Select three or four teachers, or even an entire grade level, who are willing to include media production as part of their classroom curriculum. Find a time during the school day when those teachers could send a group of students to the media center to participate in the production class while the other students work on related subject matter or perhaps language arts (reading and writing) skills. Students could rotate every few weeks, so that by the end of the nine weeks or semester, all the students in the class will have had a chance to participate.

▣ Does your school have a homeroom period? That could be a perfect opportunity to select a group of ready and willing students to start a media production class.

▣ What about meeting after or before school? This is probably a last resort, but if you and the students are willing to use this time for a production class (and parents are willing to provide transportation), it can be a viable option. Our first news-show classes (circa 1984) were done this way.

Even though scheduling and teaching a class seem like adding yet more tasks to your job list, you will find that this will actually make the job of producing the school news show easier and more enjoyable. Students will learn quickly and will be eager to use those new skills toward making the news show the talk of the school. Each semester, and each successive year, students can draw on the talents and examples of their predecessors to produce more entertaining and informative news shows.

Seek New Ideas and Information

Do not become complacent with the status quo at your school. Attend conferences and workshops in other districts and states to see what is new in this field and what other teachers are doing in their successful programs. Attend the conference's exhibit halls to speak with video and audio equipment vendors who are able to show and demonstrate new equipment and prices. Ask your colleagues during local and district meetings what they are doing about video production in their schools. Even take a day and visit some of the more advanced or successful schools to see what they are using and doing in the field of media production. Read articles and journal magazines, or seek new information now available so easily online. Many schools' Web sites contain links to their video production classes, and some even contain samples of news shows and segments from past broadcasts. Finally, universities across the nation have added new classes in their media education programs as a direct result of inquiries from media specialists in area schools seeking experience and knowledge in this field. Some of these classes are even offered online. As a professional, you want to stay current with methods and trends and keep abreast of developments in the field of media production.

Working with Students

Almost all video production projects require the efforts of a team: on-camera talent, writers, videographers, and editors. The simplest form of a production team would be required to produce an interview project. This team only needs to consist of a reporter and a videographer. In contrast, producing a documentary could require the assistance of a much larger team: writers, videographers, editors, narrators, perhaps some on-camera talent, and even a director. Producing a school news show requires even a much larger team. Depending on the size and scope of your daily news show, this team may consist of 10 to 12 students: anchors, camera operators, technical director, graphics, audio technician, teleprompter operator, videotape operator, and editors.

A successful team employs students who have the skills necessary for the jobs they choose or are assigned to do. A team is only as strong as its weakest link. Each student in the production crew must be taught the skills and components of the equipment they are operating. They should have time to learn, practice, and review the skills and operations needed to successfully produce the finished product. Students should gain confidence and ability on one component before moving on to the next. Some positions, especially the news anchors and other on-camera talent positions, are not necessarily for *every* student. Some students, and adults as well, do not feel comfortable or confidant being on camera. There are enough technical positions to place these students besides forcing them to be on camera. Still others are drawn to the talent side, enjoy being the "star," and do a good job of presenting the news in an interesting and personable fashion.

Coordinating and supervising a group of students working to produce a school news show can be an exciting and rewarding activity. Make no mistake about it, it is also challenging! The supervising teacher sets the tone and climate in which the production team interacts to achieve results. The following are some suggestions for maintaining a professional climate—and your sanity.

■ Always act professionally, and expect your students to do the same. Never criticize a student in front of their peers for making a mistake, and don't allow them to do it either. A good way to avoid that situation is to allow mistakes to be recognized as either a "technical mistake" or a "talent mistake." Students and teachers should avoid direct criticism, such as "Johnny messed up the graphics, AGAIN!"

■ Set up a schedule for rotating jobs, not just whenever someone wants to. If you are using a team of students for nine weeks, perhaps they could change or rotate job positions every three weeks. Let them submit a request at the beginning of the term that indicates their first, second, and third preferences, and then place them according to demand and skill. Not everyone will get their first choice the first rotation, but by the end of the nine weeks, usually everyone will get a chance to do the "one job" they really wanted.

■ Allow time for instruction, practice, and critique. After the show is taped or broadcast (if live), let students take time to change positions and use different components in a "practice show." Spend a few minutes several times a week to teach and demonstrate old and new techniques. Cue up older shows and point out good camera work, successful transitions, "neat" graphics, and so on. You can even replay some miscues and explain how they could have been avoided.

■ Evaluate and provide feedback for your production team. Students know when they are being "graded" and will do a better job if they know that they are being recognized for doing a task successfully. Some of the ways you can evaluate the production crew include daily journals, self evaluations, rubrics (see chapter 7 for examples), and observation checklists. Plan on evaluating each student several times during his or her term on the news crew.

News-Crew Positions

Before selecting the group of students that will become your production team, it is a good idea to list and identify the jobs or positions you need to fill. Any teacher or media specialist will tell you, *never* have more students than you have jobs! You know that saying, "Idle hands ... " It is never more true than in this situation. Likewise, never assign a student a position that is not a "real" job. For example, don't have a lighting director if you don't have any lights to adjust. If all your student has to do is flip on the light switch to turn on the fluorescent lights in the ceiling, that is not a job. A set director should have more duties than just changing the bulletin-board paper behind the anchor desk once every nine weeks. Each student in the team should have an active part in producing the news show. The more sophisticated the show, the more jobs that are needed to fulfill the positions. That said, here is a list of possible jobs you may need to produce a typical news show:

Student News Crew: Job Descriptions and Assignments

- **Producer.** Responsible for the finished news program; selecting audio and video displays, giving cues, countdowns, and so on.
- **Technical director.** Responsible for operating the video mixer during the news show. Also responsible for selecting effects and transitions.
- **Audio technician.** Responsible for all audio operations during the program, including microphone, music, and videotaped sounds.
- **Graphics technician.** Responsible for creating graphic screens and operation of the character generator during show production.

- **Digital image technician.** Responsible for creating graphic computer screens using the computer, digital still camera, and graphics resources; operating graphics computer during show production.
- **Camera operator.** Responsible for creating appropriate shots of talent, reporters, and other sources during program production and videotaped interviews.
- **Videotape operator.** Responsible for operating the source VCR during program production; playing openings, prerecorded interviews, public service announcements, and ending credits footage.
- **Teleprompter operator.** Responsible for operating teleprompter during show production, making last-minute script changes and corrections, saving script to disk.
- **Talent.** Responsible for reading the script during news-show production.
- **Reporter.** Responsible for conducting on-camera interviews, writing interview questions, scheduling videotaping sessions, and suggesting guests.

Selecting Students for the Production Crew

As we stated previously in this chapter, we believe that a school news show should be produced by a "class" taught and supervised by the media specialist or media/TV production teacher. Whether this class meets every day or just one to three days a week, the consistency and instruction will lead to a more professional broadcast. Methods of selecting students to be included in the production crew vary from school to school and district to district. Elementary media specialists certainly have different needs and activities than a high school teacher or media specialist. In an elementary setting, you may even need to involve parents in the process, especially if transportation before or after school hours is required or if students will miss part of their daily class activities. Middle schools offer a variety of activities and schedules that lend themselves to organizing a production class: exploratory classes, homerooms, and clubs. Some of the ways students can be selected could include the following:

- **Applications.** Applications can be available at the start of the school year or during the last nine weeks of the remaining school year. Students can show they are responsible and interested by completing the required forms, getting teacher recommendations and signatures, and returning the applications in good form and in a timely matter. Sample applications are included in the appendix to this chapter.
- **Teacher recommendations.** Several media specialists have been successful using "recommended" students from various grade levels. This could be just one grade level, fifth-grade students, for example, or a mixture of students from sev-

eral grade levels. Teachers select and recommend students to participate based on their academic grades, conduct, and interest. These are generally capable students who have little or no misconduct problems and who would make up any class work and assignments missed because of their participation in the production class.

■ **Clubs.** Forming a video club can be a very good way to achieve the goal of forming a production class. Clubs can meet before or after school. As an alternative, some schools have found it to be successful to implement a "Club Period" once a week for various grade levels.

■ **Individual classes.** It is not uncommon to find media specialists forming news teams composed of students from one particular class or another. If this method is chosen, we recommend that the classes be rotated by semesters or even grading periods. Letting the gifted class produce the news show every year, for example, is not really a fair way of distributing the opportunities for learning media skills and techniques.

Before deciding on one method to select the students to participate in these activities, it may be beneficial to meet with and discuss your plans with other media specialists in your district to see what works for them. It would also be a good idea to write out your plans and goals and submit them to your principal or supervisor for approval. Include any applications that students might be completing, parent letters, or other forms you will be using to assess the students and skills.

Designing the TV Studio

Once the equipment has been purchased and connected and the production crew selected, it is now time to organize and design the TV studio. The size, shape, and scope of the TV studio will depend on the facility in which it is housed. In our journeys across the country, we have seen an incredible variety of TV studios. There have been magnificent studios designed and built with video production in the forefront, and there have been redesigned book closets that only the most creative minds would call "studios." Some schools "have," and some schools "have not." It is the role of the media specialist to make the space work whatever the situation. If you have to put the video equipment together on A/V carts and roll it in and out of a closet every day, well, that's what you have to do to make it work!

Sets

This section looks at three options for designing and building a school news-show set: a typical anchor-desk set, a news-magazine set, and the "no-set" set.

The Anchor-Desk Set

Local and network news shows usually use an anchor seated at a desk as a vehicle for delivering their news and video segments. Of course, these stations have the monetary and professional resources to build a professional set. But fashioning this type of set may not be as difficult as you think. With some creative and innovative thinking, you can obtain the materials and resources you need to build a typical anchor-desk set. (See fig. 6.1.)

Many high schools have theater programs, and set building is an integral part of such programs. A simple anchor desk, curved or rectangular shaped, would not be much of a problem for a stage crew to design and build. Plywood, two-by-fours, strip molding, and some paint offer an inexpensive way to construct an anchor desk. Perhaps your school's PTA could donate the funds for materials and labor.

Professional contractors, builders, and retired grandparents are resources available to most schools. A letter or notice printed in the school's newsletter can be used to locate and recruit these people to help you design and build an anchor desk and set at your school. Many parents are more than willing to donate materials and time—they simply need to be aware of your needs. Good communication can be the start of a great relationship.

Figure 6.1 An anchor desk adds a professional touch to a school's news programs.

Local news stations periodically update their sets or build new ones. Telephone calls and letters requesting a donation of an unused set can result in a bonanza for your school. Some new paint and creative props can turn a local news station's throwaway into a prime-time news set at your school. Don't forget to contact cable operators and religious-affiliated stations as well. If you find yourself having to design and build the anchor-desk set yourself, don't despair. There are some simple, inexpensive ways to make the set appear neat and professional.

If you are using lunchroom or library tables to serve as an anchor desk, try calling some local hotels or convention centers and ask them to donate some cloth table skirts or dressings, as well as a few plastic clips to adhere them to your tables. Hotels are usually glad to fulfill a small request for one or two table dressings for your news-show set. Not only will the tables look more professional, but the cloth skirts will hide the anchors' legs and feet from the camera, as well as any cords and cables underneath the table.

One school using this type of set purchased three blazers at a thrift shop for the anchors to wear on camera. From the waist up, everyone looks very professional. Under the desk, hidden by the table's skirt, are shorts, slacks, and tennis shoes that no one sees. When you are requesting donations, try to avoid acquiring white- or black-colored material; these will cause contrast problems for your video camera. Blue, gray, maroon, or pastel colors generally look the best on video.

Cardboard can also be used quite effectively, although it doesn't hold up as well as wood in daily use. You can use duct or gaffer's tape to attach cardboard from large appliance boxes or shipping material to the anchor desk. The cardboard can be covered with wallpaper or contact paper or even painted to alter its color and appearance on camera.

Some schools have used bulletin-board paper to cover the sides and fronts of tables to give them a desk appearance. Letters and logos are simply taped or glued to the paper to give it a more-professional look.

As you begin to build and design your anchor-desk set, take some time to visit other schools in your area to see how their sets are designed. Many teachers are more than happy to share their ideas and techniques. Take along a video or 35mm camera to record some pictures for guidelines and examples. Even after you have built your set, new ideas and techniques will enable you to change and adapt your set year after year.

The News-Magazine Set

A news-magazine set differs from the typical anchor-desk format in that the news anchors are not seated behind a formal news-anchor desk. In a news-magazine format, the anchors may be seated on chairs or stools or may even be standing. The style is more casual and relaxed. (See fig. 6.2.) News-magazine shows are shown

Figure 6.2 For a more modern look, a magazine-style set can be used for school news shows.

daily in most major markets throughout the United States. Watch and record a few typical shows. Pay careful attention to the set design, anchor seating, and conversational format. For high school students, MTV offers a variety of news and information segments that use a magazine-style format.

Designing and building this type of set can be fun and exciting for you and your students. Most of the materials you will need can be purchased at area retail and hardware stores. Students can bring in props and set accessories from home or even purchase them at garage sales and thrift stores. Many magazine shows have a motif or style they exhibit in their sets. For example, one school has a "country-living" atmosphere complete with wooden rocking chairs for the anchors, who are seated on a "front porch" with a wooden facade of a cabin built behind them. An MTV-style set could be used complete with working portable black-and-white monitors, lava lamps, a fish in an aquarium, black lights, and other electronic gadgets to give the show a flashy look and a Generation X style that appeals to its high school audience.

When you begin to build and design a news-magazine set, consider the following factors.

SEATING Will your anchors be seated or standing? The types of chairs and seating arrangements are very important in this style of show. Old wooden chairs from the library do not work well. Catalog and furniture stores offer a variety of stools and chairs. Vinyl or leather stools look great on camera and fit well with this type of format. Upholstered chairs and couches can also be used to give an informal look to the show. Furniture can often be purchased inexpensively from rent-to-own stores or even furniture showrooms. Local thrift stores can also be a good source of furniture and set decorations.

BACKGROUND Two or three anchors sitting on stools in front of a curtain is not much of a set. Props and set dressings become important when you are designing and building a magazine-style set. Tables, bookshelves, knickknacks, plants, and other set decorations can be used to fill the empty spaces. Placing these decorations at an inward angle can add depth to the camera shot.

BALANCE One of the most common mistakes is to overshoot the talent and decorate too much of the background. Remember, the talent needs to remain the dominant part of the shot and not appear as little ants at the bottom of the screen. Many sets that appear large and assuming on television are in reality very small. The video camera's shot composition and angle make them look larger than life on the screen. Work with your talent and camera operators to see which angles and shots work best. Record some practice shows and review them with the technical crew. Analyze which angles, shots, and picture composition looked best. Redesign or rearrange areas of the set that looked too bare or too cluttered.

Of course, there are many strategies for designing and building magazine-style sets. Perhaps the ideas here have started your creative juices flowing. Attend workshops and seminars at conventions that focus on school news shows to get ideas and see what other teachers and media specialists are doing. Watch television shows for ideas about set design and show formats you might want to try with your school news show. And remember, just because you tried it once does not mean you can't change it. Redesigning and updating your set should be an ongoing activity. Don't allow your show to become boring or stale. New set dressings, camera angles, and show formats can keep students interested in your show and keep your technical crew excited about their productions.

The "No-Set" Set

No studio? No production room? No problem. Some of the best news shows produced in schools today are being done without a studio or production facility. Videotaping and production occur on location, whether in the media center, the principal's office, or a classroom. How can these shows be effective without the use of sets and backdrops? It's all a matter of technique and some simple strategies that can help make these shows interesting and professional. Many local and network news shows actually use this technique for their productions. Watch *CNN Headline News* and you will see the anchor positioned right in the center of the newsroom itself. News staff and electronics actually make up the background of the shot. If you find yourself in a situation where you must produce a show without a studio location, here are a few suggestions that can assist you in making your productions better.

THE PORTABLE STUDIO Organize your video equipment on rolling A/V carts. This will make it easier to move your equipment from one location to another and return it to the closet or workroom where it is stored when not in use. Try to organize the equipment logically, especially components that are used together. For example, have all your audio components (audio mixer, CD player, cassette deck) on one cart, your video components (switcher, source VCR, record VCR) on another cart, and so on. Don't be afraid to use several carts and connect them via cables when you arrive at your taping location.

LOCATION, LOCATION, LOCATION Position your video cameras and talent so you can obtain the best background possible. Avoid using bare walls, windows, and chalkboards as backgrounds. These offer nothing that can add excitement and drama to your productions. Classrooms, media centers, and even hallways that have a sense of realism and energy can be great backgrounds for taping your show. Position your talent and cameras at an angle to your background (45 degrees works well) so that your shot has depth. Avoid placing talent directly facing the camera with their backs to a wall or bookcase. Experiment with locations. Some locations will look better than others. Of course, you will need to consider time and personal constraints.

CAMERA TRICKS Try using a soft-focus or selected-focus shot for your talent. This technique is used on most news shows where the talent is located in a newsroom. The talent is sharply focused, while the background is slightly blurred or soft focused. This can be done with the following steps:

- Separate your talent and video cameras with as much as 10–15 feet of space. The more distance between them, the easier it will be to create a shallow depth of field. There should also be some distance between the talent and the background.
- Switch the camera's focusing mechanism to manual focus. Most video cameras have an auto and a manual setting. You must be on the manual setting to adjust the camera's focus with the focus ring on the front of the lens.

Figure 6.3 Professional lighting fixtures are readily available for school news production. Photo courtesy of LightTech, www.lighttech.com

▫ Using the zoom mechanism on your camera, zoom in to obtain a good bust or waist shot of your talent. Frame the shot to obtain the best picture composition.

▫ Turn the focus ring so that the talent is in clear focus and the background is slightly blurred. This is easier to see if you can look at the image on a monitor rather than the viewfinder.

LIGHTING TIPS After you have some experience with the "no-set" set, experiment with some simple lighting to illuminate the talent and set them off from the background. Professional lighting equipment is readily available, but it can be costly. Be sure to include some lighting fixtures when preparing a budget for purchasing new video equipment. Today's sophisticated lighting provides full illumination without the excessive heating that comes from halogen bulbs. (See fig. 6.3.) Inexpensive clamp lights from a hardware store can be used for this purpose. As with all lighting, be careful with heat and electrical connections.

Producing an interesting news show without a set is a challenge, but it can still be done professionally using some of the tips and techniques provided here.

Curtains, Backdrops, and Backgrounds

Watch some videotape of your recent school news program. What does the shot look like behind the anchor desk and announcers? Are your students seated in front of an off-white cinder-block wall? Backgrounds, curtains, and backdrops can add a lot to the visual appeal of your news show. Schools are often limited by monetary resources, but some inexpensive alternatives exist that can help you enhance the background of your news-show set.

Curtains

Perhaps the most widely used, colored curtains hung from the ceiling or mounted on a rod or rack offer a simple solution to taping in front of a blank wall. If you are purchasing curtains for your studio, select colors that will not present contrast problems for your video cameras. The acceptable contrast ratio for video cameras is 30:1. Avoid using black or white curtains because they quickly establish the lightest or darkest limits of the camera and thereby create contrast problems with the rest of the set. Neutral colors are best, such as blues, greens, grays, and pastels. A professional company that specializes in auditorium and theater curtains can assist you in purchasing and designing the layout for your studio.

Using a set of multiple sliding curtains can enable you to change and mix the backgrounds of your set. For example, a light gray background curtain can be used in conjunction with some red and blue curtains hung in front to produce a combination of colors to use each day.

Professional-quality curtains are expensive, so be sure to avoid damaging them. Always move and adjust the curtains by reaching around them and grabbing the back of the curtain. Avoid putting your fingers and hands on the front side of the curtain, where dirt and oils will eventually show up on camera.

Canvas Drop Cloths

If the expense of purchasing professionally made curtains exceeds your department or school budget, inexpensive backdrops can easily be made with some simple materials purchased from a local hardware store. Drop cloths used by painters can make wonderful backdrops for your sets. Cotton drop cloths (do not use plastic) can be found at most home-improvement stores for about $30. Be sure to purchase one large enough to completely cover your set. Using a latex water-based paint, you can paint the drop cloth with muted versions of your school colors. Spray paints can also be used, but only in a well-ventilated area. One video production teacher accidentally forced the evacuation of his media center while spray painting backdrops for his news-show sets. The fumes from the spray entered the air conditioning system and were funneled into the adjoining rooms and library area. Several boxes of candy and apologies to his fellow teachers and media specialists remedied the situation. The next time backdrops were made, the painting was done outside.

A textured look can be created by using sponges, feather dusters, and burlap strips as paint brushes. One school allowed the crew to paint its backdrop using hand prints and footprints in various colors all over the backdrop. Not only was this fun, but the imprints made a nice backdrop and were preserved for posterity, too. Creativity is the key. Some creations will turn out better than others, but you will learn a lot in the process about what does and doesn't work. (See fig. 6.4.)

You can hang your canvas backdrop by using a simple tool that will punch a hole and attach a grommet (metal ring) to hang and suspend the cloth from a rod or bracket mounted on the wall. (See fig. 6.5.) Ask a salesperson to assist you in pur-

Figure 6.4 Students enjoy creating drop-cloth backdrops.

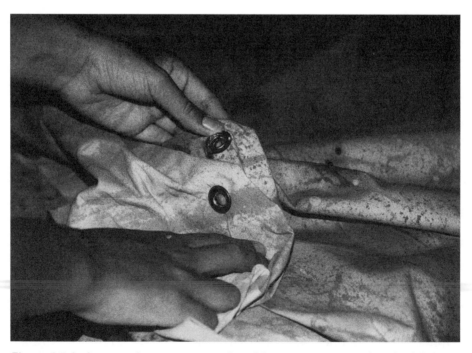

Figure 6.5 An inexpensive grommet tool positions grommets so that the fabric backdrop can be easily hung without tearing.

chasing the necessary tools and supplies to accomplish this task. When your drop cloth is hung, it is not necessary to stretch the canvas tight—the creases, wrinkles, and folds will add depth and texture to your background. (See fig. 6.6.)

Flats

Another easy way to create a background for your news set is to build some canvas flats to hang behind your desk or talent. (See fig. 6.7.) These flats are made with 1 by 1 inch strips of lumber, canvas, or muslin cloth and some paint. Begin by measuring the width and height of your set. Build a frame out of the strips of lumber. If your set is very large, you can reinforce the standard picture-frame design with an extra support in the middle of the frame. Some schools reinforce large flats with an X pattern of strips in the center of the frame. Stretch a sheet of muslin or light canvas over the frame, pulling it as tight as possible to eliminate wrinkles and creases. Use a staple gun to attach the muslin to the frame. Next, use a roller to apply white latex paint over the muslin. Repeat this last step several times. As the white latex paint dries, the muslin will become hard and tight. Apply as many coats as needed; sometimes four or five coats are necessary for larger flats. Now you have a canvas ready to be painted as a backdrop. The design is up to your imagination. Some flats are painted to look like a picture of the school or community. Perhaps the school's art teacher or even some local artists can assist you and your students with this project. Of course, you can always solicit the help of some talented stu-

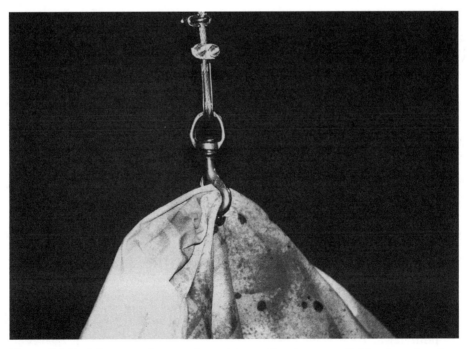

Figure 6.6 Backdrops are hung using cable and hardware available at any local hardware store.

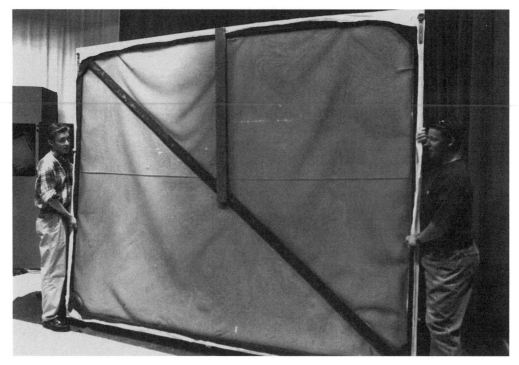

Figure 6.7 Students prepare a muslin-covered backdrop for production.

dents who may not be members of your television production crew. And don't forget to tap the parent resources available at your school. A note or letter in the school bulletin could turn up a parent with exceptional artistic talent.

Murals

Murals and photographic backgrounds are readily available through catalogs and photography stores. They can range from a beautiful beach scene to a lighted city nightscape to a professional portrait backdrop. Some are expensive, but they are easily placed on a flat wall or bulletin board to create an instant backdrop. One school received a nice donated backdrop from a grandparent who was a retired professional photographer.

Camera Strategies for Optimizing Your Set

No matter what type of set you are using, designing and building sets should be fun for you and the students. Look for creative ways to obtain materials and volunteer help. Regardless of the design and type of set, here are some basic camera strategies that can enhance your picture composition and quality:

▣ Always white-balance your camera in the light you will be taping in.

▣ Use the manual focus function of the camera rather than the auto-focus mechanism. This will eliminate focus changes throughout the course of your show and allow you to establish the depth of field for each camera angle.

▣ Be sure that your camera and talent are on the same level. This means you may have to adjust the tripod height or even build a platform or "flat" for your talent to raise them to camera level. *Never* shoot down or up with your video camera during the production of your news show.

▣ Obtain a teleprompter system so that your anchors are looking toward the camera lens instead of down at papers in their hands.

▣ Adjust lighting to eliminate shadows from the talents' faces and sets. Use a monitor to visually adjust the lighting to obtain the best image. Don't be afraid to try adjusting the iris on your video camera, too. Sometimes just a slight adjustment (open or closed) can make a big difference in the picture resolution.

Many teachers and media specialists who are producing news shows have little or no training in building and designing sets. Some learn by trial and error, others take classes at community colleges and universities, and there are always books and professional literature available. Joining professional organizations and attending conferences and workshops are also good ways to get ideas and examples.

News-Show Formats

What kind of news show will your students produce? Will it be a serious journalistic approach or a humorous and entertaining broadcast? What about show content? How will announcements be aired: read by anchors, graphics and music, or a combination of the two? How many anchors will host the show, and will any administrators be involved in the daily broadcasts? How long will the show last, and when will it be broadcast? These are all questions that you, the media specialist, need to decide before you meet with the students. Professional news organizations have in place a policies and procedures manual that governs their daily and weekly activities. As the "director" of your program, creating such a manual is also a good idea for you. There is no need to write pages and pages of policies and procedures, but it is a good idea to have in place the goals of your program, the tone of the program you would prefer, and the types of activities that you want to include in the show. This is called the show format. Each school has its own unique format, which is based on the aptitude of the teacher and students, the equipment available for production use, and the goals and direction that are set for the broadcast. Some of the aspects of the news show format could include the following:

■ **Openings.** How will the broadcast open each day? Will students produce a 30–40 second videotape with music and graphics that begins each show? Will there simply be a graphic on the screen (title and date) indicating that the show will begin momentarily? Maybe some background music can be played with the graphic so teachers can adjust the volume of their televisions.

■ **Hosts and camera angles.** How many anchors will host the show each day? Will the opening shot include both anchors and a welcome or just a one-shot of a single anchor? How many cameras will be used to record the show, and what angles will each one be using? These are all important considerations.

■ **Show content.** What kind of information will be included in each show? Will Monday's show differ from Wednesday's, which might differ from Friday's show? When will school announcements be read, and who will read them? Will teacher information be provided as well? Will there be access to an online computer to talk about and show weather maps, Internet sites, pictures, and graphics? Will the lunch menu be included? Will it just be read by an anchor, include graphics, or be hosted by "Chef Ryan" talking about the Entrée of the Day? Will interviews and video segments produced by students be shown daily, weekly, or at all? Maintaining a consistent show format assists both the production crew and the viewer. For example, watch your daily news show each day for a week. You will most likely see, in this order, the show's topics: Major news event, national news, local news, weather, and sports. Each day the format stays the same, but the content of each changes. This is a good example of how you can format the content in your show. Pick a strategy and stick to it. Start simple and build as you and your students gain experience with the equipment and techniques.

■ **Ending.** How will the show end? Will there be ending graphics, music and pictures with graphics, or a simple "That's our show for today—see you tomorrow" from the anchors?

As you begin to formulate a plan for the news show and its format, it is essential that you keep the frustration level to a minimum for both you and the students. Start with some basics, perhaps a simple opening graphic and music, school announcements with one or two graphics, and a simple ending. After your first few days, or weeks, start adding more complex content and production techniques. Add another camera, a digital image, Word of the Day, a weather map from the Internet. Just don't do it all at once! If you see that the students are at or above their competence level, reduce the size and scope of the show. Each team will be unique and different, just as each and every student is unique and different. Some production crews will move swiftly from simple to complex. Other teams, for whatever reason, may not ever make that move. Adjust what you are doing and showing to the level of competence of the students and the teacher. Don't make the production too big or too small. Keep their interest by expanding the scope of the show and their production roles.

News-show activities and formats are also included in chapter 7, "Video Production Activities."

Broadcasting Your News Show

Even though you have taken the time to schedule a daily period for broadcasting, classroom teachers will get preoccupied and forget to turn on their televisions for the news show. The first week or two of the school year, make an announcement over the intercom a minute or two before you begin playing your tape or broadcasting your show. This will remind teachers about the broadcast and also clue them in to what channel you will be broadcasting on. Most classroom teachers will find it extremely helpful to assign a knowledgeable student to turn on the news show each day. Amazingly, kids can remember to do this, and adults can't. Whenever possible, try to have a graphic (name of the show, for example) recorded on the news-show tape or on a character generator (if you are broadcasting your show live) so that the classroom teachers know they are on the right channel. It's also a good idea to have music playing so that they can adjust the volume to the appropriate listening level. You can generate the opening music and graphics each time you do your news show, or you may prefer to roll a tape for several minutes and record your news show after the graphic and music. If the news show is a live broadcast, you may want to have the graphics and music playing and just stop the tape so that the live feed will appear. It can be awkward and embarrassing to have your news-show team on the air before you're ready to begin. Playing a tape can eliminate that problem. Give the teachers a reasonable amount of time to turn the TV on and tune to your broadcast. After a minute or two, begin your broadcast.

When scheduling your broadcast, try to persuade your administration to add enough time to the appropriate class period to account for any lost class time caused by your program. For example, if your program is shown during fourth period, an extra few minutes should be added to that period. This adjusted schedule means that you are never taking up any teaching time with your broadcast. Otherwise, some teachers will decide to skip the news broadcast to squeeze in a few more minutes of teaching time. (Of course, this practice can backfire on teachers as they are called into the principal's office because none of their students heard the important school announcements.) Pad the schedule to assure adequate and equal instructional time (see fig. 6.8).

As you begin your broadcasts, questions, concerns, and adjustments to everyone's schedules will occur. This is normal. Professionals can sit down and discuss

Orlando High School Bell Schedule	
1st Period	7:15 a.m. – 8:07 a.m.
2nd Period	8:14 a.m. – 9:06 a.m.
3rd Period	9:13 a.m. – 10:05 a.m.
WDOC NEWS	10:12 a.m. – 10:20 a.m.
4th Period	10:20 a.m. – 11:12 a.m.
Lunch A	11:12 a.m. – 11:42 a.m.
5th Period A	11:49 a.m. – 12:41 p.m.
5th Period B	11:19 a.m. – 12:11 p.m.
Lunch B	12:11 p.m. – 12:41 p.m.
6th Period	12:48 p.m. – 1:40 p.m.
Teacher Planning	1:40 p.m. – 2:30 p.m.

Figure 6.8 Your school's bell schedule should have a dedicated time for your news show broadcasts.

these issues and solve the problems reasonably and amicably. Allow the classroom teachers to have some input into your broadcasts. Not only will they come up with good suggestions, but it will help them take an interest in your program and goals for the news show.

Closed-circuit systems are becoming a fact of life in schools today. The advantages of being able to play and broadcast programs schoolwide make the initial cost of the system worthwhile. The technology is affordable, easy to understand and operate, and attainable in most areas of the country. Using the system to the fullest potential becomes the task of administrators, teachers, students, and of course, media specialists.

Sample Middle School News Show Application
Multimedia/News Team Application

Thank you for showing an interest in joining the school video news crew. Before you complete the application, please understand the following:

1. Multimedia class lasts for ___ weeks. You may take the class only once per school year.
2. Multimedia class is an alternative to a section of the Vocational Wheel (art, computers, home economics). Students who are accepted into multimedia class will miss vocational wheel for one of the 9-week periods. Students may not have a choice which part of the wheel they miss.
3. Multimedia class will serve as your 1st period class during your enrollment.
4. The class will produce the news program three (3) times per week. The remainder of the class periods will be spent learning media skills like audio and video production, news reporting, computing, and so on. You will be given a letter grade for your work in this class.
5. You will need to purchase a blank videotape.

ALL COMPLETED APPLICATIONS must be returned to the media center by _____ at 2 P.M. No incomplete applications will be considered.

Student Name _____ Current Grade ____

Advisory Teacher _____ Room # _____

What were your grades on your most current report card?

Number of As _____ Bs _____ Cs _____ Ds _____ Fs _____

What are your favorite subjects/classes in school?

_____

Why are you interested in TV Production? (Hint: don't write, "It sounds like fun!") _____

_____

What are your hobbies/interests/school activities? List at least three. _____

_____

_____

Student Name _____

Recommendations

To be considered for multimedia class, you must have the recommendations of two teachers, counselors, or administrators. Please ask them to complete the section below.

Recommendation #1

Please evaluate the student named above by circling the appropriate number on the scale below. Comments are not required but may be attached to the form. Thank you.

Attendance	Poor	1	2	3	4	5	Great
Punctuality	Poor	1	2	3	4	5	Great
Conduct	Poor	1	2	3	4	5	Great
Group Work	Poor	1	2	3	4	5	Great
Academics	Poor	1	2	3	4	5	Great

Teacher Signature _____ **Position** _____

Recommendation #2

Please evaluate the student named above by circling the appropriate number on the scale below. Comments are not required but may be attached to the form. Thank you.

Attendance	Poor	1	2	3	4	5	Great
Punctuality	Poor	1	2	3	4	5	Great
Conduct	Poor	1	2	3	4	5	Great
Group Work	Poor	1	2	3	4	5	Great
Academics	Poor	1	2	3	4	5	Great

Teacher Signature _____ **Position** _____

Student Signature

"I have completed this application honestly and accurately. I understand all of the information presented in the application."

Name _____ Date _____

Sample High School News Show Application
Television Production 1 Application

Application Deadline _____

Name _____   Date _____

Current Mailing Address   _____

_____

Phone _____   E-mail _____

Current Grade Level _____   Current Overall GPA* _____
                                           *Attach copy of most recent report card.

1. Attach a typed essay (150–250 words) explaining some of the reasons you are interested in enrolling into the Television Production program. Include any previous experience in the production field, whether in school or in the community.

2. Teacher Recommendation
Please write a brief statement about the qualifications of the above Candidate in terms of responsibility, creativity, and academic standards.

Teacher Signature _____   **Position** _____
School _____

3. Television Production students are required to purchase the following materials by the end of the second week of classes: workbook, videotape, headphones.

Parent Signature _____   Date _____
All applicants will be notified by letter regarding their status and acceptance into the program. DO NOT call the school regarding this matter. Thank you.

Chapter 7

Video Production Activities

The following activities are designed for you, the media specialist, or even classroom teachers who are interested in having students work with media and technology to enhance the curriculum in the classrooms. Included in this chapter are preplanning activities, lesson plans, extension ideas, and student project plans for each activity. The activities can be easily adapted to meet your classroom levels of instruction and grade groupings.

It is important to spend some time with the students demonstrating and teaching the skills needed to operate the video and media equipment used for each activity. Although not necessary, it is a good idea to create a "sample" project to illustrate what the completed activity will look like. In successive years, you may want to save a few student-created examples to show to students and teachers.

The following activities are included in this chapter:

Video scavenger hunt. A fun way to teach students how to use the camcorder and frame shots, and how to work as a team.

Camera shots project. Used to teach and illustrate the basic shots of good videography. Students will learn the vocabulary (two shot, bust shot, etc.) and how to correctly frame their subjects.

Macro projects. A series of "still" pictures placed on videotape. Music backgrounds and narration can be added as well.

Interview projects. Ideas and plans, as well as step-by-step instructions, make these projects ideal for student instruction and use in the school's news-show broadcasts.

News-magazine shows. Sample ideas and outlines for students to design and incorporate into real or simulated news-magazine shows.

Documentaries. Video projects designed to provide visual and descriptive narrations about school or community topics.

Technology projects. Projects designed to use media technology available in most schools to enhance classroom curriculum. These include digital cameras and table-top video cameras.

These activities are designed to provide students and teachers with a framework to plan, script, and produce media projects. The finished projects will no doubt vary from school to school depending on the level of sophistication of the available equipment and media expertise. Almost all of these projects require no postproduction (editing), but many schools and programs are now equipped with editing equipment, which they can use to create a more-polished finished project. These projects will allow teachers, media specialists, and students to use the skills and knowledge gained from the preceding chapters.

Grading rubrics are included for many of the project plans.

Video Scavenger Hunt

Objective: Students will learn to use the camcorder to record a selected listing of subjects or shots. The emphasis will be on subject framing, camcorder operation (recording, not recording), and working as a team.

Method

1. Students form teams. Each team receives a camcorder, tape, and a Video Scavenger Hunt form.
2. Students will have five minutes to look over the form and develop a strategy.
3. Students have a set time frame (suggested: 25 minutes) to videotape as many of the listed shots as possible.
4. When the allotted time is up, students return to class, and tapes are viewed and scored. While viewing tapes, comments regarding shot composition, focusing, and other videography skills are encouraged.

Teacher Notes

1. Take this opportunity to teach students the rudimentary skills of using a camcorder.
2. Demonstrate how to
   - turn on the camcorder,
   - use the trigger to "record" and "stop recording,"
   - use the viewfinder to obtain information about camera functions (recording, battery power, focusing, lighting), and
   - connect the camcorder to a monitor and demonstrate some simple concepts of shot composition (headroom, lead room, background, framing).
3. Develop the idea of teamwork. Talk about the ideas of sharing and responsibility. Discuss the importance of caring for the camcorder and its monetary value, as well as the length of time it takes to get it repaired!

Student Project Plan
Video Scavenger Hunt

Team Members: _____

_____

_____

Directions (be sure to change videographer for each shot!)

1. Find your desired "shot."
2. Record each shot for 8 to 10 seconds.
3. Number in order as you record them!
4. All objects must be REAL—no pictures or photos.
5. No two-for-one shots.
6. Rewind tape and turn in with Activity Sheet.

Easy Ones (3 pts.)

1. A lunchbox ____
2. A bulletin board ____
3. A water fountain ____
4. A teacher ____
5. Two students talking ____

6. A notice ____
7. A book ____
8. Something with wheels ____
9. A flower ____
10. An office worker ____

Harder Ones (5 pts.)

1. A student reading ____
2. A teacher smiling ____
3. A parent volunteer ____
4. A cafeteria worker ____
5. Someone running ____

6. A computer being used ____
7. An untied shoe ____
8. An insect ____
9. A school bus ____
10. A blank chalkboard or dry erase board ____

Hardest Ones (8 pts.)

1. A teacher eating ____
2. Someone laughing ____
3. A bird flying ____
4. Someone doing a good deed ____
5. The principal ____

6. Students playing a game ____
7. Someone picking up trash ____
8. Student in a school shirt ____
9. A girl in pigtails ____
10. A *Star Wars* anything ____

Camera Shots Project

Objective: To teach and develop students' skills in videography. This activity is designed to teach students videography vocabulary and shot composition to assist in video projects and storyboarding.

Method

1. Distribute Camera Shots Project plan.
2. Connect the camcorder to a monitor and demonstrate each shot on the project plan.
3. Allow the students time to practice shots with the camcorder connected to the monitor. Assist and critique as needed.
4. Students complete Camera Shots Project.

Teacher Notes

1. These are the basic camera shots used in videography. It is important that your students can produce each shot and also identify them for storyboarding.
2. It is recommended that you produce a videotape with these shots so students can watch and identify them. Then you can allow time in class to practice with camcorders attached to monitors.
3. For added fun, you can add a music soundtrack to their completed tapes. This not only makes them more fun to watch but also teaches them a valuable skill (adding music to prerecorded video tracks).
4. It is advisable to pause the VCR while watching the finished tapes and point out positive and negative aspects of shot composition, background lighting, framing, and focusing techniques.
5. Students can also work in groups, taking turns and rotating while videotaping the shots.
6. Be sure the students number the shots as they record them (1, 2, 3, etc.). Sometimes it can be difficult to determine what shot you are viewing on the tape!
7. Be sure to set a time limit! This project can easily be completed in 30 minutes or less. Boundaries are also good (where to go, where not to go).

Student Project Plan
Camera Shots Project

Name _____ Date _____

Teacher _____ Grade _____

Objective: Students will be able to correctly frame and videotape a variety of camera shots.

Procedures

1. Each camera shot is to be recorded for 6 to 8 seconds.
2. All focusing, white balancing, and zooming should be done prior to recording the selected shot.
3. Shots may be recorded in any order, but assignment sheet should be numbered in the order that the camera shots were recorded.

Tips

1. Practice the assignment FIRST, and then record your shots.
2. Record 10 seconds of "black" before the first shot and after the last shot. This can be done using a lens cap, the camera's iris control, or a fade function if you have one.

Camera Shot/Description	Sequence	Teacher Comments	Points
Bust shot Framed so that only a person's head and shoulders are in the shot.			
Knee Shot Framed so that the person is cut off slightly above or slightly below the knees.			
Over-the-shoulder shot Framed so that the viewers have the perception that they are participating in the action by peering over the shoulder of the subject.			
Tilted shot Camera angle is tilted either up or down on an object.			
Unstable-horizon shot Camera angle is skewed so that the horizon line is not parallel. Often referred to as an MTV look.			
Depth shot Creates depth in a "scene" by adding objects to the foreground, middle ground, and background. A "Kodak" picture look.			
Extreme close-up Must be of a person; used to show emotion. Very tight shot of face and expressions; some part of face may even be cut out of the framing.			
Lead room Camera "follows" a moving object, keeping the object in the back third of the frame to allow the viewer to see where the object is heading.			
Macro shot Camera is positioned very close to an object to show detail. Camera is set at widest zoom position but placed extremely close to an object for framing.			
Total points awarded (possible 100)			

Macro Projects

Description: The finished project will be a one- to two-minute videotape program consisting of 8 to 15 still pictures and a soundtrack to augment the content. Pictures can be photographs, pictures from books, postcards, or even student-drawn images.

Ideas for Macro Projects

Macro projects are ideal for incorporating classroom content and media production to create a fun and easy finished product that demonstrates student learning. Here are some ideas for macro projects:

- **Growing up**. Students gather pictures from infancy to present size and age.
- **Animals.** Images from books provide good visuals for students to add narrative information.
- **History**. Make a time period or historical event come alive on videotape by capturing images and adding narration and even music from that time period.
- **Song lyrics**. Have students draw and color images that illustrate a song they have learned. The song lyrics can even be written on the bottom of the drawing paper. A wonderful example would be "Raindrops Keep Falling on My Head," in which each line is illustrated by a student artist. The accompanying music can be an actual recording of the students on cassette singing the lyrics.
- **Community topics**. Postcards and tourist magazines can provide images and information for students to use to produce a project about state or local destinations.

Method

1. The students collect images that have a central theme.
2. The students create a title for the project. This can be done with a character generator or even created on index cards with markers, crayons, or colored pencils.

3. Have the students videotape the pictures. Each image should be recorded for at least five seconds. Some camcorders have a "still" function, which works well for this project. The student will simply "capture" a still of the image and then record the captured still for the appropriate amount of time.
4. Have the student add just instrumental music or music with vocals to the soundtrack. This can be done with audio dubbing or incorporating the video into any nonlinear editing system.

Teacher Notes

1. The camcorder should be set up on a tripod to keep the shot steady.
2. It is easier for students to frame the picture if you can connect the camera's video output to a small monitor or television.
3. Focusing. Most camcorders will focus at close range (less than 12 inches) if you switch them to autofocus, zoom out to maximum, and move the camera as close as needed to the image to fill the screen. This works better than "zooming in" to get the screen filled with the image. Table-top cameras also work great for macro projects.
4. Graphics. As stated earlier, students may want to design a title with a character generator prior to recording their images. Record the title on a videotape for 15 seconds. Be sure to rewind the tape a few seconds before placing it in the camcorder so there is no "glitch" between the title and the first picture. A title card can also be made on an index card with markers, crayons, or colored pencils. This card is then videotaped as the first "picture."
5. It is nice if students can "fade in" on the first picture and "fade out" on the last picture. Do *not* have them fade in and out on every picture, which can become very distracting to the viewer watching the finished project.
6. Script. If your students are writing narration for their pictures, it is important for them to time the script and record the image for the appropriate length of time. Allow two to three seconds extra recording time for each picture so there is no need to rush the script. This is a good way to reinforce the concept of storyboarding.
7. Audio soundtracks. As noted previously, soundtracks can be added to the video through audio dubbing (your VCR or camcorder must have this feature) or by incorporating the video into a nonlinear editing system and adding the soundtrack there.
8. Have fun! Watching the finished projects on a big-screen TV or video projector can be a fun and exciting way to end this activity. Everyone claps for every project. Popcorn can be added to enhance the experience.

 **Student Macro Project Plan**
Growing Up!

Name _____   Date _____

Teacher _____   Grade _____

Project

The finished project will be a one- to two-minute videotape program
made from 10 to 15 photographs of you growing up. The first picture should be from birth or infancy; the last picture will be as you
are now. A soundtrack will be added to the finished video.

Method

1. Gather 10 to 15 photographs from your family albums or collections. Try
   to use photos that show important events in your life (birth, first birthday,
   first day at school, family gatherings or events). Number them (with pencil) on the back in the order you will videotape them.
2. Create a title for your project. Use a character generator or create a title
   card.
3. Videotape the photos. If you are adding "script" to each photo, be sure to
   record the picture for the correct length of time.
4. Fade in on the first picture; fade out on the last picture.
5. Record some "black" after the last picture. This can be done by placing the
   lens cap back on the camera and recording for 10 to 12 seconds with the
   cap on.
6. Preview the videotape to make sure there are no problems with the visuals.
7. Add the soundtrack to the tape.

Grading Rubric
Macro Project: Growing Up!

(Project Point Total: 100)

Student Name _____   Date _____

Teacher _____   Grade _____

Photo Selection (20 points)

1. Depicts life span (10)   _____
2. Variety of events (10)   _____

Title (20 points)

1. Appropriate, clever (10)   _____
2. Color balance, contrast (10)   _____

Camera Work (20 points)

1. Framed correctly (10)   _____
2. Focus, steady (10)   _____

Soundtrack (20 points)

1. Appropriateness (10)   _____
2. Sound levels, fades (10)   _____

Overall Production (20 points)

1. Smooth, glitch free (10)   _____
2. Timely, meets objective (10)   _____

Total Points Awarded (100 possible)   _____
Teacher Comments:

Student Macro Project Plan
The Great State!

Name _____   Date _____

Teacher _____   Grade _____

The Great State of _____

Step 1. Use an Encyclopedia CD-ROM, book, or the Internet to find the following state information:

History

    a. Discovered, founded, colonized (who, when)

    b. Statehood

    c. Capital

Facts

    a. Location

    b. Size

    c. State symbols (bird, flower, flag)

    d. Population

Physical Features

    a. Large cities

    b. Geography (desert, mountains, rivers, lakes)

    c. Climate

Resources

    a. Natural resources (minerals and ores, forests)

    b. Agriculture

    c. Manufacturing

Tourism

    a. Natural wonders

    b. Man-made sites

    c. Famous landmarks

Step 2. Write your script. Do not include all the facts you found, but be sure to include the most important and interesting ones. Here is an example:

The state of Washington lies in the northwest corner of the United States, known as the Pacific Northwest. Rhode Island–born sea caption Robert Gray was the first European American to arrive in the region, while looking for the fabled Northwest Passage. It was officially granted statehood in November 1889, making it the 42nd state in the Union. Its major city, Seattle, grew quickly during the Gold Rush of the early 1900s. Washington's landscape consists of mountains, coastlines, vast forests, and even deserts.

Step 3. Locate and identify pictures and images that illustrate your script. These can be from books, travel brochures, or even postcards.

Step 4. Organize your script and pictures. Time each section of your script using a clock watch with a second hand so you know how long each image is to be videotaped. Add two to three seconds of videotaping for each picture so you do not have to rush through your script. Here is an example:

Script	Time (seconds)	Picture
The state of Washington lies in the northwest corner of the United States, known as the Pacific Northwest.	:08	Map, page 12
Rhode Island-born sea caption Robert Gray was the first European American to arrive in the region, while looking for the fabled Northwest Passage. It was officially granted statehood in November 1889, making it the 42nd state in the Union.	:10	Explorer's ship, page 14
Its major city, Seattle, grew quickly during the Gold Rush of the early 1900s.	:05	Miners, page 16

Step 5. Create a title screen using a character generator or create your own using an index card and drawing materials. Record your title screen.

Step 6. Record your pictures in order, making sure to carefully time each one.

Step 7. Watch your completed tape and practice reading your script along with images. This will help you "time" your narration.

Step 8. Add music/narration to your videotape.

Grading Rubric
Macro Project: The Great State!

(Project Point Total: 100)

Student Name _____   Date _____

Teacher _____   Grade _____

Research (20 points)

1. Accurate facts (10)   _____
2. Organization (10)   _____

Photo Selection (20 points)

1. Depicts events (10)   _____
2. Variety of events (10)   _____

Title (20 points)

1. Appropriate, clever (10)   _____
2. Color balance, contrast (10)   _____

Camera Work (20 points)

1. Framed correctly (10)   _____
2. Focus, steady (10)   _____

Soundtrack (20 points)

1. Details follow video (10)   _____
2. Sound levels, fades (10)   _____

    Total Points Awarded (100 possible)   _____
    Teacher Comments:

Student Video Project
Macro Project: Guess This State Riddles!

Objective: To create a short "video riddle" about a U.S. state.

Step 1. Use a book about U.S. states to obtain information about one selected state. Information should include some physical features, famous landmarks, natural wonders, and even favorite tourist locations.

Step 2. Use this information to create a script for your riddle. **Example:** Can you guess what U.S. state I am visiting today? It may be like finding a "needle in a haystack," but this state has a very famous building called the Space Needle. This state borders the Pacific Ocean and is popular for both salmon fishing and whale watching. One more clue: this state has almost the same name as our nation's capital. Can you name this state? We will have the answer later on in our show.

Note: The topic sentence and ending sentence should be the same for ALL student scripts. These make excellent segments for school news shows.

Step 3. Locate three or four pictures that illustrate your script in the book.

Step 4. Videotape (macro) each picture. Time (in seconds) your script to identify how long each picture needs to be videotaped.

Step 5. Add narration (script) and graphics (if desired) to videotaped pictures.

Grading Rubric
Macro Project: State Video Riddle

(Project Point Total: 100)

Student Name _____   Date _____

Teacher _____   Grade _____

Information (25 points)

1. Interesting facts about state (15)   _____
2. Accurate details (10)   _____

Script Writing (25 points)

1. Topic sentence, ending sentence,
    3–4 facts (15)   _____
2. Riddle format (10)   _____

Camera Work (25 points)

1. Images illustrate script (10)   _____
2. Images fill "frame," focused (15)   _____

Narration (25 points)

1. Rehearsed, pronunciation (15)   _____
2. Read with "feeling," enunciation (10)   _____

Total Points Awarded (100 possible)   _____
Teacher Comments:

192

Interview Projects

Description: The finished project will be a one- to two-minute interview with a selected guest concerning a school or community event. The video will consist of a two-shot bust shot, and the audio will be the actual interview conducted with a handheld microphone.

Ideas for Interviews

In the school setting, there are numerous topics and interests for students to use for interviewing. Besides being fun to do, interviews are useful projects for adding to the appeal and content of the daily school news show. Here are some topics and ideas for interview projects:

- **Student of the Week.** Highlight that special student on your daily news show.
- **Teacher of the Month.** A great way to show recognition to some of the outstanding teachers at the school.
- **Athlete of the Week.** They work so hard at practice and games; here is an easy way to publicize their sport and skills.
- **Guest speakers.** They have incredible stories and have taken their time to share them with classes, so here is a great way to have them "share" with the entire school.

Method

1. Students should pick a subject or topic for their interview.
2. One student is the videographer; the other student is the interviewer.
3. Notify the interview guest concerning the time, place, and subject matter being addressed at least 24 hours prior to conducting the interview.
4. Students should prepare and *test* the video equipment prior to recording the interview. Equipment should include camcorder, microphone (handheld), videotape, tripod, and battery. If possible, connect headphones to the camcorder to monitor sound while the interview is being videotaped.
5. Students videotape interview on "location."

Teacher Notes

1. Interviewing is a skill that you must teach your students. Allow students to practice interviews with each other in the classroom before going around campus conducting interviews. Watch and critique them together, pointing out what is both positive and negative about each one. Students and teachers can all learn from watching "good" and "bad" tape.

2. A good handheld microphone is necessary to achieve satisfactory results from the interview project. Refer to chapter 2 for more information about microphones. Students should practice using the microphone and connecting to the camcorder prior to conducting interviews. Some good tips for microphone use include the following:

- Hold the microphone at least 4 to 6 inches below your mouth or the guest's mouth. The microphone should never go above the level of the chin.
- Hold the microphone in the hand closest to the guest. Don't reach across the body to move the microphone closer to the guest for his or her response.
- Be sure to hold the microphone firmly. Use a windscreen if needed for outdoors activity.

3. The videographer should also be trained to properly record the interview. Some tips and techniques include the following:

- Roll the videotape at least five seconds before the interview starts and at least five seconds after the conclusion so as to not cut off the speakers. This will also make it easier to cue up and use the interview as part of the school's news show.
- Look for a good location for videotaping. The background should add to the shot. Never use a blank wall or blackboard as a background.
- Frame the shot correctly, noting proper headroom and lighting conditions.

4. Don't frustrate students by expecting "professional" results the first few times they conduct an interview. Save some of the "best" interviews to show the next year, or make some good examples for them to watch while learning the skills of interviewing.

Student Interview Project Plan
Ask an Athlete

Name _____ Date _____

Teacher _____ Grade _____

Objective: The students will conduct a three-question interview with a school athlete.

Reporter _____

- Responsible for identifying and scheduling interview with a school athlete.
- Writes script and questions.
- Memorizes script and questions.
- Dresses professionally for interview.

Videographer _____

- Responsible for equipment checkout and operation.
- Selects camera shot location, shot composition, focusing, and microphone sound.
- Rolls videotape (at least five seconds) before and after interview.

Procedure

1. Reporter identifies athlete for interview. Completes script and questions; submits them for approval.
2. Reporter schedules interview time and date (with teacher's approval).
3. Reporter rehearses and memorizes script. Submits questions to athlete prior to interview taping. Requests that athlete wear uniform or practice jersey for interview.
4. Videotape interview.
5. Review interview. Submit for grading (if satisfactory) or reschedule interview if needed.

Grading Rubric
Ask an Athlete

(Project Point Total: 100)

Athlete Interviewed _____

Sport _____

Level (Varsity, Junior Varsity, Freshman)

Reporter _____

1. Script and questions appropriate (25 points) _____
2. Eye contact with guest and camera (25 points) _____
3. Microphone technique (25 points) _____
4. Dressed professionally, acts
   professionally (25 points) _____

   Total Points Awarded (100 possible) _____

Videographer: _____

1. Camera operation (framing, steady
   shot, rolled tape) (25 points) _____
2. Location, background, lighting (25 points) _____
3. Sound quality (25 points) _____
4. Returned equipment properly (25 points) _____

   Total Points Awarded (100 possible) _____
   Teacher Comments:

Student Interview Project
Student of the Week

Name _____   Date _____

Teacher _____   Grade _____

Objective: To highlight the accomplishments of a student in the school.

Step 1. Identify a "Student of the Week."

Name _____   Grade _____

Teacher _____

Why was this student selected?

Step 2. Write an introduction for the interview. This should be one to two sentences introducing the student to the viewers.

Example: It's time to announce our Student of the Week here at Windy Ridge School. This week, Sharon Stacy, a sixth-grade student, has been selected for her outstanding achievements both in the classroom and in the community.

Introduction: _____

_____

_____

_____

Step 3. List two questions you would like to ask the Student of the Week's teacher(s). Remember, these need to be open-ended questions, not questions that can be answered in one or two words.

Examples: Why do you feel _____ deserves to be recognized as Student of the Week?

What are some of the contributions _____ has made to our school or community?

Question 1 _____

_____

Question 2 _____

_____

Step 4. List two questions you would like to ask the student chosen as Student of the Week. Again, remember to use open-ended questions!

Question 1 _____

_____

Question 2 _____

_____

Step 5. Write an ending for your interview. This should summarize some of the information from the interviews.

Example: Congratulations to Sharon Stacy on being selected Windy Ridge's Student of the Week. Her teachers are proud of her academic excellence and the many hours she has spent volunteering in the Community Children's Center.

Conclusion _____

_____

Step 6. Videotape the introduction, interview questions, and ending of your interview.

Grading Rubric
Student of the Week

(Project Point Total: 100)

Student Interviewed: _____

Teacher Interviewed: _____

Reporter: _____

1. Script and questions appropriate (25 points) _____
2. Eye contact with guest and camera (25 points) _____
3. Microphone technique (25 points) _____
4. Dressed professionally, acts professionally (25 points) _____

   Total Points Awarded (100 possible) _____

Videographer: _____

1. Camera operation (framing, steady shot, rolled tape) (25 points) _____
2. Location, background, lighting (25 points) _____
3. Sound quality (25 points) _____
4. Returned equipment properly (25 points) _____

   Total Points Awarded (100 possible) _____
   Teacher Comments:

Documentaries

Description: The completed project will be a one- to two-minute documentary about a school or community topic. The finished project may include graphics, a sequence of video shots, narration, and a music background.

Ideas for Documentaries

Topics for documentaries abound in the school setting. Students can choose from an array of classroom topics or extracurricular activities. These documentaries are also very useful for creating segments to include on your school news shows. Some topics and ideas for documentaries include the following:

Interesting classes. Classes such as art, music, science, foreign languages, computers and technology, video production, and many others make good topics.

Clubs. Does your school have "clubs"? If so, students likely have to make choices about which club to join. Not only do clubs make interesting topic choices for documentaries, but the finished videos can be collated and played the following year when students are signing up for clubs.

Sports activities. Highlighting the work and play of your sports teams not only can be fun but can give recognition for the hard work and dedication many school athletes put in during the season.

Extracurricular activities. What are "Beach Day," "Backwards Day," "The Storybook Parade," "Earth Day," and all those other "days" and activities we have each year? These make good topics for documentaries and can help students understand what each of these "days" represents.

Student organizations. What do these organizations do and how do you join them? Groups such as Student Council, PTA, ROTC, Safety Patrols, and many others often have significant impact on the students and the school. Featuring them can help answer questions students have about their roles and organizations.

Method

1. Students should pick a topic that interests them. It should also be a topic that relates well to video projects and that is feasible for them to do during class or school time.

2. Students can work on this project in groups of two or three. Do not make the groups so large that no one has much to contribute. Each group of students should understand that they are all responsible for doing the work and completing the project. Try to avoid assigning "jobs" for each student; that way they can share in all the work and contribute in every phase.

3. Students need to understand that the script must come first. All too often, students want to run out and videotape without knowing exactly what camera shots are needed. This wastes time and makes the process much more complicated.

4. Storyboarding is an essential part of the video process. Students should be responsible for completing and getting storyboards approved before beginning the videotaping process.

5. Unedited projects. This project can be accomplished (and has been many times) without editing. In this case, students must "time" their script and record the camera shots in order for the proper length of time. Graphics are recorded on the videotape prior to recording the necessary camera shots. The narration can be added using audio dubbing.

6. Edited projects. These are excellent "beginning" projects to teach the students how to use available editing equipment. Graphics and music backgrounds can also be added easily.

7. Create an example so students can see the finished product. Save some of the better "first-time" projects to show to future groups.

8. Emphasize the important things: good scriptwriting and good camerawork. These are the skills you will be building! Disregard some minor production flaws in light of the learning that is taking place.

Student Video Project
Documentary

Objective: To produce a simple documentary highlighting a classroom, school, or community event.

Production Team (names):

_____

_____

_____

Steps to Produce a Documentary

1. Identify the topic.
   Topic: _____
   Location: _____
   Contact Person: _____
2. Research the topic: Who, What, When, Where, How, Why.
   a. Talk to the people involved in the activity.
   b. Research background information on the Internet, with books, or using CDs.
3. Write the script. This should be about 8 to 10 sentences. Total time is less than two minutes in length. Use the storyboard form that is attached to this project.
4. Identify the video shots needed for the project. Use the script to make a shot checklist. Make sure to identify the length of time needed for each shot. You can time the script for this, as in the following example.

Storyboard Example

Video Shot/Description	Audio (Script and Sound)	Time (0:00)
Title screen graphic	Music only	0:10
Follow flag as it is raised on pole.	Early each morning the Stars and Stripes, along with our state flag, are proudly raised above our school.	0:08

5. Record and preview the recorded footage using your checklist.

6. Rehearse reading the script several times while watching the completed video footage. You may have to make some minor changes to your script, either adding or deleting some words to match the time of the recorded shots.

7. Add the narration and music background (if available) to the videotape.

Production Tips

1. Record a graphic on your tape prior to videotaping the first camera shot if you are not editing the tape.

2. Add one or two seconds to each shot after you time the script. It is better if the camera shots are slightly longer than if too short.

3. Use a variety of camera angles. Don't videotape all of your shots from just one angle. Try using some over-the-shoulder shots, close-ups, and unstable horizon shots to add interest to your video.

4. Read your narration with enthusiasm! If you are excited about the topic, so will your viewers.

Storyboard for Documentary

Production Team: _____

_____

Topic: _____

Video Shot/Description	Audio (Script and Sound)	Time (0:00)

Grading Rubric
Documentary

(Project Point Total: 100)

Scriptwriting (20 points)

1. Topic details and information (10) _____
2. Vocabulary, syntax, grammar (10) _____

Storyboarding (30 points)

1. Adequate detail on visuals (10) _____
2. Variety of camera angles (10) _____
3. Timing (10) _____

Camera Work (30 points)

1. Framing, location, focus (10) _____
2. Variety of shots (10) _____
3. Variety of activities (10) _____

Narration (20 points)

1. Follows video, details (10) _____
2. Voice talent (10) _____

Total Awarded Points (100 possible) _____

Teacher Comments:

News-Magazine Shows

Description: Students will produce a news show centered around a school topic or activity.

Ideas for News Shows

The concept for this project centers around producing a news show that features announcements, segments, and ideas associated with one school topic or activity. Here are some suggestions:

1. **Back to school.** Returning to school after the long summer break is always an exciting time for both students and faculty. Segments for this show could include new teachers and faces, new school policies and procedures, welcome from the principal, interviews with students about why they are glad to be back, interviews with teachers asking what they did over the summer for their vacations, improvements in the school facility over the summer, and other topical announcements.

2. **Holiday theme shows.** Centering a show around a particular holiday or nationally recognized "day" gives the students the opportunity to research and explore what the holiday is all about and how it is celebrated. For example, let's look at Thanksgiving. A news show centered around Thanksgiving might include the following: fun Thanksgiving facts (how many turkeys will be eaten, how many people will travel on the roads, how much the average family of four will spend for dinner, etc.), the history of Thanksgiving, a small "skit" depicting the first Thanksgiving, interviews with students and faculty about how they are going to celebrate Thanksgiving or what the holiday means to them, reflections on childhood memories of past Thanksgivings, classroom activities centered around Thanksgiving, good books about Thanksgiving, a Thanksgiving joke or riddle, and other such segments.

3. **Our city.** Students grow up and attend school in their city without really understanding the history and current status of many of the landmarks surrounding them. Some ideas for a news show about their city might include the history of the city, how it got its name, meeting the mayor (interview), famous people who lived and worked in the city, historical sites and buildings, fun places to go (parks, recreation areas, museums), trivia and riddles about the city, ethnic neighborhoods with stores and restaurants associated with their ethnic background, important city buildings (Chamber of Commerce, Department of Justice, City Hall), and the tourism and industry in the city.

4. **Our generation.** Each generation of students has its own unique culture and characteristics. Think back to the 1960s, 1970s, and 1980s. What is unique about the students of this generation? Some ideas include historical events taking place as we live, their clothes and hairstyles, music of their generation, television and movies that depict their generation, facts and trivia about the decade, famous people making an impact, role models, sports and hobbies, interviews with parents about how their children's lives differ from when they were children, and many others.

Method

1. Identify a group of 8 to 12 students that you can work with to develop a topical news show or news-magazine show. This is a great learning activity for a classroom teacher or program in the school to get their students involved in creating a news show about a topic of study. Video clubs and media clubs also work well with this activity. It is a wonderful way to use the equipment that sits idle after the daily news show is broadcast each morning, as it can be used to bring the curriculum to "life."

2. Brainstorm ideas and topics with the students that they can incorporate into their show. Pick a central theme, and then associated topics and segments that follow that theme. Create a list, and let students work on topics they are interested in. Make a timeline with production schedules so they know when each piece will be recorded or finished. Students work better with timelines and deadlines.

3. Teach and instruct the students with the equipment. They need to know how to use a camcorder, microphone, and character generator. Talk about how the show will be put together: Will it be "live" or taped? Will you edit the show together after all the pieces have been recorded?

4. Have students create scripts, announcements, or complete storyboards for their projects. Have them put their ideas in writing.

5. When all topics have been identified, complete a format sheet indicating how the show will be put together. This gives everyone in the crew an outline of what the show will look like.

6. If the show is to be edited, all anchor-desk announcements and introductions can be recorded at one time and then edited together with the finished segments. If the show is to be broadcast "live," segments and video clips can be "rolled in" from a VCR during the show.

7. If the show is successful, make a few copies to put in the media center for students to check out and bring home. Sort of like your own school "Video Rental Store." This is great publicity for your school and media program.

Student Video Project
News-Magazine Show

Objective: Students will produce a News-Magazine Show centered around a central theme or topic.

Topic or Theme: _____

Segment Ideas

1. Opening for show _____
2. Segment ideas
   a. _____
   b. _____
   c. _____
   d. _____
   e. _____
   f. _____
   g. _____
3. Ending for show _____

News Crew Positions

Anchors: _____

Character generator: _____

Audio technician: _____

Technical Director (switcher operator): _____

Camera operator(s): _____

Teleprompter: _____

VCR operator: _____

Digital/computer: _____

Producer/director: _____

Editor(s): _____

News-Magazine Format: Complete News-Magazine Format Form. This is how your show will look on "paper."

Example: News-Show Magazine Format—Script and Segments

Video Segment	Script and Audio	Source/Time
News opening	Graphic (Show title) with music Example: Good Morning Windy Ridge Hosted by: Jennifer R.	Screenplay graphic "Title" Music (CD) :10
Anchor: Jen Camera/Mic	Good morning, Windy Ridge.... Today is Friday March 30th. Our show will be an in-depth look at coming back to school after the long summer break. When you returned on Monday, you saw some familiar faces and also some new ones as well. Reporter Sarah Ryan shows us just who is new in school this year....	Video camera (video and audio)
Who's New	Report with Sarah Ryan	VCR 1:30
Anchor: Jen Camera/Mic	Welcome to Windy Ridge to all those new teachers and staff. And to our new Windy Ridge students as well, especially our new kindergarten students who are in school for the first time. How did their first day at school go? We sent our ace photographer down to the kindergarten wing with a camera, and here are some of the smiling and not-so-smiling faces he saw.	Video camera (video and audio)
Digital camera	Digital photos of kindergarten	Digital camera Music: CD

Recording the Show: Practice and rehearse script and news crew positions. Record on videotape or broadcast live to school.

News-Magazine Format Sheet

Video Segment	Script and Audio	Source/Time

Grading Rubric
News-Magazine Show

(Project Point Total: 100)

Name _____   Date _____

Teacher _____   Grade _____

Video Segments (50 points)

1. Segment idea (10) _____
2. Script and storyboard (20) _____
3. Segment completed, timely (20) _____

News Crew Position (50 points)

(Position on Crew) _____

1. Learned use of equipment (20) _____
2. Performance during production (20) _____
3. Cooperation, teamwork (10) _____

Total Points Awarded (100 possible) _____

Teacher Comments:

Technology Projects: Digital Camera Projects

Description: The following activities will use digital cameras. One of the projects will actually be recorded on videotape, whereas the autobiography project uses a word-processing program and will be printed out from a computer.

Ideas for Technology Projects

These projects are ideal for incorporation into your school's classroom activities. All of the following activities can be changed and adapted to meet the needs and activities of the teachers and students in the classroom. Topics can be selected from almost any grade's subject and unit study. The digital camera projects can be adapted to show a program or show a classroom activity. The table-top camera project can be used for a variety of topics, realia, or even photographs. Some potential topics (and there are hundreds) include the following:

1. **Science topics.** Plants, hatching eggs or insects, pond water, environmental studies, rocks and minerals, electricity, and many more.
2. **Social studies topics.** Local, state, or school history, cultures and communities, monetary systems, people in the community, social change and issues, safety and health issues, and others.
3. **School and classroom topics.** A day in _____ class, art in the school, any classroom activity involving making projects and displays, special programs in the school, favorite toys and games, memorabilia that students collect, people who work in the school, and others.

Method

1. Digital cameras are fun and easy for students to use to create projects in the classroom. Most students already know how to "take a picture," but take the time to teach them how to properly use the school's digital camera. Demonstrate how to use the zoom function, how to focus (if available), and how to record the image; even playback is important so students can see the pictures they just took.

2. Spend some time teaching a few basics of good photography. Although many students know how to take a picture, very few know anything about good picture

composition. Discuss ideas and concepts such as framing, headroom, selecting a good background, even the "rule of thirds." It would be great if you had a collection of "good" and "bad" photos so they could critique them and actually see the concepts you are describing.

3. Getting the video image "out" of the camera onto videotape is easily accomplished when the digital camera has a "video out" jack. A simple cord and connection to the "video in" on the VCR accomplishes this. (See fig. 7.1.)

When recoding the images on the VCR, students should time their script, or even read it as they record the image, so that they record the images on the videotape for the correct length of time. Digital cameras using smart cards or other imaging formats may need to use a computer/video card and a software program to get the images into a VCR.

4. If students want to have a title screen prior to the images, that should be recorded first. Likewise, an ending title screen can be recorded after the images.

5. Once all the images have been recorded on videotape, students should watch the completed tape and practice reading the script. That will assist them with the timing of reading the script with the video.

6. Add the narration and background music.

7. If available, all of these projects can be done with a variety of nonlinear editing systems.

Figure 7.1 Locate the video output of your digital camera and connect it to the VCR.

Student Video Project
Digital Documentary

Name _____ Date _____

Teacher _____ Grade _____

Description of the Completed Project: The completed project will be a one-minute videotaped documentary featuring a common theme or sequence. The segment will consist of six images created with a digital camera. Each image will be recorded onto videotape for 10 seconds. The sound will consist of narration and music added in postproduction. Ten seconds of a black screen will precede and follow the project.

Equipment Needed: Digital camera, VCR with audio-dub function, monitor or television, microphone, audio mixer, music source.

Procedure

1. Select a topic for your digital documentary. You may select a class at school (e.g., chemistry), a special place at your school (e.g., the Wellness Center), or a sequence of activities (e.g., how to cover your math book). Make sure to select a topic that lends itself to a "visual" project.
2. Make a list of at least six concepts that you want to cover in your documentary. If you're creating a sequence, list at least six steps in completing the task.
3. Write one or two sentences for each concept that you've listed. This is your script. Each segment should take about seven or eight seconds for you to read slowly. Read and reread your script to make sure that it flows smoothly.
4. Make notes or draw pictures about the visual images that you would like to take to illustrate your script. Remember, think visually!

Example

Audio	Visual, Shot Description	Time
Students in the media production class brought their digital cameras to class.	A shot of students carrying cameras into class	:08
They were excited about learning how to produce a digital documentary.	A close-up of someone's excited face.	:05
First, they must identify and photograph the necessary visuals.	Students working on scripts and storyboards.	:06

5. Now, use the digital camera to create those images. You don't have to shoot them in order, but it will probably help. It's okay to take more images than you need. Just don't overdo it!

6. When you return to the classroom, review your images and decide which ones best illustrate your script. Reshoot any images that don't meet your standards.

7. Connect the digital camera to your VCR, and record each of your images for about 10 seconds in sequence. Use the VCR "pause" button while you select your next image.

8. Rewind the videotape. Review, practice, and edit your script.

9. Now, audio dub your videotape using appropriate music in the background.

Grading Rubric
Digital Documentary

(Project Point Total: 100)
Documentary Topic: _____

Production Personnel

Names   Production Jobs

_____   _____

_____   _____

_____   _____

Image selection (25 points)

1. Illustrate script (15)   _____
2. Variety of images (10)   _____

Digital photography (25 points)

1. Picture composition (15)   _____
2. Variety of angles (10)   _____

Script (25 points)

1. Details about topic (15)   _____
2. Composition, grammar (10)   _____

Narration/Music (25 points)

1. Enthusiasm, enunciation (15)   _____
2. Music appropriate, levels (10) _____

   Total Points Awarded (100 Possible)   _____
   Teacher Comments:

Student Project
Digital Autobiography

Name _____ Date _____

Objective: To create a published autobiography with digital image.

Step 1. Fill in the information below to create your autobiography.

1. Name   _____
2. Address   _____
                     _____
3. Phone   _____
4. Date of birth   _____
5. Place of birth   _____
6. Grade/teacher   _____
7. Hobbies/interests   _____
8. Favorite foods   _____
9. Favorite movies   _____
10. Favorite TV shows _____
11. Favorite books   _____
12. Favorite subjects in school _____

Complete this sentence: When I grow up I would like to

_____

_____

Step 2. Have a classmate take a digital picture of you. It should be taken so that your entire body is in the shot. To make it more interesting, add some props (maybe a basketball, skateboard, sports uniform, telescope, etc.) that illustrate some of your hobbies or interests as stated in your autobiography.

Step 3: Use a word-processing program to type in your information. Title the paper *Autobiography*. Use colons and tab settings to correct spacing. Use complete sentences for items 7–12, as in the following sample autobiography.

AUTOBIOGRAPHY

Name:	Ryan Charles
Address:	1234 Sunnyside Rd.
	Orlando, Florida 32835
Hobbies:	I like to build model airplanes. Baseball is my favorite sport.
Favorite Foods:	Pizza is my favorite food. I also like homemade cookies.
Favorite Subjects:	I really am good in math. Science is my favorite subject because I like to learn about animals.

Step 4: Insert your digital picture BETWEEN the title and your name. Resize and center your image as needed.

AUTOBIOGRAPHY

Name:	Ryan Charles
Address:	1234 Sunnyside Rd.
	Orlando, FL 32835

Step 5: Print out your completed autobiography project. Staple to colored construction paper.

Digital Autobiography
Grading Rubric

(Project Point Total: 100)

Name _____   Date _____

Teacher _____   Grade _____

Biographical Information (30 points)

1. All items completed (15)   _____
2. Accurate spelling, grammar, sentences (15)   _____

Word Processing (30 points)

1. Format, tabs, colons, spacing (15)   _____
2. Spelling and punctuation (15)   _____

Digital Image (30 points)

1. Image taken "full shot," framing,
   composition (15)   _____
2. Image inserted on document (15)   _____

Production (10 points)

1. Project finished in timely manner,
   printed, mounted (10)   _____

   Total Points Awarded (100 possible)   _____
   Teacher Comments:

Technology Projects: Table-Top Cameras

Description: Students will produce a two- to three-minute videotape using a table-top camera.

Ideas for Table-Top Video Projects

Table-top video cameras are easy to use, connect easily to existing video and audio systems, and provide a good imaging device to capture fine details from smaller objects. These lightweight mounted cameras provide a stable source for videotaping and capturing images. They are excellent for videotaping realia, which make some of the most interesting video projects. Adapters are also available for outfitting the camera to microscopes, as are peripherals and software to connect them to computers for recording for use in computer-based presentations. Here are some possible ideas for table-top video projects:

1. **Science.** How plants grow, seeds, leaves, worms and other small animals, pond water animals (e.g., tadpoles and minnows), electricity and magnetism.
2. **Art.** Clay modeling, painting, mosaic tiles, chalk, pencil drawings.
3. **Social studies.** Money and its symbols, artifacts of our civilization, memorabilia.
4. **Photos.** Any number of project can be made by recording a series of photos or postcards, pictures from books, tourist guides, and so on. (See fig. 7.2.)

Method

1. Students should select a topic that can make good use of a table-top video system. It is much more interesting to watch worms (or another moving object) crawl around on the screen than to stare at a lifeless "coin" for two minutes.

Figure 7.2 Table-top camera system

2. Research is important. Think of this project as a "mini-research paper" but on video. Students will need to find background information and details about their subject. Encourage them to use books, encyclopedias, CDs, and the Internet to find good information about their topic.

3. Students write their script after locating information about their topic. The script should be interesting to listen to, contain good facts and details, and perhaps include something anecdotal about their topic.

4. This project is "unedited." Basically, once the tape is recording, the project is started and finished without any postproduction. In some cases, the "pause" button on the VCR will enable the student to change images (if needed) and begin recording again. Students should be encouraged to read and practice their script several times before recording their project.

5. Graphics can be used before and after the recorded video project. If graphics are desired, the video output of the table-top camera should connect to the video input of the character generator. Then the video output from the character generator is connected to the video input of the VCR.

6. All narration and background music is recorded simultaneously with the video image. Remember, if the students pause the tape during recording, they must pause the music as well.

7. The diagram in figure 7.3 shows how your table-top video system should be connected.

8. If a student makes a mistake during the recording of the video project, you can simply rewind the tape and start over.

9. Adhere to the time limits. Videos that are too long tend to lose viewer interest.

10. If you do not have access to a table-top camera, a camcorder mounted on a copy stand or tripod can make a suitable replacement.

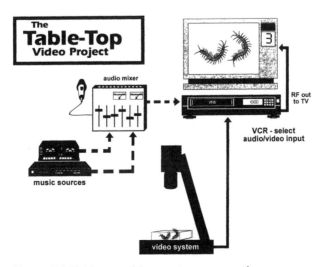

Figure 7.3 Table-top video-system connections

Student Video Project
Table-Top Video Project

Name _____ Date _____

Teacher _____ Grade _____

Project Description: The completed project will be a one- to two-minute videotape program about a _____ topic. The program will begin with a graphic screen (:10) that includes the title of your project and student(s) name(s). Following the graphic screen will be an image videotaped using the table-top video system. The audio (sound) will consist of narration and background music. Ten seconds of black screen will follow the project.

Equipment Needed: Table-top video system, VCR, monitor, microphone, audio mixer, music source, headphones (optional).

Procedure

1. Select a topic for your project. Think about a topic that will make good use of the table-top video system. Get approval for your topic from your teacher. Topic: _____

2. Research your topic. Write a one- to two-minute script with the information and details from your research.

3. Read your script aloud, and note the time. The script should take at least one minute, and no more than two minutes, for you to read. Make sure that you can correctly pronounce each word in your script. Make any necessary changes in your script.

4. Select your background music. It should complement your topic.

5. Practice reading your script aloud with enthusiasm. Practice it again … and again!

6. Record your project. Remember to include the following:
   - silent "black" (:10)
   - graphics (:10)
   - video image with narration and music (1–2 minutes)
   - silent "black" at the end (:10)

7. Watch the completed project. Redo if necessary.

Table-Top Video Project
Grading Rubric

(Project Point Total: 100)

Name(s) _____

_____

_____

Topic _____

Script (50 points)

1. Research complete, details about topic (25) _____
2. Grammar, spelling, punctuation (25) _____

Graphic (10 points)

1. Spelling, contrasting colors (10) _____

Narration (20 points)

1. Pronunciation, enthusiasm (20) _____

Production (20 points)

1. Object videotaping (10) _____
2. Music selection, sound levels (10) _____

Total Points Awarded (100 possible) _____

Teacher Comments:

Chapter 8

Presenting Your Television Programs

Video programs have become a way of life in education. It seems as if every presentation, discussion group, or skill concept involves the use of a videotape to illustrate and present information. Although we are using videotapes more, we often are not using them effectively. Presenting your programs on videotape requires some careful evaluation of equipment, audience, and room climate. Whether you're showing a video segment on "How to Study for Tests" or your daily news show, it is important to determine how the arrangement of equipment and audience seating will best accommodate viewing the video.

Showing Programs to Small Audiences

Of course, the most common equipment combination is a VCR and television or monitor placed in front of the audience or classroom (see fig. 8.1). If you are using a television, the VCR is connected by an RF cord from the VCR's output to the television's input jack. To view your program, the television must be tuned to either channel 3 or channel 4, depending on the output selection on your VCR. Most VCRs are set to channel 3, but a few models allow you to select channel 4 instead. If you are using a monitor to display your video, you will need to connect your VCR's video and audio signals with a set of RCA cords, commonly referred to as "patch cords." Simply connect the video output of your VCR to the video input of your monitor. Repeat this procedure for the audio outputs and inputs. Most patch cords are color coded so that you can easily identify which cable is connected to the video output and which cable is connected to the audio output of your VCR. Remember, use RF cable to connect a VCR to a television; for monitors, it's "video out" to "video in" and "audio out" to "audio in." Some monitors have several inputs and outputs, which are usually labeled "video 1," "video 2," and so on. If your VCR's signal is not reaching the monitor, you may have selected the wrong input to be displayed. Find

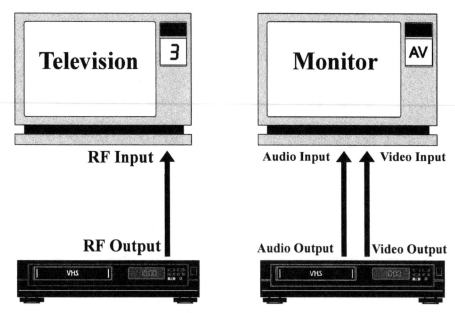

Figure 8.1 A television requires an RF signal. A monitor uses separate audio and video signals. All three signals can be obtained from most VCRs.

the input selector switch and select the input that has your VCR's signal connected to it. The television or monitor should be large enough to allow any audience member to see the video clearly. Sometimes it is necessary to place the television on an A/V cart so the screen is above eye level. That way no one has to stretch their neck to see and hear your program. The screen can be centered or even set to the left or right of the audience.

The following are some helpful tips for avoiding problems during playback:

■ Always check your system by playing the entire tape *before* the audience arrives. Adjust the volume so that the sound can be heard anywhere in the seating area. This is also a good time to check the tracking mechanism of your VCR to make sure the tape plays without any distortion. Adjust if needed.

■ Are you hearing the correct audio track? If sound has been added or "dubbed" on the tape while editing, the VCR's audio outputs must be changed to read "Normal" audio output rather than the HiFi tracks. Most VCRs default to HiFi audio output when turned on. You can usually change this by using the remote control or VCR's "Menu" options. Look under Audio or Audio Options.

■ Sit in several different chairs around the room and watch the video program. Do any lights need to be turned off so that there is no screen glare? Can you adequately see and hear the program?

■ Did you record color bars at the beginning of your video to adjust the color and tint of the television or monitor? If not, it is a good idea to adjust the color and tint by using an image or part of your program with people in it. Flesh tones should look realistic, not orange, red, or yellow.

■ Will you need to pause your tape during the program? If so, make sure you know where the "pause" button is located on the VCR. Better yet, try to find the remote, and be sure to test it. How many times have you tried to use a remote only to find that it is dead or without batteries?

■ If your VCR goes to "snow" when you push the "stop" button (this also causes a lot of loud noise), you can plug an adapter (RCA male) into the VCR's video input and trick it into thinking that another video component is connected to it. When the VCR is stopped, instead of going to static, the monitor will display a black, silent screen.

If after previewing your video you decide that one television or monitor does not adequately provide the impact or viewing capabilities you need, you may decide to connect a second screen and split your video and audio signals to both. For televisions, you can purchase an RF splitter to split one output signal into two (see fig. 8.2). These are inexpensive (less than $10) and can be purchased at any electronics store. You will also need to purchase additional RF cable to connect the televisions to the splitter. The RF output of your VCR connects to the RF input of

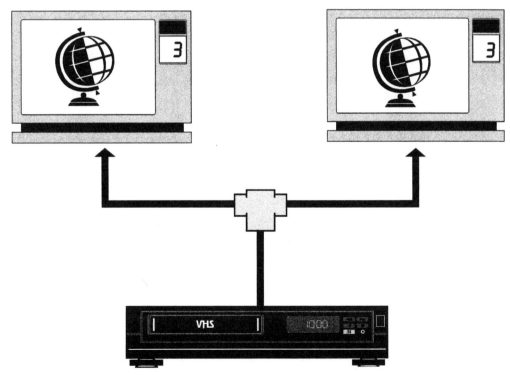

Figure 8.2 An RF splitter multiplies the RF signal so that two or more televisions can be connected to a single VCR.

the splitter. Then each television is connected to the splitter's RF outputs. When using this arrangement, be sure to bring some grip tape or wide masking tape to tape the cords to the floor so that no one will trip over them or pull them out of their connections.

If you are using monitors, many of them have not only video and audio inputs but outputs as well. This is another good reason to buy monitors instead of televisions. After connecting your VCR to one monitor, simply connect that monitor's video and audio outputs to another monitor's inputs, in a "daisy chain." You will probably need additional patch cords to do this. These are available in longer lengths at many electronics stores and A/V supply centers. Look carefully at your monitors' video jacks. Some require the use of BNC plugs and cords. There are adapters that can change an RF cord into a BNC or RCA cord. Many district media centers will supply free RF cords; consider ordering the longer cables as RF cords and using adapters in whatever configuration is required.

Showing Programs to Large Audiences

One bright spring morning, our ninth-grade class administrator swept into our television production classroom with another "Great Idea": "We should produce a video that we can show to all the middle school students during our orientation seminars at each of our 'feeder' schools." I had to admit that it was a good idea, but orientation was only a few weeks away, and this would certainly require a lot of planning, scripting, videotaping, and editing. "I have a lot of confidence in your ability to get this done," was his reply. So our class began the production process, the three-week deadline hanging over our heads and spurring us on.

After weeks of work, hours of taping, and endless hours of postproduction, the big day arrived. We were on our way to the nearest middle school, tape in hand, ready to orient those eighth graders. When I walked into the "orientation room," my mouth fell, my arms drooped, and the tape nearly fell to the floor. In the cafeteria were hundreds of loud, bouncing, hip-hopping, paper-rustling, yip-yapping, pre–high school teens. And there, almost invisible to the naked eye, was a lone 19-inch TV/VCR on A/V cart strategically placed in the front and center of the room. Did anyone see, not to mention hear, our hundreds-of-hours-of-production-work video? No! (See fig. 8.3.)

Finding the right arena and equipment to present your video is just as important as the production process. Why put in hundreds of hours of work to produce a program that cannot be watched and enjoyed because of technical or environmental constraints? Some considerations for presenting your videos should include room size, audience size and seating arrangements, lighting, sound, and availabil-

Figure 8.3 Always determine the viewing environment before the program is to be shown!

ity of video presentation equipment. If I had known how that orientation video was going to be shown, I could have offered some suggestions that would have made viewing the video an effective learning experience.

Using a Video Projector

A video presentation can be made by setting up a large screen and showing the video using a video projector. Video projectors have been in use for over a decade, and newer models have a brighter, clearer picture and require very little set-up adjustment (see fig. 8.4). Today's video projectors use a liquid crystal display (LCD) and can produce a high-resolution picture with an image size from 25 to 300 inches diagonal. Portable video projectors often are the size of a briefcase, weigh less than 7 pounds, and can be positioned at a range of distances (depending on desired picture size) from the screen. Many projectors include autofocusing, zoom lenses, built-in VCRs, rear or front projection, and remote controls. The newer models also feature longer-life metal halide lamps, which can provide an average life of 2,000 viewing hours. To save the life of your lamp and avoid a bulb burnout during your presentation, here are a few recommendations for using video projectors:

Figure 8.4 A video projector is used for large visual presentations. Image courtesy of InFocus®.

- *Never* move your projector while the lamp is on.
- Always allow your lamp to completely cool down before moving or packing up your video projector.
- Make sure you order and pack an extra lamp for emergencies. It is always reassuring to know you have a spare on hand just in case the lamp dies during your presentation.

Buying a Video Projector

Video projectors range in cost from $2,000 to $8,000. Projectors aren't cheap, of course, but their desirability and use in the educational setting have grown tremendously. Today's video projectors can be used with a variety of technology: computers and laptops, VCRs, video cameras, digital devices, and many types of cable broadcasts. The complexity of the optics and chips leads to prices in the thousands of dollars. Today's projectors use one of two imaging systems: DLP (digital light processing) or LED. DLP units use a small-scale reflective system with thousands of tiny mirrors to project the image, whereas competing LCD projectors use larger panels, prisms, and mirrors. The result is that DLP units tend to project images that are brighter overall, whereas LCD models generally deliver richer, more-saturated colors. Video projectors have really reduced in size and weight over the years. Consumers have spoken, and lighter projectors are all the rage. The portable convenience of these projectors is clearly worth the extra money.

When considering the purchase of a video projector, it is wise to think about the following aspects of its use and capabilities. How will it be used? This is certainly the first consideration for purchase. Will the video projector be moved from classroom to classroom? If the answer is yes, certainly a light portable unit will be most desirable. Because classrooms tend to be smaller and darker than most auditoriums, the unit will have less demand for larger image sizes and brightness. If the unit will also be used in auditoriums, a unit that functions in this setting (larger images, brighter images) will be needed.

What features are critical for its use in your school? Do you foresee a need to connect the projector to VCRs and computers? In that case, you must buy a projector with both video and VGA inputs. How about an S-VHS connection? If you are using S-VHS equipment and tapes in your productions, it makes sense to purchase a video projector that can use the S-VHS signal. Most projectors easily accommodate several types of inputs (see fig. 8.5).

Zoom lenses are useful for adjusting the size of the projected image for each type of situation. It makes more sense than having to physically move the projector closer or farther from the screen to adjust the image size. Try to anticipate situations and peripherals you will be using the video projector for during the coming school years.

Brightness is also critical, and it is often the area where buyers compromise when choosing one of the newer microportable projectors or when budget issues constrain available funds. The level of brightness—the amount of light hitting a screen—is expressed by a lumens rating. For a presentation in normal indoor light (and a diagonal image of about three to four feet), 800 to 1,200 lumens is acceptable. But brighter is always better.

Sound capability is another feature to look into. Video capabilities have improved greatly over the past few years, but sound remains a weak link. Many projectors have two speakers and passable stereo sound, but built-in speakers tend to have poor quality and low volume levels. For better sound, external speakers make more sense. Portable computer speakers with their own amplified sound (built-in powered amplifier in each speaker) are a simple and efficient solution, especially for classroom and smaller-venue presentations. In an auditorium, it is more bene-

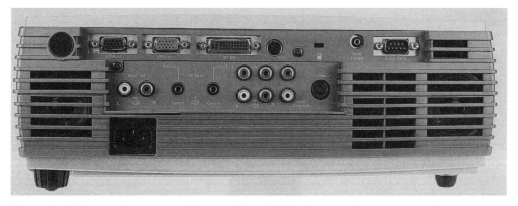

Figure 8.5 Video projectors provide a variety of video input and output selections to use with VCR's, DVD players, computers, and other video sources. Image courtesy of InFocus®.

Figure 8.6 The Bose Acoustic Wave® Portable sound system easily provides ample volume for audio/visual presentations. Image courtesy of Bose Corporation.

ficial to connect the video projector (or even the VCR playing the tape) to the auditorium's existing sound system. Portable sounds systems can also be used effectively with a video projector (see fig. 8.6).

Additional features available on many models of video projectors can make them more attractive for use in an educational setting. Some projectors, for example, come equipped with their own "Document Camera." This is an excellent tool for displaying tables, graphs, documents, and other peripherals during presentations. Teachers can display student work on the large screen for discussion and teaching exercises. A science teacher even used this document camera and projector to demonstrate a frog dissection for the biology class prior to their dissections in the lab. Remote controls have freeze-frame options, zooms, laser pointers, and in some cases, pointing effects such as boxes and markers. The best portable models also offer mouse control and USB connections. When purchasing a projector, compare features as well as prices.

There is no better way to make a purchase decision than having the opportunity to view and even use the equipment prior to purchase. Attend a conference or exhibit hall and see what video projectors are available. Many educational conferences have vendor displays with video projectors. Look at different models, compare prices, and ask for literature on the models you like best. Most school-district media centers have a video projector for use within the district. Check one out for a week, use it, and compare it with others you have seen. Perhaps there is no need for your school to purchase its own projector if the district can provide this service. Look at your state or district bid list to see if any vendors are listing video projectors. Call the vendor and see if any have been sold in your district or surrounding school districts. Get a media specialist's opinion regarding the projector, its features, and ease of operation. Some vendors are even willing to bring and demonstrate a video projector to your school!

Connecting the Video Projector

Using a video projector to display your program is a great way to give an effective presentation to large audiences. Some newer models even have a built-in VCR. Simply put in your tape, turn up the sound, and play. Other models require a separate VCR for program presentations. Connecting a VCR to a video projector is really quite simple (see fig. 8.7). Just two easy steps. First, using an RCA cord, connect the video output of your VCR to the video input of the video projector. Then, using an RCA cord, connect the audio output of your VCR to the audio input of your video projector.

Turn on the power to your video projector. Now turn on the VCR, load your tape, and play. You should be able to see and hear your tape. Adjust the picture size by either moving your projector away from or closer to the screen. Some video projectors have a zoom function that allows you to do this without moving your projector. Finally, adjust the volume. Check to make sure the video image can be easily seen throughout the hall or auditorium. You may need to dim some lights.

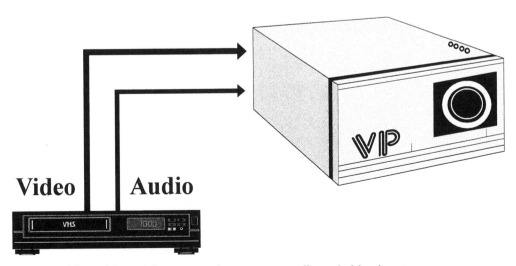

Figure 8.7 Most video projectors require separate audio and video inputs.

Audio for Video Projectors

Although most video projectors have a built-in speaker, it is often inadequate for large presentations. Try connecting the audio output of your VCR or projector to your cafeteria's or auditorium's sound system. This is relatively easy and only requires one additional cable and adapter. Instead of connecting the audio output of your VCR to the audio input of the video projector, connect it to the inputs of your school's auditorium or cafeteria sound system. You will need a cord long enough to reach from the VCR to the sound system. Also, many schools' sound systems require an XLR plug or a 1/4–inch phone plug to connect a sound component into the system. Allow plenty of time to inspect the sound system to see what type of connections you need. Electronic stores carry these adapters and cords. If you're unsure, don't be afraid to ask. Your district media center should also be able to assist you with cables or technical support. If not, the nearest high school drama department might offer to lend a hand.

Another way to achieve adequate volume and good sound quality is to connect the audio output of your VCR or projector to an amplifier and speaker system. The Bose Corporation makes a portable sound system that is easy to use and produces quality sound (see fig. 8.6). It is self-contained and easily portable, and it provides incredible sound quality with excellent sound volume. Connect the audio output of your VCR into the auxiliary input of this sound system and step back. This is a presentation with *impact*.

Any good amplifier and speaker system will certainly be better than none at all. (See fig. 8.8.) If you haven't used them before, it's really not that difficult and definitely worth the effort. A simple pair of RCA cords will connect the audio outputs of your video projector or VCR to the audio inputs of the amplifier. Most amplifiers have the inputs labeled as "tape in" or "auxiliary in." The speakers are then attached to the amplifier and placed around the room. Be sure to use grip tape or wide masking tape to tape down wires to avoid accidents or technical problems when the audience arrives.

Selecting a Screen

If you are using a video projector, you must consider the screen selection for your presentation. There are two choices: front-projection screens and rear-projection screens. Rear screens are translucent, so the video projector and other equipment is placed behind the screen, out of sight of the audience. Most video projectors made today have a switch to enable you to project either from the front or the rear. Professional presentations often use this type of system. The most widely used screens are front-projection screens, which come in beaded, matte, and lenticular styles. A glass-beaded screen is best for long, narrow rooms, and a matte screen works well in wide, shallow rooms. The lenticular screen combines the brilliance of the beaded screen with the viewing angle of the matte-screen area. When determining the screen's placement, consider the audience size, location of windows and lights (light hurts the quality of the image you will project on the screen), and room size. In planning both the screen placement and audience seating, the two-times-eight rule is often used (see fig. 8.9). This rule states that no viewer should be seated closer than two screen widths from the screen or farther than eight screen widths from the screen. When the rule is followed, the visibility of the projected images and the readability of graphic information should be adequate for all audience members.

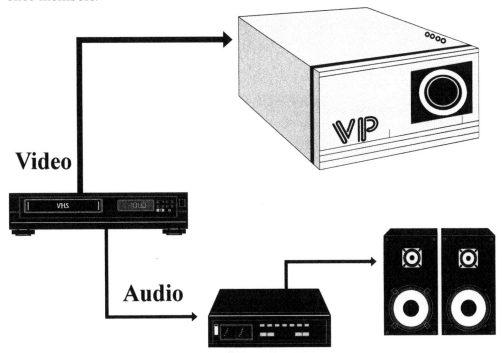

Figure 8.8 To maximize viewing impact, use a video projector and an amplified sound system.

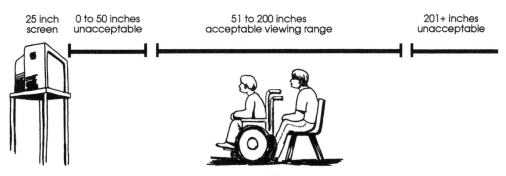

Figure 8.9 Use the two-times-eight rule when placing a television or projection screen.

Using Multiple Monitors

Large audiences can also be accommodated by using multiple monitors connected to a single-source VCR. These monitors can be strategically placed so the audience members will selectively view the monitor nearest their seated position. As mentioned earlier, you can send your video and audio signals from your single VCR into the closest monitor and then "daisy-chain" the signals from one monitor to another. Simply connect the video and audio outputs from one monitor to the video and audio inputs on another monitor, and so on. Each monitor can serve only the number of viewers who can adequately see and hear the video on the monitor nearest them. Of course, the larger the audience and room, the more monitors you need. Older-model monitors and TVs will not have this "monitor-out" feature, but you can still use multiple TVs or monitors with an RF splitter. This splitter takes the RF signal from your VCR using a single coaxial cable (like the cable TV jack in your home) and outputs the signal (both audio and video) to multiple TVs or monitors. Simply purchase a splitter with two, four, eight, or more outputs. Once again, your district media center should be able to supply you with cords, adapters, and splitters, plus some technical assistance if needed. If not, contact an electronics store for help. When using the multiple-monitor method for video presentations, you need to consider the following technical elements.

Cords

Remember, every monitor and television will need electricity, as well as a cable to carry the A/V signals. Plan on purchasing some long cables and grip tape to secure them. You need to ensure that the cables are securely taped to the floor to prevent them from being pulled out or injuring someone who might trip over them.

RF versus Video and Audio Outputs

As you know from chapter 1, RF signals are not compatible with video and audio output signals. An RF signal carries both audio and video signals in one cable. These jacks are found on most VCRs and all televisions. Video and audio jacks are found on all monitors and most professional VCRs. The video output is for the visual image only, and the audio output is for the sound. Some video jacks require a BNC cable, whereas almost all audio jacks use RCA cables. Most schools have plenty of RF cables on hand because they use these cables when connecting classroom televisions to the school's closed-circuit television system. Many district offices will even make RF cords of any desired length for use in the school. BNC cables and longer RCA cables usually are purchased from a video dealer or electronics store.

Monitor Placement

There are two options that work well for placing the monitor. You can place the monitors in the front and middle of the room or along each side of the room. How do you know which will be the most effective? Sit down and watch your video from several different seats. If you can see and hear, chances are your audience will, too. Another good option is to use a large-screen television. At our school, we are lucky to have a 60-inch television that works well for viewing videos as well as demonstrating computer applications in the multimedia lab for student training. Does your school have one? How about your district? Many local rental companies will rent a large-screen television at a reduced rate for educators. Although I would not suggest using this method routinely, it can work for a PTA open house or a once-in-a-while viewing occasion at your school. (By the way, we bought our large-screen television with some grant money.)

If you've ever attended a video presentation that featured a large screen and a good sound system, you know how effective and stimulating that can be. Conversely, if you've ever sat in the back row craning your neck and cupping your hands to your ears to watch a video presentation, you know how ineffective (and irritating) that can be. Planning your video presentation is just as important as planning your video production. You can make your video presentations just like the movies, with some technical assistance; the purchase of the right cords, cables, and equipment; and some preparation.

Showing Programs over a Closed-Circuit System

A final option might be to present your video on the school's closed-circuit television system and have the audience separated into smaller groups. For the example mentioned at the beginning of this chapter—a ninth-grade orientation video—this would have been a practical solution to the problem. The eighth-grade students could have watched the video in their classrooms prior to coming to the cafeteria for the orientation presentation.

Today's schools are being constructed with closed-circuit television systems for educational broadcasts. School news shows are often broadcast on these systems and displayed on TV sets mounted on walls or placed on A/V carts in classrooms. VCRs, laser disc players, and computer hardware are all found in school media centers. Special school staff such as media specialists, librarians, and sometimes media clerks operate these systems and maintain scheduling and control of cable, satellite, and closed-circuit broadcasts. Of course, this new technology often raises new questions. Regulations and guidelines regarding taping of network broadcasts, copyright guidelines, and strategies for implementing all this technology are being discussed and developed in school districts nationwide.

How Closed-Circuit Television Works

If your school is already wired, a basic understanding of how your system is designed and works is probably sufficient. Your school receives on-air broadcasts (from television stations) via cable or, in some instances, satellite systems. A broadband amplifier allows you to receive these broadcasts and distribute them throughout the school. An infrastructure of RF cabling throughout the building enables you to distribute your video and audio signals to each classroom. This is similar to cable reception in your own home. If your school building is large or your classrooms are located in several buildings on a campus, your broadcast system requires distribution amplifiers to boost the signal strength to the areas most distant from your main receiver/amplifier. If you want to broadcast videotaped programs on a certain channel in your system, educational videos purchased for this purpose, or even your school news shows, a separate modulator must be purchased. This modulator blocks an incoming channel from your cable system, thereby freeing that channel for broadcasts from a VCR connected to your system. Modulators are designed to block only one channel, so if you want to connect three VCRs to broadcast three different programs at the same time, you must purchase three separate modulators. Choose carefully the channels you want to block because once your modulators are installed, you will not be able to receive and distribute that television channel in your school. For example, if an educational channel such as PBS or the Discovery Channel is broadcast on channel 7, you want to make sure you do not install a modulator set to block out reception on channel 7. Obtain a list of channels and programming from your cable or satellite provider and meet with fellow teachers and administrators to select exactly which channels you want to use for your own broadcasting purposes and which television channels are to remain for educational use. Although this sounds simple, individual differences and preferences come into play, and not all final decisions meet with everyone's approval.

If you foresee a time when you would like to broadcast an event "live at the scene" from a location within your school, you may want to purchase a portable modulator. Simply connect the modulator to the RF connection at your shooting location, and you can broadcast video and audio signals via a camcorder and microphone. This would come in handy, for example, if you have a guest speaker presenting a motivational speech in the cafeteria. Not all students can sit in the cafeteria at the same time, and the speaker's time is limited to a single one-hour presentation. If you have a portable modulator, you can plug it into the RF connection in the cafeteria, connect your video camera to the modulator, and broadcast the presentation back to the classrooms for the rest of the student body to watch.

Our school has more than 4,000 students, and our auditorium can only seat 800. At the end of each year, we hold an academic awards ceremony to recognize outstanding academic achievements and award scholarships to graduating seniors. Dozens of colleges, businesses, and community organizations send representatives to award their scholarships to deserving seniors. It is a wonderful opportunity for recognizing the individuals receiving the scholarships, as well as for demonstrating school pride and fostering good academic work ethics. During this event, we set up a two-camera video system and broadcast the awards throughout the school using our portable modulator. We use our portable modulator so often, in fact, that we have mounted it permanently on a rolling A/V cart that we can easily move to any location at the school. The television production students really enjoy the excitement and recognition these "remote" live broadcasts bring. We use the modulator for pep rallies and guest speakers, and we have recently connected it to a computer to enable us to use this system as a schoolwide informational channel throughout the day.

In some districts, teams of volunteers and teachers have attempted to wire their own schools for closed-circuit broadcasts. In very small schools, this might be a cost-saving operation. In larger schools, where cable length and complicated architecture would be formidable obstacles, it's recommended that you seek professional video engineers to design and implement your installation. They will usually inspect your school and give you a bid or proposal for your broadcast system at no cost or obligation. Another option for some school districts is to subscribe to a broadcast service such as Channel 1. This company offers free hardware and installation of a broadcast system. In return, however, it requires you to watch its televised news program, complete with ads for products geared toward students. Schools must sign a contract to guarantee their obligation and viewership for a determined length of time. Your school-district officials or administrators should look very carefully at each school's educational climate before agreeing to such a proposal. An advisory board consisting of school personnel, administrators, parents, school-board members, and district representatives should be organized as your school and others in your district look into all of the options for closed-circuit broadcasting. Implementing a network in your school has an impact on students, teachers, and the community.

The Broadcast in the Classroom

After your network has been installed, each individual classroom must be configured to receive the broadcast. Televisions, electrical outlets, and RF connections
must be installed in each classroom so that teachers and students can view the
broadcasts (see fig. 8.10). Make sure the televisions are mounted within cord distance of an outlet and have easy access to the RF connection. Sounds simple, but
the fact is that if everyone is not on the same page when this installation is done,
some horrendous situations can occur. Most televisions come with a 6- or 8-foot
power cord. You must mount your television (using a standard wall-mounting
bracket) within this distance. Otherwise, you will need to buy dozens of extension
cords to reach power outlets, causing installation costs to rise and creating an eye-
sore in every classroom. Also, be sure to mount your televisions within easy reach
of your RF wall outlet. Simple preplanning avoids adding 10 to 25 feet of RF cord
tacked around the walls or baseboards in your classrooms.

Some schools purchase A/V carts for their televisions. This allows teachers to
move the televisions if needed, but it also places another piece of furniture in
already-crowded classrooms. If you are planning to buy A/V carts for this purpose,
be sure to buy carts that are 6 to 8 feet tall so that the televisions are placed well

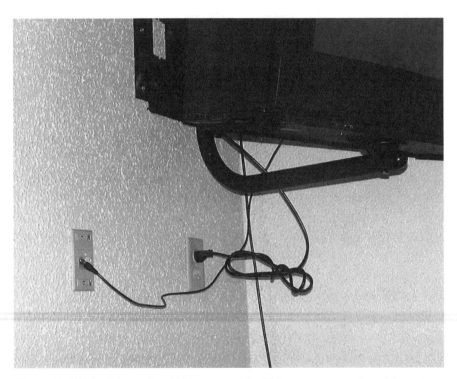

Figure 8.10 Televisions should be mounted within easy access to cable and
electrical outlets.

above everyone's head and viewing is not restricted. Also, purchase tie-down straps to secure the televisions to the cart. A dropped television can cost a lot of money, especially if it's dropped on someone's head.

Scheduling Programs

Now that you have a basic understanding of how a broadcast system is designed and operated, it is time to consider the aspects of scheduling and broadcasting your video programs. Because classroom teachers will be using this system to view various programs, you will need to have a programming schedule book and log to track what programs need to be shown, as well as the dates and times for broadcast. See figure 8.11 for a sample daily broadcast log.

A closed-circuit system enables more than one class to view a program at the same time. Not only is this convenient, but it also saves the cost of purchasing VCRs for individual classroom use. For example, if you were showing a videotape for a sixth-grade science class on weather, *all* the sixth-grade science classes could turn on their televisions and view the program at the same time. If teachers can be encouraged to plan and develop their lessons cooperatively, a closed-circuit broadcast system can facilitate instruction and relieve some financial and time-constraint burdens. And no one is spending time running to the media center and rolling the VCRs from class to class, period by period. (And we all know who that would be—*you.*)

The broadcast log not only allows you to notify teachers when a program suitable for their lessons and educational subjects becomes available, but it also enables teachers to reserve a time slot for broadcasting their tapes. If you only have one channel to broadcast video programs in your school, reserving a time and date can help avoid conflicts. If you are broadcasting a daily or weekly news show, simply block out that time slot on the log before you allow any other teachers to sign up. To save time, have the time slot for your news show printed on the log sheets before you duplicate them for the tape log book. Then, use a three-hole puncher and place them in a three-ring binder by the VCRs. Teachers should be required to sign up at least 24 hours before their program is to be broadcast, and you can request that their videotapes be sent to the media center the morning of the broadcast date. Receiving the tapes too many days in advance turns into a housekeeping chore the media specialist doesn't have time for.

Scheduling also makes it possible for the media specialist to inform teachers when their video is not legally appropriate to broadcast at the school. Yes, unfortunately, that will happen. Ask any media specialist. This occurs especially when teachers are writing lesson plans for substitutes. Having the students watch *Sixteen Candles* or *Star Wars* might seem like a good idea for when a substitute teacher is taking over the class, but it is quite illegal. Copyright guidelines for closed-circuit

DAILY BROADCAST LOG

Channel	Date	Program/Tape	Period 1	Period 2	Period 3	Period 4	Period 5A	Period 5B	Period 6	Teacher
7										
11										
13										

Channel	Date	Program/Tape	Period 1	Period 2	Period 3	Period 4	Period 5A	Period 5B	Period 6	Teacher
7										
11										
13										

Channel	Date	Program/Tape	Period 1	Period 2	Period 3	Period 4	Period 5A	Period 5B	Period 6	Teacher
7										
11										
13										

Channel	Date	Program/Tape	Period 1	Period 2	Period 3	Period 4	Period 5A	Period 5B	Period 6	Teacher
7										
11										
13										

Channel	Date	Program/Tape	Period 1	Period 2	Period 3	Period 4	Period 5A	Period 5B	Period 6	Teacher
7										
11										
13										

Channel	Date	Program/Tape	Period 1	Period 2	Period 3	Period 4	Period 5A	Period 5B	Period 6	Teacher
7										
11										
13										

Channel	Date	Program/Tape	Period 1	Period 2	Period 3	Period 4	Period 5A	Period 5B	Period 6	Teacher
7										
11										
13										

Figure 8.11 Sample broadcast log

broadcasts within a school are available from many sources, and your district's office probably has established guidelines, too. Obtain copies of these, and place them in your media-center handbook. Also, present this information to your principal or curriculum coordinator, and include a presentation of the guidelines in your beginning-of-the-year faculty meeting. Remember, the media specialist is responsible for adhering to district, state, and federal guidelines.

Preparing for Broadcasting

When your system is ready to be used, you should perform a few preliminary checks before beginning your on-air broadcasts. These measures can save some urgent phone calls to the media center during broadcasts and prevent some hectic running around looking for cords, cables, or TV remote controls. Insert a pre-recorded videotape in the VCR connected to your broadcast system. The tape should be at least one hour in length to allow you enough time to complete your check of the system. Walk around to *every* room set up to receive the broadcasts. Turn on the television, tune to the channel you are broadcasting on, and make sure the sound is turned up. Some newer-model televisions need the remote control to program the channels into the television's memory when first setting up to receive broadcasts through cable. Other features include tuning the TV from antenna reception to cable, standard cable, or even satellite reception on some of the higher channels. (Read the owner's manuals *before* you attempt to do this.) Take a notebook or clipboard to write down classroom numbers or locations that are having reception or technical difficulties. Don't expect teachers to do this for you. It won't happen unless *you* make it happen.

Chapter 9

Questions from the Floor

As presenters at national and state media conferences and as consultants to school districts, we have the opportunity to speak to hundreds of media educators each year. We always set aside a portion of our presentations for questions. In the following pages, we present some of the more frequently asked questions and our answers to them. Remember, the answers are based on our ideas, philosophies, and experiences. They are helpful suggestions, not universal truths. Our hope is that sharing these ideas with you will provide information that you can incorporate as you build your successful school video program.

Television Production Equipment and Studios

How much equipment do I need to start producing programs at my school?

If you have a camcorder, a tripod, and a microphone, you can produce any number of television production programs. Certainly, you will want to add more equipment as you become familiar with television production, but you really don't *need* any more to get started. With a camcorder, tripod, and microphone, you can produce a simple news show, create classroom videos, record school assembly programs, and even produce a simple orientation tape. Students will have fun making exciting classroom projects and interviewing their classmates for the school news show. See our *Video Projects for Elementary and Middle Schools* (Keith Kyker and Christopher Curchy [Englewood, Colorado: Libraries Unlimited, 1995]) for ideas.

Upgrading a studio by purchasing new equipment is a continuous process. Waiting for all of the equipment that you could possibly want is a waste of time and will deprive hundreds of students opportunity. Beginning television production in a school is a lot like buying a new house or returning to college—if you wait for the perfect situation, you'll *never* begin.

My "studio" is only a storage closet. What should I do?

Some of the best school video is produced in spite of the equipment or facility. You would be surprised at how many of your colleagues work in similar situations. First, remove the "Media Storage" sign from the door and replace it with your broadcast crew's moniker (e.g., "Hawkeye News Headquarters"). Then, remove all vestiges of the room's former storage function (broken film projectors, mop buckets, etc.). Apply a fresh coat of paint in bright school colors. Persuade the principal to replace the broken and stained ceiling tiles and burned-out fluorescent light bulbs. Before you know it, your "closet" will be a TV studio.

Here are some recommendations for further improvement: install simple track lighting with dimmer switchers; scavenge set decorations, such as bookshelves, tables, posters, and knickknacks; add a storage cabinet for equipment, a file cabinet for class work and equipment manuals, and tables for class work. Even though your broom-closet studio pales in comparison to a network newsroom, it will be the best studio that your students have ever worked in. This will be *their* studio, warts and all. Encourage them to take pride in their studio and their work.

Finally, don't be afraid to "come out of the closet" with your productions. Does the video equipment for your news show fit on two or three rolling media carts? If so, then go on location. Produce your news show from the art room, and interview students about their artwork. Make a news show in the science lab—the science teacher can explain the science behind television production to your audience. Video production should take place all around your school. If you have a closet studio, make it the best closet studio in the school district, and remember that the door locks on the inside, not the outside.

I see advertisements for camcorders, video titlers, audio mixers, and microphones in mail-order catalogs. They are much cheaper than the equipment described in your books. Are these bargains?

Probably not. Equipment for audio and video production continues to drop in price, and a category of very inexpensive equipment has emerged. Typically, equipment in this ultra-low price range does not have the features described in chapters 1, 2, and 3 of this book. For example, a bargain-basement camcorder can now be purchased for as little as $250. This camcorder will probably use the VHS-C format, which is average quality at best. There will be no microphone jack, no headphone jack, and no way to focus the camera manually. The viewfinder will be tiny and in black and white and accessed via the eyepiece. The installed microphone will be low quality, and you may have to purchase many of the desired accessories separately. So, is this a useless camcorder? No! It is probably a good choice for the video hobbyist on a limited budget who wants to record family re-unions, softball games, and vacations. It would also be a great "starter" camcorder for young videographers, and if they drop it or accidentally run over it with their skateboard—well, you're only out 250 bucks. But it's not suitable for a school pro-duction facility. Many of the features described in chapter 1 do not appear on this camcorder.

Similarly, a video titler that sells for $150 will allow you to type a few charac-ters on the screen but will meet neither the demands of your program nor the ex-pectations of your students. Save your money, explore funding sources, and buy only the equipment that will perform adequately at your school.

When is a tripod necessary?

You and your students should use a tripod when a shooting assignment lasts more than two or three minutes or any time a steady shot is required. A tripod probably isn't necessary for that one-minute interview with the principal or the series of 10-second shots around school. However, tripods are critical for assembly programs, news shows, and election speeches.

How many times can I reuse a videotape?

This questions pops up at almost every conference and school visit. Budget-minded educators are looking for the threshold at which a videotape begins to lose its abil-ity to record a crisp picture, or worse, when another playback puts a big glitch in your video program.

Videotape is basically a thin strip of plastic covered with metal particles. The metal particles are glued to the plastic, and a coating is applied to prevent the metal from falling off. However, when a tape is used many times, the plastic coating be-gins to break down, and metal particles are shaken loose from the plastic strip of videotape. The absence of metal particles creates the white flashes, or "drop-outs," on your TV when the tape is played.

You've probably watched rental videotapes at home. Notice how the video pic-ture gets fuzzy lines and bright flashes as the ending credits start to roll. This is the point where most people press the "stop" button on the videotape. Continuously abusing this small section of tape has resulted in the "drop-outs" that you see. The same effect is produced with any tape that is used repeatedly.

Understand two things at this point: 1) videotape has a tough life and 2) video-tape is cheap. The tough life of a videotape begins when it is inserted into a VCR. The trap door at the top of the tape opens, and a comparatively long section of videotape is pulled from the videocassette and wrapped around several rubber pulleys and metal recording and playback heads inside the VCR. The search function on the VCR pulls the tape through even faster and adds more friction to the rubbing of the tape against the guts of the VCR. With friction comes heat, and the sealer used to coat the tape begins to wear. The heat of the VCR (most VCRs *don't* have built-in fans) begins to melt the glue, and particles begin to drop off. *Voila.* We have a drop-out.

This brings us to the second point: tape is cheap. A high-quality consumer-brand VHS videotape can be purchased at a discount store for a dollar or less. Schools can also buy videotape from tape dealers, as explained in chapter 4. Considering the wear and tear placed on videotape and its low price, it doesn't make sense to expect a large number of recordings from a single tape.

But how many is a large number? Rather than the condition of the videotape, think about the value of the program that you are recording. Simple classroom video projects can probably be recorded on a used tape. However, valuable recordings (school plays and concerts, video movies, contest entries) require a new tape. Remember, a tape glitch is an imperfection in *the physical tape,* not the program recorded thereon. Rerecording on a tape with several drop-outs will not make the drop-outs go away. No one wants his or her hard work ruined just to save a small amount of money. When possible, use new tape.

What about new developments in television, like HDTV (high-density television)? Wouldn't it be best to wait until the new technologies are "written in stone" before buying new equipment for my school?

Unfortunately, technology never seems to get "written in stone," does it? Just a few years ago, an IBM 486 computer was considered fast, and we couldn't imagine ever filling 1 gigabyte of hard-drive space. Waiting for technology to find a resting place will deny thousands of students access to video production. It is better to make informed choices based on available information and accept that upgrading is an inherent part of educational technology.

Television will change—no doubt about it. The picture will get sharper, the colors more vivid. The screen will get wider, and the sound will be digital quality. And, as one comedian astutely observed, "There probably still won't be anything on worth watching." Walter Cronkite became a crackerjack newsman before videotape was invented. *I Love Lucy* was filmed in black and white. Teach your students how to make good television programs using technology currently available. Don't let the prospect of future developments in the television industry foil your school video plans. Equipment that you buy today will become worn out before it becomes obsolete. By the time new television standards become widely accepted, that middle schooler sitting in your media center will be a doctor or an airline pilot.

I've been reading about television production in other countries, and the terms PAL and SECAM keep popping-up. What do they mean?

In simplest terms, TV signals around the world are not compatible with each other. The three standards are NTSC, PAL, and SECAM. The signals are produced and recorded differently in each system. TVs and VCRs made for one system won't work with the other systems. (The differences are the number of lines of resolution, the number of frames per second, and the frequency at which color is processed.)

Remember that TV was invented by different people in different places about the same time. It is only natural that the systems are different. NTSC is used in the United States, Japan, Korea, and some other countries. PAL is used in most of Europe and Africa (think British influence). SECAM is used in France and most of Asia (including China and the former Soviet bloc countries).

What is the best way to clean my VCR?

The best way to clean the VCR is preventative cleaning. In other words, try not to let the inside of your VCR get dirty! We recommend that only high-quality blank tape be used in your school VCRs and camcorders. This tape should be new (when possible) and dedicated for school use. Don't let your students record their projects on old, abused videotape that has been used at home. Provide storage for these tapes so they don't "live" in the student's book bag or car.

Occasionally, however, VCRs get dirty. The best way to clean a VCR is with a new, high-quality blank videotape. Do not use a consumer head-cleaning tape. Most of these products contain abrasive cloth, which can damage your VCR. Your VCR's video head is in a recessed slot only 4 microns wide! A hair or speck of dust can clog this slot. A high-quality tape will gently wipe over the head and remove the debris. Put the tape in, and let it play for 2 or 3 minutes (of course, you will just see "snow" on the TV). Then insert a recorded program, and check the picture quality. Repeat if necessary.

If, after several repetitions, your picture quality is still poor, take the VCR to your local video repair shop for cleaning. Most shops will perform a thorough cleaning for less than $50.

My friend and I have a small wager riding on this. Before recharging our camcorder's batteries, should we run them until they are dead? I say "yes," and my friend says "no." Who's right?

You both are. It all depends on what kind of batteries you are using.

There are three types of batteries used in camcorders today: the nickel-cadmium (ni-cad) battery, the lithium battery, and the lead (say "led") battery. They are all rechargeable. First, determine the type of batteries that you use. Generally speaking, the smaller the camcorder, the greater likelihood that you're using a ni-cad battery or a lithium battery. Larger camcorders usually use the lead batteries. Check your owner's manual or read the label on the battery.

If you're using a ni-cad battery, then discharge the battery totally before recharging. In other words, a ni-cad should be dead when it goes on the charger. (Some new chargers automatically discharge the battery before they begin charging your battery. Once again, check the owner's manual.)

The lead battery can go on the charger after every use. If a lead battery is left around for a few weeks without a charging, it can die beyond the point of charging and must be discarded. That's why so many educators find themselves buying new lead batteries in August. They haven't been charged since June! Take the lead batteries and the charger home over the summer, and periodically charge the lead batteries. Remember, a lead battery is the same type of battery used in your automobile. If a car is abandoned for a few weeks, it will not start when the ignition is turned. The battery is dead. That's how lead batteries work.

The lithium battery, which is now the battery of choice in small digital cameras and camcorders, can also be charged after every use.

So, in summary, run down the ni-cad, but charge the lithium and lead batteries frequently. Good question. Now buy each other lunch!

Someone told me that I have to use green for my chroma key background. Is this true?

Not true, but it makes sense. When you engage the chroma key function on your video mixer, you are telling the mixer to ignore a certain color (or range of colors) and replace that color with the second video input (the desired background). Therefore, anything that color will be replaced. As long as no one wears green clothes, you're safe.

But why not red? Some flesh tones have a pinkish hue that can appear red on camera. Blue? Very black hair can have bluish tones when lighted. And some folks have blue eyes, which can make for a very spooky video. So green is a natural choice.

How can I get my video mixer's chroma key function to work better?

Chroma key is tricky. No doubt about it. Lighting is very important in the chroma key application. The background must be very bright. The lighting must be even, with no shadows or dark spots. An adequate amount of light should be used with the talent. The camera's iris control may have to be adjusted. Also, make sure your talent is not wearing clothing or jewelry the same color as your background. Those items will become invisible in the shot!

Finally, be sure to read the equipment manual before attempting a chroma key. Often the manual has tips on creating a good chroma key situation. Most schools who use chroma key on a regular basis have a special chroma key set that is used. When students desire a chroma key application, they can simply turn the cameras to the chroma key set. This reduces the lengthy process of chroma key set-up and illumination tweaking.

Keep trying!

Television Production and the School Media Program

My students are making great computer multimedia presentations and surfing the Internet. Is television really needed anymore in schools?

Television is still an important spoke on the audiovisual wheel that should be part of our total media program. Remember that older technologies can still be very useful, even though newer technologies exist. Students will get excited about anything a good teacher gets excited about.

School video production has some real benefits that can't be overlooked. Students can make quick, yet meaningful projects. An interview with the principal can be produced in about a minute and be viewed and critiqued about a minute later. How long would it take a group of three students to produce a computer multimedia presentation about the school principal? Hours? Days?

This brings us to another important benefit of school video production. The basics of video production can be learned very quickly. After about 10 minutes of instruction, a team of students can videotape a pretty good interview or minidocumentary. Audio dubbing and simple graphics creation are also quickly learned.

Also, don't forget the performance aspect of school video production. Students who conduct interviews and host your news show gain valuable experience communicating with an audience. Their success also builds their self-esteem.

Should I teach a video production class?

If your school is involved in video production (news-show production, entering video contests, etc.), someone should be teaching a television production class. Unfortunately, we often hear about schools (elementary, middle, and high schools included) where there is no class time for television production. The students run in to the media center to quickly produce the news show and then run back to first period. This is usually a frustrating experience for everyone involved. And why shouldn't it be? The program never seems to get better because new skills are never taught. The media specialist is there to educate, and this is *not* education. (See fig 9.1.)

Plan to offer television production class as an elective at the middle, junior high, and high school levels. The class can be taught by the media specialist or any other interested teacher. (One school we visited had an excellent television production class taught by the physical education coach.) The students could produce the news show during the first half of the class period and then learn the skills of television production during the remaining time. (Recommended texts include Keith Kyker and Christopher Curchy, *Television Production: A Classroom Approach* [Englewood, Colorado: Libraries Unlimited, 1993], Keith Kyker and Christopher Curchy, *Television Production for Elementary and Middle Schools* [Englewood, Colorado: Libraries Unlimited, 1994], and Keith Kyker and Christopher Curchy, *Video Projects for Elementary and Middle Schools* [Englewood, Colorado: Libraries Unlimited, 1995].) Many high schools teach several television production classes, with beginning and advanced levels. It is common to find a full-time television produc-

Figure 9.1 "That's the show. Have a great day! On your mark, get set … "

tion teacher in medium and large high schools. Middle school and junior high school television production courses may be only a semester long. Many schools at that level successfully integrate production classes into an elective "wheel," which alternates the class with others such as art and home economics.

Elementary scheduling may be a bit trickier, but it is certainly realistic to select a crew of 15 to 20 elementary students and meet with them during the school day several times each week. Crews can be rotated throughout the year. Most media specialists find that their news shows dramatically improve after they have taught the skills of television production to their students. Sounds basic, doesn't it? Teach the students and their performance will improve. You would be surprised to know how many schools do not follow this basic educational process when it comes to television production.

How much time should I commit to school video production?

This is an important question. In fact, we begin many of our workshops by asking this question to our audience. The only correct answer is, "An amount of time that is realistic and comfortable for you." Ask yourself, "How many hours each week can I dedicate to video production?" If you are a middle school media specialist, the answer may be "five hours." A high school video production teacher may answer "38 hours" because school video is her full-time job.

The important thing to remember is that *you* get to choose the amount of time. You may only have one or two hours per week to work with video production. If so, give your students the best two hours you can. There are two traps that you must avoid. Trap number one occurs when the media specialist performs television production tasks to the detriment of other school media functions. Should you cancel story hour so you can spend more time with video production? No. Should one-on-one information service to students be cut back so the media specialist can work on video? Of course not. Integrate television production into your media program. And make sure it doesn't push out another equally important component.

The second trap occurs when you commit to more video production than you can reasonably perform. A high school media specialist in a neighboring county decided to immerse her school in video production. She had no experience but scheduled a full-year television production class and promised the principal a daily news show. She also committed her students to production of a video yearbook, a school orientation video, tutorial tapes for all departments, and videotaping of all athletic events. All of this was to be done in addition to her regular duties as the school's only media specialist. A few months into the school year, she was hopelessly behind on all of her tasks and worked at least 60 hours a week for the entire school year. Exhausted, she approached her principal at the end of the year and informed him that she needed to decrease the amount of video work planned for next school year. The principal congratulated her for her yeoman duty, stated that he really liked her video work, and said he wanted her to continue it each year. Rather than endure another impossible year, she switched schools and hasn't picked up a camcorder since. Who created all this work? She did. Instead of beginning slowly, developing a dedicated crew of students, and adding services each year, she started with a complete program. Start slowly, and then progress.

If you ask yourself how much time you can realistically commit to video production and avoid the two common traps just described, you can probably determine your level of commitment.

How can I get my principal to support my television production program?

Our experience with principals tells us three things. First, principals support teachers who make them look good. Make a simple orientation tape for your principal to show at open house. Create a news show that makes your principal proud. If your principal doesn't always get to watch the show, make a tape and leave it on his or her desk. Ask your principal for ideas. When your principal is proud of your work and sees him- or herself as a stakeholder in the process, support will likely follow.

Second, principals support programs that don't create problems. Much of an administrator's job consists of fixing small problems before they become big problems. Don't create small problems, and if you do, fix them yourself when you can. Don't allow your students to jump off the roof with a camcorder. Don't let your students leave campus without going through proper channels. Don't put the school's "loose cannon" on the live news show. You get the idea.

Finally, principals like plans. Write down three or four simple objectives for your school television production program, and share the list with your principal. Typical goals could include featuring interviews in the news show, teaching students how to use the camcorder, producing a brief orientation video, and so on. Use this book and others like it to show your principal how you are educating yourself about television production. Make sure your principal knows that you have some great ideas about buying new equipment.

How can I learn more about video production in schools?

Most states have a media organization. Join it, even if you're not a media specialist. This small investment gives you access to educational-media materials and information about media conventions. Plan to visit a convention, even if it means an overnight trip. Encourage your district media specialist to host a meeting or conduct in-services about television production. Read this book and others like it. Read

Videomaker magazine, which can be found at most newsstands. Visit your audio/video vendor. Ask questions and read catalogs. Investigate educational opportunities at local colleges, vocational schools, and adult night schools. Search the Internet for other school video production teachers (we're out there). Learning about school television production is a gradual process. Don't be overwhelmed by what you don't know. Instead, focus on adding a few new skills and building on your experiences.

I know that you speak at several media conferences each year. How do you select which ones to attend?

Several factors go into our decision to attend a conference. We always attend our state media conference. In addition, we try to attend at least one national conference each year (examples include the National Educational Computer Conference and the Florida Educational Technology Conference). The rest of our conference schedule depends on invitations we receive. Typically, we are invited to conduct preconference workshops and concurrent sessions. In some cases, we participate in book signings and receptions. It's really up to the host.

Our involvement in a conference usually begins with one or two educators making such a request to the committee that plans their media conference. Give your association officers a call, and ask them to invite us to your next conference.

For more information about our conference participation and rates, please visit our Web site, www.SCHOOLTV.com.

Working with Students

How should I enroll students in my program? What criteria should I use?

We've already stated that we believe a television production course should be offered at every school program. But how are these students selected to be part of the program?

Most teachers working with video production find that more students want to take the class than the media specialist can accommodate. Two choices exist. Either a full-time video production teacher is hired to teach an elective course in video, or the media specialist must select students to be a part of the program. High schools generally take the former approach; middle and elementary schools the latter. However, many full-time television production teachers select the students who enter their program as well.

To ensure a fair selection process, some sort of application process is needed. The most natural strategy is to require students to complete a written application. Here are some topics that should be included:

Student's name, grade level, and homeroom teacher.

A statement that describes the course and the instructor's expectations.

Materials or lab fees associated with the course.

List of student's grades on the last report card or perhaps a copy of the report card.

Student hobbies, interests, and activities.

A paragraph or brief essay on why the student wants to be in the class.

At least two teacher recommendations. Teachers can be asked to evaluate students on criteria such as attendance, punctuality, conduct, responsibility, and ability to work in groups.

A student signature section, just like a real job application.

The teacher or media specialist may want to speak briefly with recommending teachers or review grades and discipline records in the office. The teacher or media specialist may even conduct brief interviews with the applicants to help in the selection process.

How much control and leadership should students have?

Obviously, your personal experience carries more weight than a recommendation from a book. However, simply put, students should be given control of your school news show and exercise professional leadership when they are ready. You can help by setting ground rules. For example, when a student makes a mistake during news-show production, there are only two possible comments: "talent problem," which means the announcer made a mistake, or "technical problem," which means that someone on the crew made a mistake. No eye rolling, no screaming, no criticism, no flaring nostrils. Just two simple words. (Everybody already knows who goofed. There's no reason to crush the student's self-esteem.) Recue the tape; then try it again. A good student leader gets the show rolling.

Although students may have control of your news-show production, make sure that you maintain control of your content. A nightmare situation happened at a local high school. Before the end of the first news show, just about everybody in the audience was offended. God and country were both insulted. An obscene gesture was thinly veiled, and two vulgarities were uttered. But who was in the principal's office? The teacher, of course. Student control ends when poor judgment takes over.

How about after-school video clubs?

Many schools have fine after-school video clubs. Students often meet in the media center one afternoon each week to talk and learn about video production. Club membership (and sponsorship) can be very enjoyable. But remember—students join clubs for social reasons more than content reasons. Don't expect the same type of environment and production from a club as you have in a class. In a class, the activities are more instructor driven, and student expectations are higher and more content oriented. An after-school club will probably find making a Claymation video or an action movie more fun than producing a news show or recording the chorus concert. And when it stops being fun, they stop coming to the meetings. If you remember these important differences, then sponsoring an after-school video club can be fun and rewarding. However, don't make it a substitute for a television production class during the school day.

I teach my high school TV production class with a heavy emphasis on the technical aspects. Across town, the TV production teacher teaches mostly acting and drama. Should we get together and standardize our curriculum?

It's the nature of education that every teacher teaches a little bit differently, regardless of the standards, course design, or textbook. It doesn't really matter if the teachers are across the hallway or across the continent. Most teachers focus on what they like to do and what they think is important.

Differences in course content can be good. We, as teachers, bring more than our training to the educational table. Most course outlines in the United States are written to allow for such diversity. We are provided with standards and competencies, not daily lesson plans. We don't need to "homogenize" education by making sure everyone teaches the same thing. If one teacher spends more time on a topic of television production than another teacher, what difference does it make? It's probably because they're good at it! As long as both teachers are teaching the basics and covering their school system's course requirements, everything is fine.

What's a good way to evaluate video projects? These things tend to be a group effort, but I like to give grades on an individual basis.

Grading video projects can be difficult, especially when several students are working on the same project. Here are three ideas to consider. First, give work-in-progress grades. Every time an important step in the production process is completed (storyboarding, script, raw footage), give a grade. Don't base the entire grade on the final video submission. This way, you can evaluate each individual's progress as the project is produced. This also keeps all the students involved in every step of the process.

Second, give both an individual *and* a group grade. This is especially important when specific tasks are assigned. If the video project is worth 100 points, think about 50 points for the individual grade and 50 points for the group grade. This encourages everyone to do their part and also encourages group success.

Finally, realize that students perform at different levels. Even your best students will struggle at times. Make sure that everyone tries their best. Grade process, not product.

My students' video projects look like home movies. What's the problem?

First, let's think about what we mean when we say "home movies." The videographer starts the tape and then pans, zooms, and looks for a good shot as the tape rolls. If nothing meaningful happens, tape rolls anyway. Zooming and panning may lead to some good footage. But probably not.

When your students produce video projects, they should plan each shot. They should create the shot in the viewfinder and *then* begin recording. If a UFO lands in the commons area, then they can pan and zoom. If not, they should stick to the storyboard and shot list.

I am a junior in high school right now, and I am taking TV Production. Next year I will be taking the Broadcast Journalism course, where we learn every job of producing a television show. I am very interested in communications for a career, and I was wondering what are some good communications colleges.

"Where should I go to college?" That's a big question—one that will have a profound impact on the rest of your life. It's a tough decision, and I'm assuming that you're also seeking the input of your parents, your teachers, and your school guidance counselor—people who know you.

Also, remember that there are many factors involved in selecting a college. Location is very important. You may want to stay close to home, or you may want to make a big move. Price is also a consideration.

As far as the communications and TV production classes, we would look for four things in the selection process: 1) your access to hands-on training, 2) your place in the program, 3) other departments at the school, and 4) internships and placement programs. First, when you visit the school, take a look at their equipment, and ask how it is used. If you already know how to use it all, then you may not learn much during the next four years. Look for a *real* campus TV studio. Many colleges have PBS or cable TV stations that regularly produce massive hours of TV. This, of course, increases your chance of getting some serious experience.

Which leads us to the second part: your place in the program. Will you be able to get some individual attention if you need it? Are freshmen allowed to work on real video programs? Or are you just expected to wait until your senior year?

Third, pay attention to other programs at the school. Most reporters also have strong backgrounds in political science and government, as well as a working knowledge of business, literature, and other topics. Make sure that you will have the opportunity to develop in these areas. A vocational school prepares you for a job. College prepares you for life.

Finally, look at internships and job placements. Part of that life is getting a job! Colleges frequently offer internships for their students and placement services for their graduates. Ask around. Call the local TV stations, and find out where those people went to college. Most schools are proud to put their graduates in the field. Internships and placements are critical.

Finally, realize that you are the most important part of your college education. In broadcasting, you make your own breaks. No one will knock on your door and offer you a job. Even if you don't end up at a "powerhouse" college, you can still be successful if you (say it with us, parents) APPLY YOURSELF!

School News Shows

How can I improve the look of my school news show?

Many media specialists are disappointed with the way their news show looks and sounds. Here are some tips that will allow your students to emulate the broadcasters on real television.

Use an external microphone. Many schools rely on the camcorder-mounted microphone to capture the sound of the student reading the announcements. The camcorder microphone is probably omnidirectional and does a poor job of recording your announcer's voice. A lavaliere (tie-pin) microphone is the obvious choice; however, a handheld microphone on a desk stand or a PZM microphone works well, too (see chapter 2).

Make sure that the camera lens is eye level to the announcer. This is probably the easiest way to improve the video picture of your news show, yet it is hardly ever done. Why? Because teachers are big and kids are little. Big teachers set up camcorders on tripods so *they* can see into the viewfinders without bending over and getting back pain. But unfortunately, their news readers are almost always sitting at children's tables in children's chairs, resulting in a camera angle that looks down at the children rather than at them. Your video camera should be *level* with your news readers. That may mean that your camera operators are bending over or even seated, but the shot will look great.

Use a teleprompting system. A teleprompting system electronically displays the news-show script in large letters. A student operates the prompting system, and the news anchor reads along. Most teleprompting systems are computer driven. The scriptwriter types in the announcements and saves the script just like any word-processing file. Then a function key is pressed (for example, F9), and the script is displayed in a very large font—about five or six lines of text on a computer monitor. The script can easily be viewed 10 or 15 feet away. The student operating the teleprompter presses up-arrow or down-arrow keys to roll the script at a comfortable pace.

Where is the computer monitor placed? The monitor must be placed very close to the camera lens—below the lens or just to the left or right works well. This way, the news reader can look in the general direction of the camera and still read the script. A more-complicated arrangement has the computer monitor placed *below* the camcorder lens and facing the ceiling. A one-way mirror or coated glass placed in front of the camera lens displays the script. (Most teleprompting software offers a mirror-image display.) If you're just beginning, stick with the beside-the-lens approach.

The results are astounding. Students can look right at the camera as they read the announcements. No more shuffling papers or stumbling over scribbled announcements. Some teachers will say that typing a new script every day is a real hassle. But think about it—you saved the script as a word-processing file. Simply load yesterday's show, delete old announcements, add new announcements, and you're ready to roll. A teleprompting program actually saves time by cutting down on news reader mistakes. Your student media assistants can update the script throughout the day on the day before show production so that very few changes are made the morning of the actual taping. Just type in the sports scores, and you're ready to roll.

Unfortunately, computer teleprompting programs designed for broadcast-news programs can be quite expensive and complicated. To remedy this problem, we have developed an inexpensive, user-friendly prompter program for schools. Computer requirements are quite low—the program will easily run on an older (donated or obsolete) computer. The program is distributed by a professional software business. For more information, visit our Web site, www.SCHOOLTV.com.

White balance your camera. White balancing adjusts the color response of the video camera by showing the camera the color white. The camera makes adjustments based on the lighting environment. Don't forget this simple operation when you produce a news show. This also gives your camera operator an important task during news-show production. Before the show begins, the news reader can hold a white piece of paper, and the camera operator can white balance the camera.

Plan some simple backdrops and set decorations. The scene is set for your news show. Your seventh-grade news reader is sitting at a table, ready to read the script from the teleprompter. Her hair is styled, her face is clean, her teeth are brushed. She wears a lavaliere microphone. The camcorder is adjusted so that the lens is at her eye level. Everything looks great. Except that behind our well-groomed, well-prepared news reader is an off-white cinder-block wall. Decorate that set so that the viewer enjoys looking at the entire picture. Set decoration doesn't have to be complicated; it just takes some thoughtful planning. First, turn your video camera on, set the news reader at her usual post, and establish your shot. (Displaying the video picture on a large television will be helpful at this point.) The area of the shot is the only area that you need to decorate. That area may be as wide as 6 or 7 feet or as narrow as 3 or 4 feet. You don't have to hire a professional artist to paint a room-size mural. Consider a section of attractive wallpaper or make a backdrop as described in chapter 6. Bookshelves, posters, and student artwork also make great backgrounds. Avoid overly busy backgrounds. Keep it simple. Even though the news reader remains the focal point of your show, the background should still be attractive.

The students say my news shows are boring. How can I enliven them?

Let's face it, they could be right. Your student audience compares your news show to the programs they see on TV at home. Although you don't have the big budget of major news programs, there are some ways to enliven your show. The easiest way to do this is to feature more students on your program. Should students be pulled from the hallways at random to read announcements on the air? No. Try the opposite approach. Take your camcorders and microphones out into the school. Interview students, coaches, club sponsors, teachers, and administrators about upcoming school events. Roll these interviews into your news show. End your news show with rolling tape of a school basketball game or chorus concert. At one elementary school, the news show begins with the national anthem sung by a classroom of students. The media specialist tapes the anthem in the classroom and rolls the tape into each show. The best way to improve your show is to feature the people at your school.

My elementary school has recently purchased video equipment, and we are making plans to produce a news program and video projects with all grades (K–6). Another school in our district started off with only six students involved for the entire year. My principal is adamant that this not become an elitist activity but try to involve as many students and teachers as possible. How should I proceed?

School television production certainly doesn't have to become an elitist activity. Your question mentions two types of production: 1) news-show production and 2) video-project production. Let's tackle the news-show production issue first. Make a list of jobs that need to be performed each day on your news show. Nine or 10 students will probably be needed. Add a couple to cover absentees, and you'll probably need a crew of 12. Most TV teachers use some form of written application. We like to use character and citizenship as our criteria for selection, with a heavy emphasis on teacher recommendations. We repeat this process three or four times a year, giving us an entirely different crew every few weeks. This way, dozens of your students will get a meaningful, extended television production experience. Even younger children can lead the pledge or provide the "Word of the Day."

Which leads us to your second type of production—video projects. As your students complete elementary video projects, feature the projects on your news show. Perhaps language arts students are interviewing storybook characters or making video book reports. These are great news show features! We offer 25 curriculum-based video projects in our book *Video Projects for Elementary and Middle Schools*.

Carefully select your news crews, and make the news program an outlet for student creativity and success. This approach will allow many students of all ages and levels to contribute. A student doesn't have to be in the TV studio to contribute to the school news show.

I am doing morning announcements for the first time at my school. We've had some fun so far and taped our first show for Monday. We have previously created a "live" production, but I want the kids to do the news more carefully. Any thoughts about live versus taped presentations?

Both of us prefer taped shows. There are several reasons, which I'm sure you've discovered in your efforts. Personally, we think a taped show is only fair for the kids. Everyone makes mistakes. There is a certain security in being able to rewind the tape and start over. Our students deserve that security. In addition, we can attempt more-complex show elements (rolling in segments, creative graphics, etc.) when we know that we can try again (and again) if our initial efforts are not successful.

Glossary

adapter. A device used to achieve compatibility between two items of audio/video equipment.

aperture. The opening of the camera lens, as controlled by the iris.

audio. The sound portion of television production.

audio dub. An editing technique that involves erasing the existing audio track on a videotape and replacing it with a new audio track.

audio mixer. An electronic component that facilitates the selection and combination of audio signals.

audio/video mixer. A single electronic component that consists of an audio mixer and a video mixer. Also called an A/V mixer.

automatic focus. A feature on most camcorders that automatically makes minor focal-length adjustments, thus freeing the videographer from focusing concerns.

automatic gain control. A feature on most video cameras and camcorders that, when engaged, boosts the video signal to its optimum output level.

automatic iris. A feature on most video cameras and camcorders that automatically creates the lens aperture that allows the optimum amount of light to reach the imaging device.

A/V mixer. *See* **audio/video mixer.**

BNC. A video connector characterized by a single shaft enclosed by a twist-lock mechanism.

buy-out music. Production music purchased for a one-time fee, as opposed to a lease or per-use fee schedule. *See also* **production music.**

camcorder. An item of video equipment that uses a video camera permanently attached to a video deck to create and record video signal.

cardioid. Another name for the unidirectional microphone pick-up pattern. The name *cardioid* comes from the heart shape of the pick-up pattern. The terms *super-cardioid, hyper-cardioid,* and *ultra-cardioid* describe more-narrow pick-up patterns.

CCD. *See* **charge-coupled device.**

character generator. A video component that allows the typing of words and simple graphics onto the television screen.

charge-coupled device (CCD). An imaging device used in most video cameras and camcorders.

chroma key. A video mixer-based electronic effect, in which a second video source is substituted for a color (or range of shades within a color) within a video shot. For example, a weather reporter stands in front of a green screen. A weather map (the second video source) replaces the green background using the chroma key effect.

condenser microphone. A microphone that contains an element made of two small vibrating magnetized plates.

contrast ratio. The comparison of the brightest part of the screen to the darkest part of the screen, expressed as a ratio. The maximum contrast ratio for television production is 30:1.

crawl. Graphics that move across the bottom of the television screen, usually from right to left. The weather alert that moves along the bottom of the TV screen is a crawl.

cue (n.). An audio mixer function that allows the user to hear an audio source (usually through headphones) without selecting that source for broadcast or recording; the audio counterpart of a preview monitor.

cue (v.). The act of rewinding or fast-forwarding a video- or audiotape so that the desired section is ready for play.

digital editing. *See* **nonlinear digital video editing.**

digital zoom. A feature found on some camcorders that electronically increases the lens zoom capability by selecting the center of the image and enlarging it digitally.

dimmer switch. A control used to gradually increase and decrease the electricity sent to a lighting fixture, thereby affecting the amount of light it gives.

dissolve. A video transition in which the first video signal is gradually replaced by a second video signal.

distribution amplifier. An electronic device that boosts the strength of audio, video, or RF (radio frequency) signal and facilitates disbursal of the signal to several outputs.

dolly (n.). A set of casters attached to the legs of a tripod to allow the tripod to roll.

dolly (v.). A forward/backward rolling movement of the camera on top of the tripod dolly.

DV8mm. A digital videotape format that consists of magnetic tape 8 millimeters wide in a small plastic videocassette shell. DV8mm is superior in quality to both 8mm and Hi-8.

dynamic microphone. A microphone that contains an element consisting of a diaphragm and moving coil.

8mm (eight millimeter). A videotape format that consists of magnetic tape 8 millimeters wide in a small plastic videocassette shell. *See also* **Hi-8.**

editing. The process of combining, adding, and deleting audio and video elements to create a television program.

F-connector. A video connector characterized by a single metal wire. F-connectors may be either push-on or screw-post.

fade. A video technique in which the picture is gradually replaced with a background color.

fader bar. A vertical slide controller on audio and video equipment.

FireWire®. Apple computer's registered name for IEEE-1394 digital cable and connectors. *See* **IEEE-1394.**

flying head. A video head that engages when the video deck is on "pause," providing a clear still-frame image.

focus. Adjustment made to the focal length of the lens in order to create a sharper, more-defined picture.

font. A style of type. Many character generators offer the user a menu of several fonts.

frame. A complete video picture. NTSC televisions (as used in North America, Japan, and many other countries) display 30 frames each second. Other standards (most notably, PAL and SECAM) display 25 frames each second.

frequency response. The characteristic of audio equipment that describes the lowest and highest frequencies (pitches) that the equipment can receive, record, or play back. For example, a microphone might have a frequency response of 22–18,000hz. (Human hearing has a frequency range of 20–20,000hz.)

gain. An increase in the output of audio or video signal.

glass-beaded screen. A projection screen covered with minuscule glass particles, which help create an extremely bright image in a darkened setting.

head. A magnet used to record or play signal on a magnetic medium, like videotape.

head (tripod). *See* **tripod head.**

Hi-8. A videotape format that consists of magnetic tape 8 millimeters wide in a small plastic videocassette shell. Hi-8 offers a higher-quality image than standard 8mm.

high-speed shutter. A camcorder feature that allows detail enhancement of fast-moving objects by electronically dividing the charge-coupled device into imaging sections.

IEEE-1394. A connecting device used to connect digital video camcorders to personal computers and nonlinear digital editing systems. The IEEE-1394 signal carries audio and video tracks and is capable of speeds up to 400 megabytes per seconds. *See also* **FireWire** and **i.LINK.** (IEEE is the Institute of Electrical and Electronic Engineers, a technical and professional society.)

i.LINK®. Sony's registered name for IEEE-1394 digital cable and connectors. *See* **IEEE-1394.**

imaging device. The part of the video camera or camcorder that converts light into electrical signal.

impedance. A resistance to signal flow. Microphones and audio mixers are rated for impedance and can be categorized as high impedance or low impedance.

import, importing. The process of recording audio and video segments onto a hard drive (or other storage medium) for use in nonlinear digital video editing.

iris. The mechanism that controls the lens aperture.

jack. A receptacle for insertion of audio or video cable on audio or video equipment. For example, headphones plug into the audio mixer's headphone jack.

jog. Frame-by-frame advancement of a videotape in a VCR or video deck.

jog/shuttle wheel. A dial on many video decks and VCRs that controls jog and shuttle functions.

lavaliere microphone. A small condenser microphone used in television production. Also called a tie-pin microphone.

learning curve. A geometric metaphor for the amount of time one needs to learn a new task (such as operating an item of television production equipment).

lens. The curved glass on a video camera or camcorder that collects light.

lenticular screen. A projection screen that is silver in color and scored with thin vertical indentations, allowing bright projection in a semidarkened room.

line-out monitor. A monitor that is connected to a recording device to show how the finished product will appear or sound. A line-out monitor may be a video monitor (video product), an audio speaker (audio product), or a television (both audio and video).

logic control. An operational feature on higher-quality audiocassette player/ recorders, in which the tape functions (play, fast-forward, rewind, etc.) are achieved electronically, rather than mechanically. Logic controls eliminate the "clunk" sound associated with operation of an audiocassette player/ recorder and reduce the wear and tear on the equipment.

loop. A brief, repeatable audio segment (usually one or two measures long) used as a building block of a song created using music-creation software. Such a song might include a drum loop, a bass loop, a keyboard loop, and a guitar loop, all of which are combined and repeated to create a song.

lux. A measurement of light. Lux is used in television production to determine the minimum amount of light (lux rating) needed for camera operation. Hence, a 2-lux camcorder requires less light than a 4-lux camcorder.

macro lens. A lens used for videography when the camera-to-object distance is less than 2 feet. The macro lens is usually installed within the zoom lens of the video camera or camcorder.

matte screen. A projection screen with a flat white surface.

microphone. An audio component that converts sound waves into electrical energy.

minidisc. A digital audio format characterized by a small, optically recorded disc housed within a 2–1/2-inch square plastic shell. A minidisc can store 74 to 80 minutes of digital-quality audio.

MiniDV. A digital videotape format that consists of magnetic tape 1/4-inch wide in a small plastic videocassette shell.

minitripod. A small three-legged mounting device used to hold 35mm cameras, digital cameras, and small camcorders. Minitripods are about 6 inches tall, and are usually used on a tabletop.

modulator. *See* **RF modulator.**

monitor (audio). A speaker or headphone set.

monitor (video). A video screen. A video monitor accepts video signal and does not have a tuner.

monochrome. A video picture consisting of different saturations of a single color, usually gray. Technical term for black-and-white television.

monopod. A one-legged mounting device used to help the videographer steady a handheld camera shot and reduce fatigue.

MP3 (MPEG-1 Audio Layer-3). A digital audio format for compressing sound into a very small computer file, while preserving the original level of quality. MP3 uses an algorithm to achieve this compression, reducing data about sound that is not within the normal range of human hearing. (MPEG is the Motion Picture Experts Group.)

nonlinear digital video editing. Postproduction work using audio and video elements saved as digital files on a computer hard drive or some other storage device. Nonlinear digital video editing is characterized by the ability to work on segments in any sequence (as opposed to traditional linear editing, which requires working from the beginning of the production straight through to the end).

nonlinear editing. *See* **nonlinear digital video editing.**

omnidirectional. A microphone pick-up pattern in which the microphone "hears" equally well from all sides.

1/8-inch mini. A small audio connector used frequently in consumer electronics.

1/4-inch phone. A connector used in audio production that is characterized by its single shaft with locking tip.

on-screen display. A function on many VCRs and televisions in which operational functions (tint, brightness, VCR function, programming, etc.) are displayed graphically on the television screen.

pan. A horizontal movement of a camera on top of a tripod.

phantom power. Electricity provided by audio mixers for use by condenser microphones connected to the audio mixer. Some microphones require phantom power and must be connected to audio mixers that provide it.

phono (RCA). A connector used in audio and video components, characterized by its single connection post and metal flanges.

pick-up pattern. The description of the directionality of a microphone. The two dominant microphone pick-up patterns are omnidirectional and unidirectional.

pixel. A single section of a charge-coupled device capable of distinguishing chromanance (color) and luminance (brightness); professional slang for picture element.

postproduction. The phase of television production that includes all activity after the raw footage is shot.

pressure zone microphone (PZM). A microphone consisting of a metal plate and a small microphone element. The PZM collects and processes all sound waves that strike the metal plate.

preview monitor. A video monitor that displays the picture from a video source. The technical director uses the video monitor to evaluate a video source before selecting it.

production music. Musical selections created specifically for use in audio and video programs. When customers buy production music, they also buy copyright permissions not granted with standard music purchases, thus averting copyright violations.

quick release. A system for mounting a camcorder on a tripod. A quick release system provides a metal or plastic plate that is attached to the bottom of the camcorder. That plate easily attaches and locks into the tripod head.

RCA connector. *See* **phono (RCA).**

rear-projection screen. A translucent screen onto which a reverse image is projected. The audience sits facing the opposite side of the screen.

record review. A feature on many camcorders that allows the videographer to see the last few seconds of video recorded on the videotape.

RF modulator. An electronic device that converts audio or video signal into RF (radio frequency) signal.

RF signal. Modulated composite (video and audio) signal produced by television stations and VCRs and processed by televisions.

RF splitter. A device that multiplies an RF signal. A person could use an RF splitter to send the signal from one VCR to two or more televisions.

resolution. The sharpness of the picture. Resolution can be measured numerically by establishing the number of scanning lines used to create each frame of video.

scroll. Graphics that roll from the bottom to the top of the screen (e.g., end credits).

shotgun microphone. A microphone with an extremely directional pick-up pattern.

shuttle. A variable-rate search, forward or reverse, of a videotape using a VCR capable of such an operation.

signal-to-noise ratio. A numerical value, expressed in decibels (dB), that represents the strength of a video signal as compared to the amount of video noise present.

studio address system. An intercom system that allows communication between control-room personnel and personnel working on the studio floor.

surface-mount microphone. A microphone that is flat on one side, has no handle, and lies flat on a tabletop or other surface. Surface mount microphones are designed to be used in group discussions, workshops, and other situations in which subjects are seated around a table.

surge protector. An electronic device that protects electronic equipment from power fluctuations.

S-VHS. A video format that uses VHS-sized cassettes and 1/2-inch S-VHS tape and produces a signal with more than 400 lines of resolution. S-VHS is not just high-quality VHS. S-VHS signal cannot be recorded on a VHS tape or recorded or played on a VHS VCR.

S-VHS-C. A video format using S-VHS videotape in a compact shell (*see* **VHS-C**). S-VHS-C records an S-VHS quality signal. The tape can be played in an S-VHS VCR using an adapter.

television. A combination tuner, RF (radio frequency) modulator, picture tube, and audio speaker that converts RF signal into picture and sound.

tilt. A vertical movement of a video camera or camcorder on top of a tripod.

time-base corrector (TBC). A video component that digitizes inherently unstable analog video signal and converts it into rock-solid video. A TBC usually has controls for manipulating the output signal's color, brightness, and strength. The advent of digital video has reduced the need for time-base correction.

tracking. The video control that allows proper placement of the videotape across the video and audio heads.

trim. The editing technique of eliminating part of the beginning and/or part of the end of a video or audio clip used in the nonlinear digital video editing process. Trimming a clip allows the editor to select exactly where the imported clip will begin and end.

tripod. A three-legged mounting device for a video camera or camcorder that provides stability.

tripod dolly. A combination tripod and dolly.

tripod head. The topmost part of a tripod. The tripod head provides the mechanism for mounting the camcorder on the tripod and facilitates panning and titling motions.

tuner. An element of a television set that allows the user to select specific signals and frequencies (channels) to be shown on the picture tube and played through the speaker.

unidirectional. A microphone pick-up pattern in which the microphone processes most of its signal from sound collected in front of the microphone, and very little from the sides and back.

VCR. *See* **videocassette recorder.**

vendor. A person or business that sells audio or video equipment, supplies, or services.

VHS. A videocassette format characterized by a plastic shell and 1/2-inch-wide videotape. VHS is an abbreviation for "video home system" as created by the JVC company. VHS is the dominant videotape format for home VCRs, video rentals, videotape program sales, and blank videotape sales.

VHS-C. A videocassette format characterized by a plastic shell and 1/2-inch-wide videotape. VHS-C-recorded tape is compatible with VHS if an adapter is used. VHS-C was developed as a way to create VHS signal with a smaller videocassette, and thus a smaller camcorder, than VHS.

video. The visual portion of television production.

video camera. A video component consisting of a lens, a viewfinder, and at least one imaging device that converts light into electrical video signal.

video deck. An electronic component used for recording and playback of videotape. It consists of a video/audio head assembly, a mechanism for transporting videotape past the heads, and operational controls.

video mixer. A video component that allows the selection of a video source from several source inputs. Most video mixers allow the technician to perform wipes, dissolves, and fades.

video noise. Poor-quality video signal within the standard video signal. Also known as snow (slang).

video signal. The electrical signal produced by video components.

videocassette. A length of videotape wound around two reels and enclosed in a plastic shell.

videocassette recorder (VCR). An electronic component consisting of a tuner, an RF (radio frequency) modulator, and a video deck used for recording and playback of a videocassette.

videographer. A person who operates a video camera or camcorder.

videography. Operation of a video camera or camcorder in video production.

videotape. A thin strip of plastic material containing metal particles that are capable of recording and storing a magnetic charge.

viewfinder. A small video monitor mounted on a video camera or camcorder that provides a view of the video image to the videographer. Viewfinders may be presented as eye-pieces, as small screens mounted on the side of the camcorder, or as larger video monitors mounted near the top of a studio camera.

volume unit (VU) meter. A device used to measure the intensity of an audio signal.

white balance. The process of adjusting the video camera or camcorder's color response to the surrounding light.

wipe. A video transition in which one video source replaces another with a distinct line or lines of definition.

wireless microphone system. A microphone system consisting of a microphone, an FM transmitter, and a tuned receiving station that eliminates the need for long runs of microphone cable.

XLR. An audio connector characterized by three prongs covered by a metal sheath.

zoom lens. A lens with a variable focal length.

Index

~~~~~~~~~~~~~~~~~~~~~~~~~~~~~~~~~~~~~